THE *SECRET* WAR

This was a secret war, whose battles were lost or won unknown to the public. . . . No such warfare had ever been waged by mortal men.

SIR WINSTON CHURCHILL, *The Second World War*, Vol. II

P.A.C. ROCKETS ARE FIRED AT THE ATTACKERS AS GERMAN AIRCRAFT
CARRY OUT A LOW-LEVEL RAID ON AN EAST COAST CONVOY

Fr. *By permission of "The Sphere"*

GERALD PAWLE

THE
SECRET WAR
1939-45

With a foreword by
NEVIL SHUTE

*With 23 plates in half-tone
and an endpaper map in colour*

GEORGE G. HARRAP & CO. LTD
LONDON TORONTO WELLINGTON SYDNEY

To
MARY
who bore so patiently with the long months
of research before this book could be written
and to
J. H. D. C.
in grateful memory of the Mediterranean
years which followed my service with the
'Wheezers and Dodgers'

940.541242
P 339 s
153155

First published in Great Britain 1956
by GEORGE G. HARRAP & CO. LTD
182 High Holborn, London, W.C.1
Copyright. All rights reserved

Composed in Intertype Baskerville type and printed by
Western Printing Services Ltd, Bristol
Made in Great Britain

FOREWORD
by
NEVIL SHUTE

Looking back over the years to the exploits of the Department of Miscellaneous Weapon Development in the Admiralty, I think it is the personalities of the people concerned that now interest me most. What sort of people were they who did the things described so excellently in this book? If any future war should come and make a similar department necessary again, what sort of people should the Admiralty seek to staff it?

Well, first of all, I do not think that such a department is likely to be created again in just that form in any future war. It was the child of Goodeve, and it was amazingly lucky for the Admiralty that Goodeve happened to fall into their lap at the commencement of the War. He was a scientist of some repute, though only thirty-five years old in 1939, but he was much more than that. He was born a Canadian, and visits to the United States in his youth had infected him with something of the vigour of their scientific and commercial enterprise; although a scientist he thought like an American project engineer, with a quick, instinctive flair for picking out of half a dozen schemes the one which could be driven through to practical success in terms of hardware. His travels between Canada, the United States, and England had given him a breadth of outlook denied to those who are constrained to spend their lives in one country, and he had immense vigour. In addition, he was passionately devoted to the Navy. From early youth his reserve service in the Navy had been practically his only recreation, his one hobby. Apart from his work and the Navy, his only relaxation lay in ice-skating. When the War came it must have been a secret joy to him; it meant that he could give his whole life to the Navy instead of just his holidays. The Admiralty would be lucky indeed if any such man fell into their hands at the right time in any future war.

Without a Goodeve the department could never have come into being. No doubt in any future war the Admiralty could make as wise a choice of a captain to command such an unusual department as they did when they appointed G. O. C. Davies. He was a burly R.N. captain with a strong sense of humour who intended to retire from the Navy anyway at the conclusion of the War, having some private means. He was therefore quite prepared to blot his copybook and to incur the disapproval of his seniors if by doing so he could advance the War effort, a fitting commander for this crowd of turbulent civilians in uniform who had no future in the Service either. Two or three times a week an R.N.V.R. lieutenant accustomed to civilian ways of doing things would return from a visit to a firm and plunge Captain Davies straight into a procedural mess. "They said they thought it would cost about three thousand pounds, sir, so I told them to go right ahead. I said we'd let them have a letter by the end of the week. They've put fifteen men on to it already. They're really very keen." To his eternal credit Captain Davies would laugh heartily before he plunged into the appalling paper-work involved in Admiralty contracts that had been started off in so unauthorized a manner.

If any one quality was a common requirement for the officers in this unusual department I would say it was imagination—the imagination to look forward and to visualize what might happen. When the Petroleum Warfare Department set up a flame barrage to prevent invading boats from landing upon beaches that consisted of a line of oil discharged from pipes under the sea, igniting on the surface to make a wall of fire twenty feet high and twenty feet wide parellel to the beach, it appeared to be an impregnable defence. It needed imagination for somebody to say, "I don't believe that thing's much good after all. I think the bow wave of the boat would push the oil aside. I don't think you'd get burnt up. Let's get a boat and try it." We did, we weren't, it did, and it wasn't. This quality of imagination came into everything we touched; without it little could have been created.

Next to imagination I would say that the most useful officers were those who had a knowledge of some industry. The objective in practically every case was to produce a piece of hardware which would be of service to the fighting man, and the detailed design and manufacture had to be carried out by some firm. Knowledge of one sector of industry and personal acquaintance with the people in it were invaluable to an officer in this department, imposing a handicap upon the younger officers straight from a university or college that had to be countered by the greater energy of their youth. Technical journalists, such as that valiant little man Menhinick, were good members of the department. Their work in peace-time brought them into contact with civilian firms, they were accustomed to taking a bird's-eye view of an industry, and they could express themselves clearly and concisely.

The Law played a surprisingly effective part in the activities of D.M.W.D. Terrell and Lochner were both barristers, though the latter had an engineering background, and these were two of the most successful officers in the department. Perhaps the ability to analyse and check evidence and to extract the truth from several conflicting stories may make it easy for a barrister quickly to gain a knowledge of an industry or a technique, added to the feature of a first-class mind. However that may be, experience has shown that the legal mind can be most effective in the activities we carried on; it may be that in Patent law there lay some technical and analytical resources that we might have used but didn't.

Pure scientists, such as Guggenheim, Penney, and Purcell, were invaluable to the department, but I think we may have had too many physical chemists straight from college. These men did first-class work, but not as physical chemists; they were very keen and very brave in trials, but they learned their job as they went along, and so made many mistakes that could have been avoided with more engineering knowledge. However, engineers are very scarce in time of war; we raked in every one that we could lay our hands on, and in that time of man-power shortage Goodeve was no doubt correct to bring in anybody technical, in any field, that he could get hold of.

Lastly we come to the men with no apparent qualifications at all for work on the design of weapons. Some of these were ineffective on creative work and drifted off to other work in other spheres of the Navy. But others, and there were quite a number of them, revealed a dormant aptitude for work on weapons to Goodeve at an interview; he had a flair for detecting this quality. Lane, the expert on tree culture, was to be the man who succoured and encouraged B. N. Wallis in his frustration, and brought him to the department and organized the trials of the weapon which resulted in the breaching of the Mohne Dam. It was Brinsmead, who made furniture in peacetime, who became our expert on shaped charges; it was Eades, the young auctioneer, who crowned his work on the development of rocket weapons with the exploitation of the rocket grapnel, and so lost his life in the invasion. And there were many others.

When I was first sent from H.M.S. *King Alfred* to be interviewed by Goodeve in the Admiralty I was furious. The War seemed to me, in June of 1940, to be desperately serious, and England in imminent peril of invasion. I had just abandoned technical experiment and research on gliding torpedoes to go and fight, as this book tells. Now I was threatened with a posting to a new experimental department, the king of which was interviewing me. I was not reassured. The man was young, but he had snow-white hair, very blue eyes, and a nervous, restless manner. I knew nothing of him at that time. Since he was interviewing me my opportunities for interviewing him were limited, but in my time I have met many cranks, and this man bore all the external hallmarks. Here, I thought, was a crazy inventor who had sucked in the simple admirals to the point when they were allowing him to set up a staff to mess about with graph paper and slide rules instead of fighting the Germans. If I got involved in this, I thought, I should be very safe, but other men would win or lose the war within the next three months. If I didn't, if within the three days of joining the Navy I refused point-blank to do what the Navy wanted me to do, I might well find myself cashiered before I got my uniform.

This book shows how very, very wrong I was in every single particular.

PREFACE

THE writing of this story of D.M.W.D., the Admiralty department described in Chapter 1, had its genesis in an article entitled "Highly Explosive" which I contributed to *The Sunday Times* in 1953. Not until I began the detailed research for this book did I realize, however, the problems of giving shape and form to a record of such varied endeavour while attempting at the same time to preserve some chronological sequence.

Work on many of D.M.W.D.'s projects overlapped by considerable margins, and I have therefore aimed to introduce each new enterprise at the point of its greatest significance to the war effort.

While initiating ideas of their own, D.M.W.D. also helped to develop many weapons and devices for which they were not themselves responsible at the outset. In many instances, too, other Admiralty departments and individuals continued to contribute valuably and constantly to every phase of evolution from the drawing-board to the final production. I stress this fact because, inevitably, the story of any one particular unit engaged in such a field as research and development cannot convey an adequate impression of the part played by other organizations working in parallel.

D.M.W.D. had many successes—and many failures. But it should be emphasized that the latter were often failures only in the sense that the swift march of war removed the need for some strange and resourceful invention before its development was fully completed.

Although I have had generous co-operation from many quarters, the views expressed in the pages which follow are entirely my own. I have not sought to produce an 'official history,' but rather to give a picture of certain facets in the life of a unique organization now no longer in existence. At the same time every attempt has been made to ensure accuracy of fact, and my grateful thanks are due, first of all, to the many former members of D.M.W.D.—too numerous to mention individually—who submitted themselves to cross-examination at all hours of the day and night. Without their ungrudging help this book could not have been written.

Captain A. W. Clarke, C.B.E., D.S.O., R.N.(ret.), Chief of Naval Information, and Mr H. G. O. Cross, M.B.E., his deputy at the Admiralty, readily placed facilities at my disposal for inspecting material in the Admiralty archives. Rear-Admiral R. M. Bellairs,

C.B., C.M.G., gave me the freedom of the Admiralty's Historical Section, and Mr G. H. Hurford, F.R.Hist.S., and Commander F. Barley, R.N.V.R., of his staff, went to much trouble to check countless details concerning the naval plans for the assault on Normandy.

From many sources unconnected with D.M.W.D. I have received valuable assistance and advice, and I should like to express my gratitude to Admiral Sir William Tennant, K.C.B., C.B.E., M.V.O., who as Flag Officer, Mulberry and Pluto, played a leading part in the events described in the closing stages of this book; Admiral of the Fleet Lord Fraser of North Cape, G.C.B., K.B.E., a former First Sea Lord, and Controller of the Navy when D.M.W.D. was formed; Admiral Sir Harold Burrough, G.C.B., K.B.E., D.S.O.; Admiral Sir Alexander Madden, K.C.B., C.B.E.; Marshal of the Royal Air Force Sir John Slessor, G.C.B., D.S.O., M.C.; Sir Steuart Mitchell, K.B.E., C.B., Controller of Guided Weapons and Electronics at the Ministry of Supply; Major-General Sir Millis Jefferis, K.B.E., M.C.; Vice-Admiral John Hughes-Hallett, C.B., D.S.O., M.P.; Surgeon Vice-Admiral Sir Alexander Ingleby Mackenzie, K.B.E., C.B., M.R.C.S., L.R.C.P.; Sir Arthur Whitaker, K.C.B.; Commander Norman Holbrook, V.C., R.N.(ret.); Mr E. G. Bührle, head of the Werkzeugmaschinenfabrik Oerlikon of Zürich; Captain Basil Jones, D.S.O., D.S.C., R.N.(ret.); Mr A. T. Holman, O.B.E., chairman of Holman Brothers, Camborne; Mr Antoine Gazda, head of the engineering organization at Providence, Rhode Island, U.S.A., which bears his name; Mr R. E. Stubington, managing director of the Merryweather Engineering Works, Greenwich; Lieutenant-Colonel L. V. S. Blacker, O.B.E.; Commander Peter du Cane, O.B.E., R.N.(ret.); Lieutenant-Commander Peter Scott, C.B.E., D.S.C., R.N.V.R.; Mr J. M. Waldram, of the General Electric Company's Research Staff; Mrs Ronald Hamilton; Commander J. S. Mulock, O.B.E., R.N.V.R.; Mr J. S. Herbert, M.A.; Mr C. R. Thompson, of the Schermuly Pistol Rocket Apparatus, Ltd; and Mr R. J. S. Crowe.

Mr Francis Marshall has kindly allowed me to reproduce his diverting drawing of Mulberry Harbour, now in the possession of Admiral Tennant; and the illustration for the menu card of D.M.W.D.'s first reunion dinner—another engaging flight of fancy— is the work of Mr Russell Brockbank, of *Punch*. In respect of Chapters 11 and 20 I am indebted to Kemsley Newspapers for permission to use material published in *The Sunday Times* and other journals under their control.

GERALD PAWLE

ST MAWES
September 1956

CONTENTS

PART I: *The Enemy in the Sky*

PART II: *The Enemy under the Waters*

PART III: *Keys to the Fortress*

ILLUSTRATIONS

PLATES

IN THE TEXT

KEY TO ENDPAPER MAP

1. Phœnix Units: A concrete breakwater in sections.
2. Leviathan: The ship which filled the Phœnix Units with sand to give them extra weight.
3. Corncobs: Old merchant ships sunk as a breakwater.
4. Gooseberry: Code name of the breakwater formed by Corncobs.
5. Spud Piers: The landing wharf at which material was unloaded.
6. Whale: The bridge connecting Spud Piers to the shore.
7. Beetles: The pontoons on which the Whales were supported.
8. Headquarters: Naval officer in charge.
9 and 10. Mulberry 'B': the full code name of the artificial harbour.
11. Golden Arrow: Arrow, the code name for the port of Arromanches. Gold, the code name of the beach sector.
12. Liberty Trot: Trot of buoys for Liberty ships.
13. Liberty ships anchorage.
14. Rhinos: The power-driven pontoons on which cargo was brought ashore.
15. Ducks: The D.U.K.W.'s, amphibious vehicles.
16. Duck cushions: Assembly point for Ducks.
17. Planter: The code name for officer in charge of sinking arrangements for Phœnix and Corncob.
18. Western entrance to harbour.
19. Northern entrance to harbour.
20. Eastern entrance to harbour.

... and, mark you, our scientists are not surpassed in any nation in the world, especially when their thought is applied to Naval matters. ...

SIR WINSTON CHURCHILL,
in his Victory broadcast

PART I: THE ENEMY IN THE SKY

I

THE CANOE LAKE

THIS is the story of a group of naval scientists, the story of a department in the Admiralty which had no exact counterpart in the whole complex Allied machine which waged the Second World War against Germany and her confederates—the story of the Wheezers and Dodgers.

The Wizard War, as Sir Winston Churchill has termed the cease-less struggle for mastery between the Allied and enemy scientists, involved moves and counter-moves often 'unintelligible to ordinary folk.' And for long after the war was over a detailed description of some of those moves, which would have made them intelligible to the layman, was inadvisable on security grounds.

To-day, however, most of what was attempted and achieved by the Royal Navy's Directorate of Miscellaneous Weapon Development—to give the Wheezers and Dodgers their official title—is no longer on the secret list. It has remained untold only, one presumes, because D.M.W.D. was essentially a clandestine organization, its triumphs and failures unknown to all but a relatively small circle of Servicemen and civilian scientists.

The Wheezers and Dodgers were a research and development team. They were formed in the shadow of defeat in Europe, and their activities reached flood tide with the Allied landings on the coast of Normandy four years later. In those four years they were destined to tackle some of the strangest tasks in the history of warfare.

ON the last Sunday in May 1940 there was intense activity in the Admiralty. The British Expeditionary Force, with four of its divisions in imminent danger of encirclement outside Lille, was fighting its way back to the French coast, and Operation Dynamo was on.

The first significant move in this naval plan for the evacuation from France had wisely been made a full week earlier. When the German Army broke through at Sedan an immediate request went from the Admiralty to the Ministry of Shipping for all available

B

coasting vessels to proceed to the Downs, but as late as May 24 it was still not certain that a major evacuation would be feasible. Since then the situation had deteriorated alarmingly, and no one on the naval staff expected more than 45,000 men to be brought away from the beaches. But now the die was cast. The operation named Dynamo was to be attempted.

A severe ordeal faced the array of little ships massing in the Downs. The Germans had already reached the coast near Calais, and were shelling any vessels which tried to approach Dunkirk direct. H.M.S. *Wolfhound*, carrying the imperturbable Captain William Tennant and his staff to Dunkirk, where he was to act as the Navy's Master of Ceremonies at the evacuation, had to make a sixty-mile détour to avoid a minefield, and was dive-bombed all the way, a final stick of bombs straddling her as she reached the inner harbour.

For the individual protection of the hundreds of coasting vessels now awaiting the orders of Vice-Admiral, Dover, there was little that the Admiralty could provide against the mounting air attack. The threat of enemy mines was another matter, however, and as the unceasing stream of trawlers and colliers, yachts and drifters, barges and paddle steamers, neared the assembly area they were diverted to one of three South Coast ports and shepherded through a strange ritual.

As ship after ship made fast, working parties of sailors swarmed on board. Heaving-lines were thrown to them by men in boats alongside, and then, sweating and straining, they began to haul a huge cable of copper wire slowly up the ship's side. A whistle shrilled, and for a few seconds the cable clung to the hull. Then it slid slowly back to rest under the water. A brief pause for mysterious calculations, and the ship was cleared for sea, another heading in immediately to take her place.

Hour after hour, through daylight and the confusion of darkness, this selfsame performance was repeated. In four days four hundred ships destined for Dunkirk underwent this baptism by electricity surging from enormous submarine storage batteries ashore. To the older men in the crews of the trawlers and small coasters ordered forward for these strange attentions—men whose lives had been bound up with the simpler science of wind, tides, and stars—the whole business must have savoured of black magic.

They knew about the magnetic mine. The Germans had been sowing them by parachute in the shallow waters of the shipping channels and harbours, where they lay inert and invisible till some poor devil took his ship over them. They had seen escorting destroyers and the bigger merchantmen, their hulls festooned with coil upon coil of cable—some sort of protection against these magnetic

mines thought up by the scientific chaps. That might be all right for
ships with enough power to keep the coils charged; for the rest—
and that meant the greater part of the civilian fleet waiting to head
for Dunkirk—there was nothing to hope for in that line. Nothing, at
least, till now, though what good could come of wiping a wire against
the hull and taking it away after less than half a minute was difficult
to understand. There seemed little sense in it.

To the team of naval scientists from H.M.S. *Vernon*, the Torpedo
and Mining establishment at Portsmouth, who had been roped in
en bloc to supervise this urgent operation, and toiled with little rest
for four days and nights, this 'wiping' technique had, however,
developed well beyond the realm of experiment. They were now
applying a proved and brilliantly simple answer to the problem
first studied in the *Vernon* six months earlier, after Lieutenant-
Commanders Ouvry and Lewis had retrieved from a mud-bank in
the Thames the first magnetic mine to fall into British hands intact.

When that first mine was dissected it was found that if a ship's
natural magnetic field could be reduced by some artificial means to
a certain point the steel hull would no longer set the mechanism of
the mine in motion.

Two initial tasks, therefore, faced the men in *Vernon's* Mine
Design Department. They had to find a practical way of demagnetizing or 'degaussing' ships so that the lurking mines remained
inert on the sea-bed when approached. And they had to discover
how these mines could be swept.

It was a race against time, and the team of scientists anxiously
pursuing their own lines of research in *Vernon* were called upon to
investigate the wildest schemes put up to the Admiralty by well-
meaning individuals who had thought up their own dramatic
counter-measures. Typical of these was the following plan, forwarded
officially to the Admiralty by an influential member of one of the
Navy's most famous shore establishments.

> It has been suggested [said the writer] that a means of causing
> magnetic mines to explode harmlessly may be found by attaching
> small but strong permanent magnets to flat fish, and distributing
> these fish over the sea bottom. The fish, moving in search of food,
> would, at short range, bring mines under the influence of a magnetic
> field and consequently cause explosion. The questions are (1)
> Whether the influence of a magnet which could be carried by a fish
> would be effective; and (2) Whether the scheme is possible from the
> 'fish' point of view.

The writer plainly had doubts about "the 'fish' point of view,"
but he had, he confided, been encouraged by an optimistic opinion

expressed to him by a marine biologist. The latter favoured catching skates and rays, "which are large, hardy, and will survive much handling." The biologist had, it appeared, offered any help necessary to put "this excellent idea to immediate use," and the author of the plan added: "Mr —— has lately been employed on research into the habits of skates, so his knowledge of that aspect of the question is recent and first-hand." He ended his memorandum to the Lords Commissioners of the Admiralty on an encouraging note: "It would appear that if a suitable small magnet will do its work, then the skate can be induced to do the rest."

Rear-Admiral Wake-Walker had been appointed by the First Lord of the Admiralty, then Mr Churchill, to supervise all technical measures for defeating the magnetic mine, and to him this memorandum was passed. The cares of office had not robbed the Admiral of his sense of humour, and in due course the author of this imaginative scheme received the following formal reply:

1. The suggestion contained in your 191/D 478 is considered of great value.

2. As a first step in the development of this idea it is proposed to establish a School for Flat Fish at the R.N. College, Dartmouth. Candidates for this course should be entered in the first place as Probationary Flat Fish, and these poor fish would be confirmed in their rank on showing their proficiency by exploding a mine.

3. A very suitable source of candidates to tap would be the Angel Fish of Bermuda, which, though flat, swim in a vertical plane.

4. With the success of this scheme it may be necessary to control fried-fish shops.

5. It is requested that you will forward, through the usual channels, proposals as to the necessary accommodation, and a suggested syllabus of the Course.

The sponsor of this novel plan reluctantly concluded that the Admiralty were unable to recognize a good idea when they saw one, and the skates and rays never contributed to the war effort after all!

Within a month, and despite such well-intentioned distractions, the team at *Vernon* had established the principle of degaussing vessels by passing current through cables permanently fixed to their hull. Devising a practical technique for sweeping the mines presented much greater difficulties. Professor B. P. Haigh, Professor of Mechanical Engineering at the Royal Naval College, Greenwich, was the first to hit on the idea of two minesweepers towing floating parallel cables through which violent pulses of electricity could be discharged to detonate the mines, but his scheme involved the use of so many thousand horse-power of electricity that special power plants would have been needed.

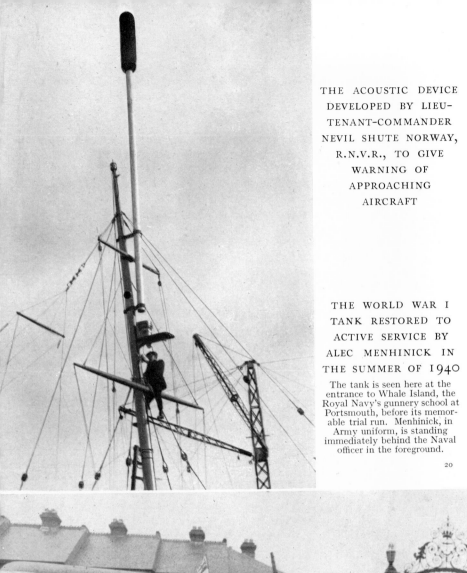

THE ACOUSTIC DEVICE
DEVELOPED BY LIEU-
TENANT-COMMANDER
NEVIL SHUTE NORWAY,
R.N.V.R., TO GIVE
WARNING OF
APPROACHING
AIRCRAFT

THE WORLD WAR I
TANK RESTORED TO
ACTIVE SERVICE BY
ALEC MENHINICK IN
THE SUMMER OF 1940

The tank is seen here at the
entrance to Whale Island, the
Royal Navy's gunnery school at
Portsmouth, before its memorable trial run. Menhinick, in
Army uniform, is standing
immediately behind the Naval
officer in the foreground.

20

PLASTIC ARMOUR MARK
III, KNOWN AS P.P.P.
(PLASTIC PROTECTIVE
PLATING), FITTED TO
THE BRIDGE OF A
MERCHANT AIRCRAFT-
CARRIER AS PROTECTION
AGAINST BOMB
SPLINTERS AND CANNON
GUNFIRE

Imperial War Museum

A LANDING-CRAFT USED
IN THE DIEPPE RAID IN
1942 AFTER THE EX-
PLOSION OF A MORTAR
BOMB

Although the damage appears
considerable, the Plastic
Protective Plating prevented any
penetration, and many lives were
saved.

Imperial War Museum

21

At this point of stalemate a young lieutenant-commander R.N.V.R. who had been serving for some weeks in *Vernon* as Staff Technical Adviser to Captain Denis Boyd,[1] the establishment's commanding officer, and had been following the progress reports, made a significant discovery.

Charles Frederick Goodeve was a Canadian, now in his middle thirties. He had come to England twelve years earlier on an Empire scholarship, and when war broke out he was Reader in Physical Chemistry at University College, London. He had also made rapid progress as a private consultant in chemical and electrical engineering. If science absorbed Charles Goodeve's working hours the Navy was his dominant interest outside them. One of five children, he had been brought up in Winnipeg, on the Red River, which flows north to 300-mile-long Lake Winnipeg, with its fascinating, picturesque islands and beaches. His father was a Church of England parson, and his parents, always hard up, solved the holiday problem by building a cottage on the lake. There the children spent months every year, eating the lake fish they caught and the abundant fruit. Charles, an unsociable boy older than his years, would disappear for weeks on end, covering hundreds of miles in boats or canoes with his Husky dog as his only companion.

As soon as he could he joined the Canadian Navy's Volunteer Reserve. In those early days he had no interest in the technical side. For him the Navy spelt excitement and adventure, and every year he spent three golden summer months afloat, either in the *Patrician*, an ancient destroyer, or in a minesweeper, where he soon found himself, to his intense pride, second in command. At that time two old destroyers, discarded by the Royal Navy after the First World War, and four minesweepers comprised the entire Canadian Fleet, but its youngest commissioned officer was given a thorough grounding in navigation and seamanship.

In spite of these halcyon days as a naval reservist, life was far from easy for young Charles Goodeve. His father's health broke down, and, with the family hard put to it to make ends meet, he left school early and apprenticed himself to a firm of Chartered Accountants in Winnipeg. His mother was determined that after a while he should return to college; Charles, tasting the first delights of financial independence, had no intention of surrendering his freedom. But Mrs Goodeve was an astute tactician. As soon as the family's resources permitted she got him fired from the job, and back he went to study electrical engineering. Soon he switched to science.

[1] Now Admiral Sir Denis Boyd, K.C.B., C.B.E., D.S.C., principal of Ashridge College.

He proved an apt pupil. His naval training had increased his self-reliance, and he was beginning to shed the unsociability and intro-spection of his boyhood years. Already he had an astonishingly clear, analytical mind which quickly rejected the non-essential and gave perspective and ready significance to what remained. At nineteen he was lecturing at the University of Manitoba, mightily relieved that his hair was prematurely grey! At twenty-three he held the degree of Master of Science and the Gold Medal of the Engineering Institute of Canada, awarded for spectacularly successful research work into the cause of a disastrous explosion in the city central-heating system.

In the same year he won a scholarship to University College, London. There he was destined to spend the next twelve years. Before leaving Canada, however, there was one goal which he desperately wanted to attain. He had been long waiting for a chance to take his final Navigation test, and a few weeks before sailing for England he was ordered to report at Esquimalt. He was to take the ancient *Patrician* to sea, carry out certain manœuvres, and anchor her in the Bay. After sleepless nights, going through every detail of procedure and word of command, the great day had come. The *Patrician* had been undergoing major repairs to her engines, a not infrequent occurrence, but when Goodeve went on board and asked anxiously whether she would be ready for sea he was told that all was well. "They've patched her up again. You're to take her out of harbour at 0900," said the captain to the nervous candidate.

At 0857 Goodeve gave his first orders.

"Let go after springs!"

"All lines clear aft, sir."

"Fifteen port!"

"Fifteen port on, sir."

He then ordered "Slow ahead, port" to swing her stern out, but hardly had he uttered the words when there was a colossal explosion and clouds of steam billowed from the engine-room hatch. It was the end of the veteran. *Patrician's* main engine connexions had burst asunder.

Young Goodeve climbed sadly down from the bridge. He was never again to have the opportunity of gaining the "N" that he coveted, but England, which offered vastly greater scope to the scientist, widened the experience of the sailor too. Goodeve transferred to the R.N.V.R., and in the decade before the war he went to sea in submarines and minesweepers, served in four battleships and three destroyers, and began to specialize in the electrical side.

By 1935 the wardroom talk was of war. Up till then Goodeve had been content to regard his naval training as an absorbing hobby—

the complete relaxation from his research work and the lectures he gave to young scientists and medical students.

Now he sensed a changing atmosphere during his spells afloat, an awareness of the approaching storm which gave a new urgency to the training programme. Dissatisfied with his old complacency, Goodeve started planning to use his scientific proficiency. He qualified as a Torpedo specialist in the *Defiance* at Devonport: by the time war broke out he had been right round the Navy, studying tactics, investigating technical problems, and arguing long into the night with any senior officers he could provoke into debate on the part which science would play in the war at sea. In peace-time the average serving officer tends to look upon change with ill-concealed suspicion, and Goodeve's theories startled the conservatively minded members of many wardrooms. But he made friendships which were to stand him in good stead. Two regular officers in particular, Commander C.N.E. Curry and Willie Dallmeyer, the Instructional Commander at H.M.S. *Vernon*, took the young Canadian under their wing. Curry, sharp-featured and *staccato* of speech, was an electrical specialist with a supreme contempt for orthodoxy. He was an all-rounder, intensely keen on technical progress and a fine seaman, who taught Goodeve much about the finer points of sailing a dinghy. Captain Denis Boyd was another whom Goodeve found particularly receptive to new ideas, and it was a happy chance that sent Goodeve to work under him at *Vernon* when the war was still only a few hours old.

When he arrived at Portsmouth a team which included Dr A. B. Wood, of the Naval Mine Design Department—later to be joined by Dr Edward Bullard[1]—was hard at work on magnetic-mine counter-measures. In the early stages Goodeve himself was more closely concerned with a projected screen for countering magnetic torpedoes, but when the snag developed in Haigh's design of the Double L Sweep—the plan for towing electrically charged cables astern of a pair of minesweepers—he was brought into the discussions.

Sifting through the mass of intricate calculations passed to him, and wondering how Haigh's ingenious plan could be made to work, he came across a paper by a young scientist named Tuck. This suggested a means of reducing the power needed for the Double L Sweep very substantially. Here was a vital clue. If Tuck's scheme could be modified, applied to Haigh's basic idea, and combined with the electrodes used in the torpedo screen they had the answer to the magnetic mine.

[1] Now Sir Edward Bullard, lately Director of the National Physical Laboratory.

Greatly excited, Goodeve searched through his address book and put through a call to a man named Guggenheim,[1] whom he had often worked with at University College.

"Can you pack your bag and come down to Portsmouth straight away? I've got a problem here which is right in your line."

"What's it all about?" said Guggenheim, surprised.

"I can't explain on the 'phone, but I'll ring the Admiralty and get their security people to give you a clearance. Pick up a rail voucher, and I'll meet you off the train which gets into Portsmouth at 2124."

Guggenheim, a brilliant mathematician, joined Goodeve a few hours later. After four days of trial and error on paper, checking and counter-checking calculations, they thought they had the answer. Now it was a question of giving the apparatus they had designed a practical test. Would the current flowing back through the sea from the Double L Sweep cancel out the current still coming from the cables? That was the first thing Goodeve had to be certain about; Guggenheim, checking his figures for the tenth time, was encouragingly confident.

For the trial they needed a calm stretch of water where they could work undisturbed—and it had to be sea water. Right on the spot in Portsmouth was the ideal place—the Canoe Lake, where small boys sailed their model yachts—but security was the snag. The Canoe Lake was in full view of the public, and overlooked by near-by houses. Any attempt to screen it off would undoubtedly *attract* attention, and it was important that the sailors helping with the trial should not realize what was happening. So Goodeve thought up an ingenious cover-plan. In the deepest of confidence the sailors and police were told that a new secret device for detecting enemy ships was being tried. A large number of models were launched on to the waters of the lake, some floating proudly as the schoolboys' yachts, and some mounted on pieces of wood.

It was a bitterly cold winter day, and ice had to be swept aside before the trial could start. Then the sailors began towing their model ships backward and forward across the lake, watched by an ever-growing crowd of housewives, small boys, and policemen.

Of all the gathering on the lake-side only Goodeve and two assistants knew what was afoot. They had brought with them a large box. In it was the mechanism of the German magnetic mine which Ouvry had brought from its resting-place on the mud-bank at Shoeburyness. This could not be placed on the bed of the lake; the water was too shallow. So they decided to reverse the normal procedure, the Double L Sweep wires being strung out along the bottom of the

[1] Since 1946 Professor of Chemistry at Reading University.

lake. The mine itself, hidden in its box, was lifted into one of the rowing-boats, and as the sailors hauled their model ships to and fro the boat carrying the mine and three tense observers moved slowly among them.

When they had been afloat, ostensibly engrossed in the movements of the models, long enough to allay any interest on the part of the spectators they pulled towards the head of the lake. Goodeve bent over the instruments connected to the mine mechanism.

"Tell them they can switch on now!" he ordered quietly. At a signal from the boat the current began flowing through the submerged cables. And as they paddled slowly back down the lake a spasmodic flickering on the dial in front of him announced the firing of the mechanism of the German mine at all corners of the sweep. In the freezing cold wind, which whipped up small waves on the grey waters of the lake, Goodeve found himself sweating with excitement. It had worked! The magnetic mine on which Hitler had based high hopes of securing Britain's blockade could be destroyed just as certainly as the ordinary moored mine.

Making his way through the crowd still staring fascinated at the little wooden models, Goodeve hurried back to *Vernon*. On his desk lay an envelope marked "Top Secret," and he extracted a brief, emphatic memorandum with a Whitehall note-heading:

> You should discontinue any research on the lines you have indicated in your latest report. It is clear to me that the method you suggest will prove self-cancelling, and cannot work.

The triumph on the Canoe Lake was doubly sweet!

Early in the following cheerless February of the "phoney war," when the only bright gleam of achievement to stir a chilled and somewhat apathetic public was provided by Captain Philip Vian and the *Altmark* rescue, there was a private celebration in the *Vernon*. The Double L Sweep had its first operational success. By then Goodeve had applied his keen mind to another worrying problem with equally happy results.

The Admiralty had set up a vigorous organization under Vice-Admiral Sir Richard Lane-Poole to cope with the degaussing of Allied shipping. In terms of time, labour, and materials it was a colossal task, for every ship—and there were over 10,000 vessels on Lloyd's Register—had to be put through a special test to determine its magnetic field; vast lengths of special copper cable had to be fitted; and men had to be trained to use the new equipment.[1] Some-

[1] In the first two years of the war 50,000 miles of degaussing cable were fitted to Allied ships by Admiral Lane-Poole's organization. In this period degaussing equipment cost an estimated £20,000,000. Between May and June 1940 (the time of Dunkirk) 2000 ships were degaussed, and a further 1000 were 'wiped.'

thing much quicker and much simpler was needed to make the ships safe against the magnetic mine—particularly the smaller ships, which had not enough power available to use the degaussing system even if it could be installed.

"We don't seem to be making headway fast enough. There's another meeting to-morrow afternoon, and Admiralty have been getting on to Boyd again." It was a day early in January, and Good-eve had Richardson[1] with him—a fair-haired, thin-featured sub-lieutenant R.N.V.R. wearing the green stripe of the Special Branch.[2] Richardson had been a student of Goodeve's in the early thirties. Before he won a Commonwealth Scholarship to Princeton in 1937 they had done a good deal of research together on torpedo problems. For one still in his twenties he had an unusual maturity and balance; in addition, Goodeve noted with particular admiration his tenacious unwillingness to accept defeat, either technically or administratively. That meant a lot in the kind of work they were now carrying out. They had formed a good team on the Double L Sweep, and now, to refresh his mind, Goodeve went over the ground already covered in the degaussing calculations, thinking aloud while his deputy traced abstract patterns on the blotter in front of him.

"The only way to speed things up is to find some means by which the steel can degauss itself."

"Is there anything in the French idea?" Richardson asked.

"Too elaborate. Besides, it would cost about half a million . . . but that's obviously the line of attack. We've got to introduce negative magnetism into the ships without having to build a vast installation."

The French Navy had put forward the suggestion that ships should be passed through a gigantic coil, reversing their magnetism by this means. Poring over his notes and figures once again, Goodeve felt he was very close to the solution. It seemed like the Double L Sweep stumbling-block all over again. If only he could cut down the current needed for this demagnetizing process the rest was easy. For most of that night he stayed in the office, worrying at the problem like a terrier.

By next morning he had produced a formula which satisfied him. It employed in a very simple equipment only one-hundredth of the current used in the huge French coil. If this worked, all that was now necessary to protect ships against the magnetic mine was to 'wipe' their hulls for a few seconds with a copper cable charged with electric current. This roughly cancelled out the ship's own vertical magnetism, and although the effect was not permanent—the vessels

---

[1] Now Dr F. D. Richardson, Director of the Nuffield Research Group at University College, London.
[2] Non-executive officers specially recruited for their technical qualifications.

would have to be 'wiped' again at intervals of so many months—the whole process would take only a few minutes.

Goodeve's calculations were rushed to London and fed into the Admiralty machine—but for some time there was complete and galling inactivity. After two decades of peace the machine still moved with ponderous and cautious deliberation in matters of research and development. Goodeve had no say in the arrangement of the trials. These were to be 'laid on' by another department, but as he passed through the barrier at Waterloo Station one morning later in the month he ran into the man responsible for rushing the experiments through.

"How are you getting on?" he asked.

"Oh, all right. . . . I've put in a request for a destroyer, but nothing much has happened about it yet. I expect it'll turn up some time, and then we can get on with the job of checking your figures."

"Look here," said Goodeve, startled to realize that nothing at all had been done, "would there be any objection to *us* doing the preliminary work?"

"Oh, none at all, old man. . . . You carry on by all means." Plainly relieved to be rid of his responsibility, the Admiralty official hurried away. Goodeve, cursing the wasted days, went to a 'phonebox and rang up Richardson at Portsmouth. When he got back to *Vernon* that night he found that Richardson, with a borrowed Woolworth's compass, had carried out a complete series of trials on destroyer plates and merchant-ship steels. He had even cajoled the Dockyard into hoisting a steel lighter for him to work on, and by hammering the plates and reversing the current supplied by a generator in one of the machine shops he had demonstrated that he could restore the magnetism which the wiping had faithfully cancelled out. From now on it was plain sailing.

If there had been delay in testing Goodeve's theory, no time was lost in applying this new and brilliantly simple form of protection to the hundreds of ships unable to use the cumbersome degaussing gear. It had a tremendous effect on morale.

> Aged mariners came up to scientists in the street and shook their hands for saving their lives. Confidence in wiping even became excessive and myths arose. One captain reported, after his ship had been wiped—"Why, my dear chap, you could see torpedoes going harmlessly in all directions!"[1]

For all the myths, however, there was soon solid proof that Goodeve had made a major contribution to the defeat of the magnetic mine. And though on this eve of Dunkirk the men of the coasters

J. G. Crowther and R. Whiddington, *Science at War* (H.M.S.O., 1947), p. 171.

watched sceptically while the huge cables were hauled from the
water to perform their strange rites, they, too, readily acknowledged
their debt to the scientists in the hectic days which followed.

Out of the 218 ships lost during Operation Dynamo only two of
them—the armed boarding steamer *Mona's Queen* and the Fleet
Air Arm yacht *Grive*—were claimed by magnetic mines.

2

A JOURNEY TO DOVER

IRONICALLY enough, the eve of Dunkirk found Goodeve out of a job and viewing his next appointment with ill-concealed anxiety. In the first few weeks of the war he had discovered that without a knowledge of Admiralty procedure any relatively junior R.N.V.R. officer working on research and development at one of the outlying shore establishments had little chance of securing quick decisions. His investigations into circling torpedoes and the magnetic mine often took him to London, and when he had ferreted out the technical information he wanted from the files in D.S.R.'s department[1] in Archway Block South, close to the Mall, he often stayed on, chatting to the Admiralty civilian officers, until it was time for him to catch the train back to Portsmouth.

From them he learnt much that was to stand him in good stead—the organization for dealing with the dockets bearing suggestions, recommendations, and information which circulated in a constant stream through the "In" and "Out" trays of the various departments; the precise responsibilities of each Staff Division; and just where these sometimes overlapped or failed to meet.

Charles Wright,[2] the Navy's Director of Scientific Research, was a tall, alert man with the wrinkled, weatherbeaten look of the Arctic voyager; he had been physicist to Scott's South Polar expedition before the First World War. Goodeve found him an ally from the start, but a few of the people in Whitehall were frankly critical of the 'interloper from the *Vernon*' who kept on wandering into the department and asking questions. Set in their ways, they liked things to be done through the Right Channels, and they had a strong suspicion that this self-assured young two-and-a-half ringer who drifted into their rooms uninvited, and was always hobnobbing with the civilian officers, would disregard the Right Channels whenever it suited him.

[1] D.S.R. was the Director of Scientific Research.
[2] Now Sir Charles Wright, K.C.B., O.B.E., until recently Director of the Marine Physical Laboratory.

Their resentment of Goodeve, with his impatient, unorthodox approach to problems which, after all, they argued, would be solved perfectly satisfactorily sooner or later by the routine methods, mirrored an attitude of mind not uncommon in Whitehall. In many departments of the Service ministries there were men whose whole lives had been devoted to the strange, abstract ideal of service to a machine. Loyal, hard-working, and conscientious to a degree, they believed implicitly in the routine laid down for them.

All their working lives the machine they served had run at a set tempo, producing after suitable periods of gestation new ships, new aircraft, and new weapons ... new batches of young gentlemen at Dartmouth; new and often impetuous Commanders, who had to be taught on arrival at the Admiralty that the machine had only one strict tempo; and new First Sea Lords, who already knew this from painful experience. It all took time, and if people like Goodeve thought they could short-circuit long-established procedure they would have to be shown that the machine did not take kindly to attempts at acceleration.

Goodeve declined to be shown. The contacts he was making enabled him to speed the progress of various projects he was still supervising at H.M.S. *Vernon*, and he could therefore afford to ignore any hostility he encountered from the minority. It was, after all, a relatively small minority. Many of the Admiralty civilian staff were pleasantly surprised to find a naval officer genuinely interested in their work and problems, and Goodeve's easy informality made him a welcome visitor.

One morning towards the end of May he had a 'phone call from a man he knew in the Admiralty.

"You've just about finished your job at *Vernon*, haven't you?"

"I'm clearing up now," said Goodeve. "Know any interesting jobs going in my line?"

"No," said the voice, "but I know one which *isn't* in your line, and if you don't move fast you'll find yourself landed with it. Harington's put in for you! Just thought I'd warn you."

"Thanks for the tip," said Goodeve ruefully.

He knew Harington well, and he knew just what the job meant. For the rest of the war he would be shackled to an endless, monotonous round of inspecting electrical gear and putting up with Harington's constant browbeating. Harington had a genius for upsetting people, and rumour related that one of his distracted subordinates had thrown a steel filing-cabinet at him!

Goodeve's one hope was Wake-Walker, the pivot round whom all the anti-magnetic-mine measures had centred. At their last meeting Wake-Walker had mentioned a new department which the

Admiralty were setting up under Vice-Admiral Somerville.[1] Unable to get Wake-Walker on the 'phone, he took his courage in both hands and rang up Somerville, only to find he had left for Dover; he had been temporarily detached to assist Admiral Ramsey with Operation Dynamo. It was to Dover that Goodeve went that night.

James Somerville was one of the great characters of the Navy. Just prior to the war he had been Commander-in-Chief, East Indies, and he was already a Vice-Admiral when he was 'invalided' with suspected lung trouble. Whatever the doctors thought, Somerville himself was belligerently certain there was nothing wrong with him, and he supported his views with such power of invective that a later Medical Board quakingly pronounced him fit for limited employment. When he came rampaging back into the Service the Admiralty were looking for a strong personality to speed up the introduction of the greatest brainchild of the military scientists prior to the atomic bomb—the detection and location of aircraft by radar. Somerville, a radio signals specialist, filled the bill, and he was given the imposing 'cover' title of Inspector of Anti-aircraft Weapons and Devices —I.A.A.W. & D. for short.

Goodeve met him in Ramsey's house above the fortress at Dover, and took to him immediately. Behind his bluff manner was a shrewd, wide-ranging mind, and as they snatched a hasty meal they mulled over ideas for anti-aircraft measures, passive defence, and rocket warfare. The mounting German air offensive against Allied shipping and the desperate shortage of close-range weapons to combat it was a theme to which Somerville returned again and again. He was convinced that the danger was not fully appreciated; dive-bombing attacks on coastal traffic and long-range assaults by heavy bombers on the Atlantic convoys could strangle Britain's war supplies. Back in the Dynamo operations room they talked with many interruptions right through the night, Somerville plying the scientist with questions. It was after daybreak when Goodeve walked down the hill to catch the first train for London. In his pocket was a request to the Admiralty scribbled in Somerville's strangely boyish handwriting on a sheet torn from a signal pad. It asked for Goodeve's immediate attachment to I.A.A.W. & D. "Collect a small team and get to work on some of those ideas of yours," were Somerville's parting words. "You'll have a free hand, but I want results, and I want them soon."

A free hand! Goodeve suddenly thought of Harington, and felt again in his pocket to make sure that his new passport to freedom was still there. Then he fell asleep in the crowded carriage, and the train jolted on towards London with hundreds of other men who

Later Admiral of the Fleet Sir James Somerville, G.C.B., G.B.E., D.S.O.

slept too, their rifles and packs strewn in motley confusion about
them—the men snatched overnight from the beaches and shattered
quays of Dunkirk.

Oblivious of this shaping of their destinies, the members of Goodeve's team-to-be were scattered far and wide in this first week of
June 1940.

Nevil Shute Norway, an engineer who wrote increasingly successful novels in his spare time, had been connected with flying all his life.
He had helped to build the airship R.100; he had been managing director of a famous pioneer firm in the light-aircraft industry; and since the
war he had been working with his old chief, Sir Dennistoun Burney,
on the design of a gliding torpedo which the Fleet Air Arm were
interested in. When the Germans overran the Low Countries Norway threw down his slide-rule. What was the point of experimental
work now? England would only be saved by people going off to
fight—not by able-bodied men sitting in offices and designing equipment for use a year or more hence. Norway was forty—too old to
fly on operations, but he had sailed a boat ever since he was a boy
and was well versed in celestial navigation. So he wrote to the
Admiralty, offering his services to the R.N.V.R., who were calling
for "Elderly Yachtsmen," and was promptly accepted.

In the same week the R.N.V.R. acquired another Elderly Yachtsman named Currie. Donald Currie had been through Osborne and
Dartmouth, but left the Royal Navy after the First World War because, as he would often remark to his friends when pulled up for
some minor infraction as a lieutenant R.N.V.R. in the Second War,
he had "found the regulations so boring."

Between the wars he had managed with great success to avoid
regulations and routine of any kind, burying himself in the heart of
Devon, where he painted water-colours, developed a rare culinary
skill (which he inherited from a French mother), and philosophized
over the follies of his acquaintances who chose to fetter themselves
to City stools. When the war came it took some time to persuade
their Lordships that active employment should immediately be found
for an artist from Devon, and even a strong recommendation from
Admiral of the Fleet Lord Cork and Orrery, who remembered the
untidy but resourceful 'snotty' serving under him in H.M.S.
Repulse in 1917, produced no tangible result. Then Currie heard the
call for yachtsmen, and found himself on the parade ground at
H.M.S. *King Alfred*, the vast municipal swimming-bath on the front
at Hove where embryo R.N.V.R. sub-lieutenants were put through
their paces. Like Norway, he was happy at the thought of getting to
sea at last.

HINTS ON THE HARVEY PROJECTOR

Lieutenant Ian Hassall, R.N.V.R., drew this cartoon to warn Harvey Projector crews of the danger from rocket blast. The 'victim' here caricatured is Admiral Sir Frederick Dreyer, one of the Navy's most famous gunnery officers.

32

A HARVEY PROJECTOR MOUNTED ON A COASTAL-GUN SITE

Imperial War Museum

COMMANDER SIR CHARLES GOODEVE, O.B.E., F.R.S., R.N.V.R.

Goodeve, the guiding genius of the Wheezers and Dodgers, later became Vice-Chief of the Naval Staff, Research and Development.

The R.N.V.R. had already rejected a young Cornishman named Menhinick for war service on account of weak eyesight, which rankled not a little with him, for he had joined the London Division of the R.N.V.R. at sixteen. And only a few weeks before the war he had set up a world motor-cycle speed record. Since this achievement involved propelling himself down the Royston–Newmarket road at well over a hundred miles an hour he felt that the Navy were taking an unduly cautious attitude. The Army, to his even greater annoyance, agreed with the Navy, and said he would not make a safe dispatch rider, but they gave him a commission in the R.A.S.C. and put him in command of four 4-inch naval guns, for which they were providing the transport. In this month of June 1940 Alec Menhinick was reasonably content, for, although he was undeniably a 'pongo,' he found himself unexpectedly attached with his four guns, twenty-six soldiers, and a daily rum ration, to a naval establishment, H.M.S. *Excellent*. His immediate task was to await the invasion, and then repel it with his four ancient pieces of ordnance, but he felt that if he remained attached to *Excellent* for long enough there was a sporting chance that the Army would forget all about him.

Some of the others destined to find their way early on into the strange, secret world of Charles Goodeve were already on the reserved list, like Tolman, a cheerful roly-poly young schoolmaster teaching science at Wallasey, and Coulson, a physicist whose researches for the Shirley Institute had led to a directorship of a Cheshire textile firm in his early twenties. Others, like Lane, a dark, restless, intense man who was one of the L.C.C. experts on tree culture, and Terrell, the barrister, were chafing at civilian tasks which had lost their significance. Brinsmead, in peace-time a furniture manufacturer, was already off the beaches with his own 40-foot motor-cruiser. And ashore at Dunkirk, where he had been sent to fly kites in an effort to deter the strafing German fighters, was a retired Commander R.N., John Dove, who could perhaps claim to be the first recruit of all to Goodeve's team of experimenters. For when Goodeve got his new appointment Dove was already serving under Admiral Somerville in the room in the Admiralty Arch which was soon to be the birthplace of some of the strangest activities in the whole war.

C

3

THE ROOM IN ADMIRALTY ARCH

IN addition to speeding the development of radar—the uncanny device for tracking the movements of ships and aircraft—Admiral Somerville was charged with wide responsibilities in meeting the threat of the mounting enemy air offensive against Allied shipping. His mandate covered the whole field from the devising of new weapons and protection of ships to the training of crews.

His department, only now taking shape, came under the Third Sea Lord, Vice-Admiral Bruce Fraser,[1] whose kingdom ranged over all matters of research and production, the supply of everything from ships and guns to ammunition and torpedoes, and the running of the great naval dockyards.

Somerville's little department had as its immediate parent the Admiralty Signal Division (D.S.D.). All the smaller bodies in the Admiralty were placed under the broad supervision of one or other of the permanent Staff Divisions, but Goodeve soon found that D.S.D.'s control over its new and puzzling offspring was purely nominal. So far, few of D.S.D.'s officers had been able to fathom precisely what the Inspector of Anti-aircraft Weapons and Devices was meant to do; he certainly did not appear to have much connexion with Communications. So I.A.A.W. & D. were left in splendid and satisfactory isolation.

Goodeve was in no doubt about his own immediate task. The Navy was desperately short of close-range weapons, and in this high summer of 1940 many merchant ships faced the long hours of daylight with a single machine-gun as their sole armament. One report to reach the Admiralty told of the crew of a coaster, the ammunition of their only Lewis gun exhausted, hurling lumps of coal at an attacking aircraft in impotent defiance. The ships had no means of detecting an approaching 'plane, and attacks were often over in a flash, the German fighter-bombers swooping out of low cloud to spray the unprotected bridges with cannon-fire.

There was no escape in the narrow waters, and every ship leaving

[1] Later Admiral of the Fleet Lord Fraser of North Cape, G.C.B., K.B.E.

the Tyne for London ran the gauntlet with little chance of hitting back. Soon it would be the same far out into the Atlantic, for the enemy were adapting their heavy Focke-Wulf long-range bombers for shipping attacks.

As a first step Goodeve realized that a close study of enemy tactics must be made. And orthodox ideas of naval weapons were of little use; there was no time and not enough raw material to produce elaborately finished breech mechanisms, gun-mountings, and barrels, quite apart from the ammunition problem. If the lifeline was to be held, and the morale of the merchant seamen kept high, the ships must be quickly fitted with new devices altogether for striking at their attackers.

At Somerville's request Richardson had been released from *Vernon* to join the new department, and Goodeve asked the Drafting Commander at H.M.S. *King Alfred* to find him some one with technical knowledge of aircraft. This produced Nevil Shute Norway, still in civilian clothes and in a state of almost apoplectic indignation. Before he had even been in the training-ship long enough to order his uniform he had been pulled out of the ranks and asked several awkward questions about his activities in peace-time. Less than a fortnight after the slide-rule had been cast aside for active service at sea its dejected owner was being told to retrieve it and go to work on some abstruse calculations of the angle of attack of enemy dive-bombers. It was some time before Norway recovered his usual sangfroid.

Another sub-lieutenant, Harwood by name, arrived from *King Alfred*, and Goodeve, still casting round for somebody to collect and analyse information on enemy tactics, discovered Terrell, a man of forceful presence and inventive turn of mind—he was, incidentally, a K.C. and Recorder of Newbury—in search of a job and demonstrating to the head of the Admiralty's personnel branch various gadgets he had made, including an unspillable ink-bottle! So he was roped in too.

Somerville's department proved, on closer inspection, to house a surprising number of people, all crammed into one large room over the Admiralty Arch. There was the Admiral's personal assistant, a retired R.N. Commander named Millar—a tallish, greying man with a pleasant but quietly authoritative manner—and the entire Kite Balloon Section of the Navy, under Commander P. J. M. Penney, R.N., already hard at work organizing the supply of balloons and winch gear to merchant ships. In the early months of the war a project was afoot to send a large naval force into the Baltic, and as some protection against air attack it was decided to fly a mass of balloons above the fleet. Nothing came of the plan at the time, but later balloons proved a useful deterrent to low-flying aircraft, and Somerville, seeing possibilities in the kite as a simpler form of protection for merchant ships, took the section under his wing.

Dove, who was initially a member of Penney's team and had recently been conducting some intriguing experiments at Helston with the only really large kite in the country, which had belonged to Colonel Cody, the original Buffalo Bill, well remembers the sudden invasion of their office by Somerville's new protégés. "There was only one vacant desk, and that really belonged to an Australian Engineer Commander named Ross, then away on sick leave. Goodeve, whom we all regarded as an extremely suspicious character, promptly appropriated this, and before long Richardson, Norway, Terrell, and Harwood were all sitting round it, their papers overflowing on to the floor and quite often on to the adjacent desk of the long-suffering Commander Penney."

Lack of space to work in was, however, the least of Goodeve's immediate worries. Science had played all too little a part in the life of the Navy before the war, and research and development took such a back place that there was a year's wait in the queue for sea trials of new equipment.

The scientist dealing with Service ministries in peace-time had a hard row to hoe, and Goodeve recalled an experience of his own just before the war. A new kind of torpedo, designed to explode immediately beneath its target instead of striking the ship, was about to undergo trials, and an indicator was needed to show the precise position of the missile at the moment of functioning.

Recalling the peculiarity of a gas called phosphine, which explodes on contact with the air, Goodeve devised a means of employing this to advantage. He planned to fit a container filled with phosphine to the head of the torpedo; when the detonator fired the pocket of gas was released, and, rushing to the surface, it would then flare up in a puff of red flame and smoke.

Finding a solution to a problem like this and gaining any support for it were two entirely different matters, however, and to attract attention to this particular proposal Goodeve eventually decided on a ruse. He made a deliberate mistake in the plans he submitted to the Admiralty, his drawings showing the phosphine cylinder fitted the wrong way up inside the torpedo. At this angle the gas would only have dribbled out, and there would have been a fatally long delay before it reached the surface of the sea.

Although it was peace-time and there was no special urgency about the matter Goodeve was promptly summoned to the Admiralty. He was lectured on the extraordinary mistake he had made, and there and then he was offered a substantial sum to continue the development of the apparatus.

Not long afterwards he went to H.M.S. *Vernon*, where his indicator was being tried out, and, to his surprise, he learnt that on the staff there was a man who only a short time earlier had put up a very good suggestion for just such an indicator as the Admiralty were now demanding.

It had consisted of a number of small red rubber balls, inserted in the head of the torpedo. When these shot to the surface they marked the position far longer than Goodeve's puff of phosphine, and Goodeve saw at once that the device was simpler, safer, and cheaper than his own. To his astonishment, he heard that it had been rejected on the grounds that there was 'no staff requirement' for an idea of that kind.

Happily, belated justice was done. The scheme was resurrected and eventually put into operation—but not before Goodeve and others had wasted a great deal of time on evolving what would have been an inferior substitute.

There was, too, the strange case of the French inventor. In the early thirties a series of submarine disasters shocked the nation, and an Admiralty committee was formed to investigate possible safety measures. The French Navy had already adopted the use of sodium peroxide to provide an emergency air supply, and the originator of this system, a certain M. Descartes, offered it to the Admiralty.

Sodium peroxide performs three functions which can be of vital importance in a submarine. It takes up carbon dioxide, which the lungs give out. It absorbs water vapour, which also comes from the lungs. And in doing both these things it gives off oxygen, thus restoring the air.

The Admiralty committee were not noticeably impressed. After much deliberation they sent the papers to the experimental establishment at Porton. There the proposal was closely examined. Back to the committee went a report praising the system highly, and recommending its adoption. No further action was taken for a year, and then, when the committee did bestir themselves, they merely passed the whole matter to the Admiralty Chemist for a further investigation of a minor technical point. The Admiralty Chemist also reported in glowing terms, but another year passed by. The proposal was sent to the Submarine experts, who were invited to have a further look at it. Again opinion was favourable, but the committee, still loath to take any decisive step, were now fighting a stubborn rearguard action. They forwarded the details of M. Descartes' system to the Director of Naval Intelligence.

In due course this department reported that some years earlier M. Descartes had submitted another invention to the Admiralty, entirely unconnected with the proposal under review. And it had proved unsuccessful.

This irrelevant disclosure so alarmed the committee that they dropped the sodium-peroxide idea like a hot brick. The war came, and in the fullness of time it was found that Germany's U-boats were equipped with just the sort of installation which the Admiralty had turned down. Submarine officers, who knew nothing of the background to the whole affair, waxed wrathful and asked what on earth the scientists had been doing for years past. Why, they demanded, had such an unconscionable time been taken to produce similar benefits for the crews of British submarines.

It was the old story of peace-time inertia and reluctance to take any action in any direction. Too many people considered it safer to follow a policy of masterly inactivity, and Goodeve was well aware that a scientific 'ideas unit' composed mainly of R.N.V.R. officers would be none too popular. It would not be easy, either, to recruit the type of officers he now needed.

In the few months before the war it had become increasingly obvious that the armed forces would need scientists in uniform, and unsuccessful efforts were made to form a pool of volunteer scientists who would receive training in the seagoing side of naval service. This would have given them a broad practical training for 'development' work in war. The supporters of this plan did not suggest that uniform was either necessary or suitable for people working in experimental laboratories or drawing-offices, but they insisted that it *was* necessary for officers carrying out trials at sea. War-time trials, they pointed out, had to be controlled by the naval organization working in the area concerned, and had to be co-ordinated with all the other requirements of the war. An officer in uniform would fit more smoothly into such an organization. Goodeve, who had given a lot of thought to this question, argued that, since all wars brought a shortage of manpower and an even greater shortage of executives, the latter ought not to be handicapped by lack of authority or facilities for doing their job. The sort of executive he was looking for now would have to assume heavy responsibilities. He would have to assess the purely naval requirements of some weapon or device, consider the scientific and technical viewpoints, the view of the manufacturer and that of the sailor as well. A uniform, even if it represented no higher rank than a sub-lieutenant R.N.V.R., tended to give its wearer more authority and self-confidence, he contended—but, although the R.A.F. adopted the idea, the Navy was strongly opposed to 'technical people in uniform,' and the pre-war move had been firmly turned down by the Senior Service. The Battle of the Magnetic Mine completely reversed this attitude.

So far Goodeve had now, in addition to Richardson, secured three recruits—Norway, already wrestling with counter-measures for low-level and dive-bomber attacks; Harwood, working on lethal improvements to the first of the 'stop-gap' weapons (a rocket-propelled cable and parachute); and Terrell, immersed in secret intelligence reports. It was obvious that more officers must come from somewhere, for the report which Somerville had approved on his return to the Admiralty launched the new section on to a far wider programme of invention and research. It envisaged a number of highly unusual anti-aircraft devices in which monster rockets and wires played their part; there was to be an investigation of types of explosives and armour; and immediate work on an idea already put up by Norway for detecting aircraft by acoustic means.

For a while Goodeve continued to comb the ranks of *King Alfred* for men with technical training. Other recruits were tracked down in the universities and in industrial firms, and were hurriedly commissioned as officers in the R.N.V.R. Special Branch. In theory all Special Branch officers—distinguished by a band of green cloth between the gold 'rings'—were required to undergo a short course of naval training; often there was only time to teach them how and when to salute, and dissuade them from referring to "the sharp end" when on board ship for trials!

Admiral Somerville and his assistant, Commander Millar, gave every encouragement to their rapidly expanding band of scientists. Millar, who was destined to remain with them throughout the war, had arrived in his present appointment through a confusion of identities. After collecting a Distinguished Service Cross as a sub-lieutenant, fighting against the Turks at Alexandretta in the First War, he was unable for long to conceal the fact that he was colour-blind, and he had to leave the Navy. He then turned to coffee-planting in Kenya, but was called back in 1939 and posted to Kirkwall, where one day he received orders to report to the Admiralty and relieve an experienced Gunnery officer, Commander Sir Charles Madden.

Madden was busy clearing up his papers when Millar reached the Admiralty.

"You're taking over as the Admiral's personal assistant," said Madden.

"There's a mistake over this somewhere," said Millar. "I've never been a Gunnery officer in my life."

Madden, impatiently waiting to turn over to his relief and get to sea, looked at him in astonishment. "Why, you *are* G. D. Millar, aren't you?"

"No. . . . I'm F. Millar, and I don't know the first thing about gunnery."

When he repeated this to the Admiral, Somerville exploded with laughter. "Fine," he roared. "I know precious little myself. We'll make a bloody good pair!"

As it turned out, neither Millar nor Goodeve was destined to serve under Admiral Somerville for long. Hardly had he told the new section to go ahead with their plans when the Admiral called Goodeve into his room one morning.

"You'll have to get on as best you can without me," Somerville said. "I'm off to sea. They want me for some special job."

"What happens after that? Are you coming back, sir?"

Somerville straightened up from the drawer he was emptying and grinned like a schoolboy.

"If you ever see me in the Admiralty again, Goodeve, I reckon I'll be a damned failure! You needn't worry. Admiral Fraser's very interested in what you are doing, and he'll see no one shuts down the department."

In an hour the Admiral was gone. It was ten days later, on the evening of July 2, that the Prime Minister instructed the Admiralty to send to the Flag Officer Commanding Force H, in the Mediterranean, the following signal:

> You are charged with one of the most disagreeable and difficult tasks that a British Admiral has ever been faced with, but we have complete confidence in you and rely on you to carry it out relentlessly.[1]

The melancholy objective of Force H was Oran; its resolute commander, who was later to distinguish himself so greatly at sea in tasks more congenial to him, was James Somerville. The "Instigator of Anti-Aircraft Wheezes and Dodges," as his ghost was to be known, never returned to the Admiralty, but, though they had lost their influential sponsor, his "Wheezers and Dodgers" were now getting well into their stride.

[1] Sir Winston Churchill, *The Second World War*, Vol. II, *Their Finest Hour* (Cassell, 1949), p. 209.

4

FLAME ON THE WATERS

As the days lengthened in that summer of 1940 the threat of invasion loomed. Strangely enough, the Germans made no real attempt to conceal their intentions, and, since pictures taken on photographic reconnaissance at a height of 30,000 feet were often clear enough to show cattle grazing in the fields, it was easy to distinguish the large new ammunition dumps at Antwerp and Terneuzen and the growing concentration of barges in the French and Belgian ports.

On the British side of the Channel preparations were hastened forward to give the barges a warm reception. Second-Lieutenant Menhinick drilled his guns' crews with increasing fervour at Portsmouth, and, after a War Office conference had decided that the problem of transporting and mounting scores of other naval guns which were lying idle presented almost insuperable difficulties in the time available, a man in a bowler hat called on Captain John Hughes-Hallett at the Admiralty, announced that he came from Pickford's, the furniture-removers, and said that his firm could quite easily do the job over the week-end!

Goodeve had made it known that his team of experimentalists were ready to tackle anything. The main purpose of his scientific section was to put up ideas for new weapons and devices and see them through the development stage. But by showing a readiness to try out ideas which might be discarded by more conservative and less energetic departments the section would keep others on their toes. This often meant looking at some of the well-intentioned but wildly impractical technical proposals which flooded ceaselessly into many departments of the Admiralty. Already a man had found his way into Penney's room with plans for a death-ray. This, he suggested, could be mounted in one of the Navy's balloons, and he gave detailed specifications of what the operator in the basket would need in the way of provisions, protective clothing, and signalling devices.

"This is all very well," said Penney, "but what about the death-ray apparatus?"

"Oh, you don't want to worry about that," replied the inventor; "the Admiralty have access to the Secret Archives. . . . There are bound to be several death-rays there, and you can take your choice."

There were cranks who planned to rout the night bombers with searchlight beams which solidified at the appropriate moment; the aircraft was then to be belaboured with the beam until it dived to destruction, but the sponsors of this ingenious weapon were equally vague over the actual method of solidifying the searchlight rays, which, they claimed, was "merely a matter of research and development." Others submitted plans for firing thermite into the air to 'seize up' aircraft engines, and designs for machine-guns fired by centrifugal force, the lightest of which, unfortunately, would have weighed several tons.

Not surprisingly the invasion threat produced a rich crop of fanciful suggestions, among them a plan to electrocute the Germans as they waded ashore, by means of high-tension cables laid on the sea-bed. The protagonists of this idea overlooked the colossal amount of power required; the sea would have boiled before a single invader died of electrocution.

Of all the less orthodox methods put forward for discouraging German visitors the use of flame in various forms seemed to hold a special fascination for naval minds. Perhaps it was an obsession springing subconsciously from the far-away days of Drake and his fire ships. At any rate the view was widely held in naval circles that 'England will again be saved by fire,' and technical objections were brushed aside.

At first the new department kept clear of the flame controversy. Goodeve had never been a great believer in flame for coastal or harbour defence, but the Petroleum Warfare branch of the Ministry of Supply were both energetic and enthusiastic, and the South Coast became ringed by flame traps and weapons of all kinds. Eventually Goodeve's team were drawn into experiments with fire when someone discovered that a flotilla of M.T.B.'s at Felixstowe were anxious to project jets of creosote at German E-boats.

Then two more promising proposals were put forward. A special weapon was needed to defend naval airfields against attacks by glider-borne troops, and Admiral Sir Frederick Dreyer, a famous gunnery officer who was organizing the training of Merchant Navy gun crews with characteristic vigour and foresight, suggested that a flame-thrower mounted on the poop of ships on the East Coast run might be very disconcerting to enemy dive-bomber pilots. If the flame-thrower was designed to fire directly upward the pilot would either have to abandon his line of attack or fly straight through a pillar of fire which might destroy him. The department therefore began to take an active interest in incendiarism, and flame found a passionate advocate in one of Goodeve's new recruits—a certain Lieutenant Parker.

Parker, a tall Irishman with unruly hair, had one consuming enthusiasm, which he lost no time in bringing to Goodeve's notice. He wanted to engineer the greatest holocaust in the history of the world. "Do you remember the explosion at Halifax in 1917, sir?" he said to Goodeve one day. "If you'll let me do a little more research I think I could lay on something much bigger than that in one of the French ports and destroy every German craft in the place."

Goodeve remembered the Nova Scotia disaster. An ammunition ship with 2000 tons of high explosive had blown up and caused terrific damage.

"It's quite simple really," said Parker persuasively. "All we have to do is to get hold of an old tanker, load her with 3000 tons of oil, and sail her unescorted down the Channel with a skeleton crew. The Germans would capture her and take her into port. We would then send another ship, a wooden one, up Channel towards this port, loaded with a thousand tons of liquid oxygen——"

"Half a minute," said Goodeve. "The Germans would hardly fall for this twice in one day off the same port."

"They might if the second ship is disguised as a neutral. She can appear to be about to enter the port, and then change her mind and make off. The Huns will be bound to go after her and bring her in. You could have time-fuses in both ships so that the crew can get away. If the tanker blows up first it will cover the whole harbour with oil. When the second ship goes up and the liquid oxygen is ignited by the oil you'll get the biggest explosion there's ever been. It would destroy the port and everything in it."

Goodeve thought for a minute. It seemed just another wild-cat scheme, but it did have an awkward vestige of plausibility, which made him reluctant to turn it down out of hand. And Parker seemed so fanatically bent on the plan that he didn't want to discourage him too sharply.

"How on earth do you think we're going to lay on a thousand tons of liquid oxygen, for a start?" he asked.

"We could order it from British Oxygen, sir."

Goodeve thought it highly unlikely that British Oxygen would have anything like that amount to spare, but he reached for the 'phone.

"I think the whole idea is impractical," he said, "but I'll ring them up and you can hear for yourself."

He put in the call, expecting that British Oxygen's flat rejection would be audible to Parker, standing in front of his desk. To his astonishment, a brisk voice at the other end said, "A thousand tons? Certainly. Where would you like it delivered? We can get it to any port you name in three days."

"I'll let you know," said Goodeve unenthusiastically, and went to talk to Richardson. Discussing the plan, they had to admit that there *might* be something in it. Liquid oxygen was easy to keep in bulk, for it would not lose more than 2 per cent. of its efficiency for each day it was in the ship. "It looks as if we shall have to let Parker do some further tests before we shoot it down," Goodeve decided. "Tell him to get on to the Fuel Research people at Haslar and ask for facilities."

As a start Parker gained permission to stage a small-scale trial under the supervision of the Admiralty Fuel Research staff. He proposed to flood Haslar Creek with several tons of oil and a ton of liquid oxygen, and set fire to it to see what might happen—an experiment promptly vetoed by the Commander-in-Chief, who said he could not accept the risk of Portsmouth being razed to the ground!

After impassioned entreaties by Parker the authorities relented, and, not without misgivings, he was allowed to conduct a very small-scale experiment on condition that he used only two buckets of the liquid oxygen. So one morning he borrowed a dinghy, and, arming himself with a box of matches, some oil, and his two buckets, he pulled out into the centre of the creek.

Parker was a man who liked doing things on a large scale. Now that the trial had been reduced to such niggling proportions he announced that he would not bother with any remote-control system for setting off the explosion. He poured the oil and oxygen over the side and told the apprehensive watchers ashore that he proposed to throw a lighted match on to the spreading pool. This came as no surprise to the spectators, who knew that Parker had already volunteered to swim from a submarine on actual operations and ignite the fuel himself if there was any difficulty in starting the conflagration. They held their breath, but the first match fizzled out as soon as it hit the surface. Parker paddled a shade nearer and lit another, which he cast right into the centre of the pool. Instead of a deafening explosion, all that happened was a tiny puff of white smoke!

When the crestfallen incendiarist returned to the Admiralty to report his failure he asked eagerly if he could try again with much larger quantities of oxygen. By then, however, Goodeve was certain the scheme had no chance of success.

"If you had failed to come back we would probably have carried your experiment a stage further," he said jocularly. "As it is, I'm

afraid we shall have to concentrate on other more promising methods
of inconveniencing the enemy."

As a means of protecting inadequately armed merchant ships and
the shore bases of the Fleet Air Arm flame did, however, seem to have
possibilities. The Petroleum Warfare team had already produced a
large flame-thrower, and Norway and Lieutenant Jack Cooke,
R.N.V.R., another newcomer destined to do much experimenting
with explosives and strange devices in the years ahead, went to a
small farm called Moody Down, not far from Winchester. Here the
projectors were being developed by the Army with the technical
assistance of research workers from the Anglo-Iranian Oil Company.

"It was a terrifying apparatus," Norway recalls. "The most effective model was one produced by the Lagonda Car Company, which
fired a mixture of diesel oil and tar and had a range of about a
hundred yards. It had a flame thirty feet in diameter and used eight
gallons of fuel a second. In later models made by other companies
the range went up to nearly two hundred yards, with a corresponding increase in fuel consumption. When demonstrated to admirals
and generals it usually appalled and horrified them, and they
ordered equipments in far greater numbers than their tactical use
justified."

The department's first task was to adopt the Lagonda flame-
thrower for airfield defence. Airborne troops landing by glider
require a time of about one minute after touch-down to get out with
their equipment and open fire. In this minute they had to be destroyed. Norway saw that if the flame-gun could be mounted on a
truck with a special fuel tank it could be driven at high speed to the
middle of the airfield, and the enemy could be enveloped in fire before they had time to destroy the truck. Cooke went to work on the
problem, and produced the "Cockatrice"—a two-and-a-half-ton
Bedford lorry armoured to make it invulnerable to rifle-fire. It had
a tank holding two tons of fuel; and the flame-thrower itself,
mounted in a turret behind the cab, could be operated by a gunner
within the turret.

The trials of this awe-inspiring weapon were impressive. They
began with an informal demonstration on Basingstoke Golf Course,
where a small tree was removed at a range of a hundred yards and
an interested spectator from the department, standing fully thirty
yards beyond the target, had the whole of the front of his naval
uniform charred to an unbecoming shade of khaki. Then Cooke gave
the Cockatrice a thorough trial in a blitzed area of East Ham, where
the Army had a street-fighting school.

The Cockatrice was a formidable vehicle, weighing over twelve tons,
and took a lot of stopping when travelling at any speed. On the day

Cooke brought it back from London by road Army manœuvres were being held in the Basingstoke area, and Corporal Mitchenor, one of the Royal Marine team which Cooke was training, found his path suddenly blocked on a bend in the road by a temporary barrier. Quite unable to stop, he charged straight through the road block, whereupon the soldiers guarding the barrier opened fire. Highly incensed, Mitchenor trained round the turret and retaliated with a fierce jet of flaming oil. What with the flying débris from the barrier, the fusillade of shots, and the return fire from the Cockatrice they had an eventful few moments!

The seal was set on the Cockatrice's reputation when three Russian officers arrived at Basingstoke, armed with special passes and permission to watch a demonstration. They made an immense fuss of Cooke, whom they took to be the inventor; here, they kept telling him exultantly, was the perfect weapon for killing "Fascist brutes" in large numbers!

With the Cockatrice a success—though the need for testing it in action in an airborne landing happily never arose—some one suggested to Norway that he should apply flame to the problem of low-flying aircraft. Information on enemy tactics now coming into the department showed that the German pilots specializing in shipping attacks were working to a set pattern. They would approach low over the water, hoping to escape detection from the ship's bridge by merging the 'plane with the sea, particularly at dawn or dusk. They would then zoom up, just clearing the masts, and drop their bombs. For bombing to be accurate, however, the aircraft had to pass right over the target.

The first flame-thrower to go to sea looked rather like a large incinerator, with its round tank and long funnel protruding upward. It was installed on the poop of a very old French trawler called *La Patrie*, whose task it was to attend to the buoys in the swept channel in Spithead. As she was large and slow, and was conveniently based at Portsmouth, where she returned every night, she was ideal for experimental work.

First of all, Norway had to find what deterrent effect the device was likely to have on an aircraft. Fired vertically, it seemed to the watchers on *La Patrie's* deck far more terrifying than the Cockatrice, for the length of the flame was increased by its own heat, and at sea the pillar of fire was now reaching an altitude of at least four hundred feet. The R.A.F. agreed to provide an aircraft for dummy attacks on the trawler, but at this stage Norway's team, much impressed with their early experiments, began to worry about the danger to the pilot. The latter was therefore brought aboard *La Patrie*, and the working of the flame-thrower was carefully explained

to him. Norway told him to make his first dummy attack on the ship
passing well ahead of the bow, where he would be quite safe from
the flame; on succeeding attacks he might venture as close as crossing
the waist of the ship, but he was to come no nearer than that.

The trawler then put to sea, and as the aircraft came out from
the Hampshire coast up went the roaring column of fire. The pilot
crossed the bow, returned, and flew over the waist of the ship; then
he did another couple of runs much closer to the flame, until his
wing-tip was practically passing through it.

"He doesn't seem to think much of it," said Norway to the
trawler's captain as the 'plane disappeared. "Still, we can't do anything in the way of modifications until we've had his report."

The report reached Goodeve two days later. The pilot did not
consider the device very effective as a deterrent, but he thought the
trial had been biased by the fact that he knew exactly what to
expect. The R.A.F. recommended that the dummy attacks should
be repeated with a pilot who had no previous knowledge of the
flame-gun at all; he would not even be told that the weapon incorporated the use of flame. "We have complete confidence that you
will have the flame-thrower sufficiently under control to avoid
destroying our aircraft," the report ended.

This seemed to Norway a very bold proposal, but two days later
he again took his team to sea. This time the aircraft came in low
over the water, making straight for the waist of the ship. When it
was two hundred yards away the pillar of flame shot skyward, but
the pilot never wavered for an instant. He came straight on across
the ship, brushing his wing-tip in the flame. Then he circled and
came back, this time taking half his wing through the inferno of
burning oil.

Much depressed at this second obvious failure, they sent a message
inviting the pilot on board for a drink, to see whether they could get
any line on the mystery.

"It *was* a bit alarming at first sight," he said, "but I can't say I
think it would put off a really experienced chap who was determined
to sink the ship."

"You don't think it's worth going on with it?" some one asked.

"Oh, I don't say that . . . but it might be fairer to try it out on
some one else. I've had a bit of experience of this sort of thing."

"How do you mean?" asked Norway. "What were you doing pre-
war?"

The Flight-Lieutenant looked slightly embarrassed.

"As a matter of fact, I had an odd sort of job. . . . Used to drive
Dodge cars through sheets of plate-glass and walls of fire for a stunt
firm," he said sheepishly.

Norway's team went back a little happier about the flame-thrower's prospects. They had no doubt that the R.A.F. had picked their man for that demonstration, and it came as a shock to them to learn, a few days later, of the death of the flight-lieutenant who had seemed so unconcerned by danger. Flying in thick weather, he had hit a barrage balloon cable.

As it was felt that the Luftwaffe were unlikely to have many pilots with circus experience, the naval flame-thrower went into limited production, and a number of them were mounted in coasters plying between the Thames and the Forth. They were difficult to keep in order, as a very high pressure had to be maintained. And unless the device was expertly handled the ship and her crew were liable to be smothered in tar and oil. Intelligence sources, however, reported one dividend. News of the mysterious new weapon on the poop of some British ships soon got back to Germany, and, whether or not it was cause and effect, the average height of attack soon lifted far above two hundred feet—the level at which the enemy aircraft had hitherto been securing 47 per cent. hits.

Intelligence also revealed that the enemy were having their own setbacks with flame-projectors, and after a very discouraging experience at Le Havre they were believed to have abandoned the struggle. Their own experimental vessel had a long pipe and nozzle running up the mast. On the day they had chosen to demonstrate the device to an impressive array of high-ranking officers in the French port the ship was moved into the centre of the basin for safety. Nevertheless, when the firing key was pressed the entire assembly ashore was deluged with torrents of thick black oil, and no ignition took place at all. Cooke, who had more than once caused similar consternation on board a Methil-bound coaster, was particularly delighted with this report.

The department was destined to have only one further encounter with flame weapons. This came much later in the war, when advanced anti-aircraft guns had long removed the need for flame-throwers at sea, and no invasion of Britain was likely to call the Cockatrice into action.

Studying a forthcoming operation, Combined 'Ops' H.Q. were anxious to find out whether an assault landing-craft entering a harbour loaded with infantry could safely pass through the fire of any flame-thrower which might be mounted on the breakwater. To Goodeve's department came an inquiry about the form of canopy which would be needed to cover the well of the craft.

Norway said flatly that no protection at all was needed. He explained the difficulty of firing a flame-thrower (with its horizontal trajectory, or, if anything, slight upward curve) at an angle of

LIEUTENANT-COMMANDER
L. H. M. LANE, R.N.V.R.

Lane was one of the founder members of the department and an intrepid handler of explosives.

ADMIRAL OF THE FLEET
SIR JAMES SOMERVILLE
ON THE BRIDGE OF
HIS FLAGSHIP

With him is his Chief of Staff, Captain M. J. W. William-Powlett.

Imperial War Museum

48

THE HOLMAN PRO-
JECTOR READY FOR
TRIALS ON THE
MOOR AT PORTH-
TOWAN, NEAR
CAMBORNE

A CORNWALL COUNTY
COUNCIL STEAMROLLER
IS BROUGHT TO THE
MOOR TO AID TRIALS OF
THE FIRST STEAM PRO-
JECTOR, MARCH 1940
Earlier Holman guns were operated
by compressed air.

depression. And he maintained that if the soldiers lay down in the boat they would be safe.

This view was hotly challenged by the Petroleum Warfare branch, who said that the Admiralty did not know what they were talking about, and trials were therefore arranged at Portland, where a large flame-thrower commanded the harbour entrance.

The master of ceremonies at these trials was Robin Byng,[1] a stockily built R.N.V.R. lieutenant who had played a prominent part in developing many weapons and devices for the department. Before the war Byng had owned a Brixham trawler, the *Arthur Rogers*, and he spent the summer of 1939 in her as a member of Dr Edward Bullard's team investigating the Atlantic Shelf. Later, as a civilian, he joined Bullard at H.M.S. *Vernon* to work on the magnetic and acoustic mines, and then, by a masterpiece of bluff (for he had had to leave the Royal Navy many years before owing to weak eyesight), he got himself passed A1 by a Service doctor who failed to notice his contact lenses! To his delight, he was now back in uniform.

For the trial at Portland he procured an old landing-craft, and arranged for it to be towed through the harbour entrance, where the flame-thrower was to fire at it. In the bottom of the craft he placed three dummies, clad in battledress—one at the bow, one amidships, and one at the stern. Inside the battledress of each dummy he put strips of paper coated with greenish-yellow anti-gas detecting paint, which changes colour if heated to the temperature at which skin is scorched.

Admirals and generals turned up in force to watch the trial, and after the landing-craft had passed through the flame Byng extracted the papers from the tunics of the dummies. Not one showed the slightest sign of scorching.

The Petroleum Warfare observers protested that the flame-thrower had not been aimed quite right. Again the landing-craft was towed through the wall of fire without any effect at all, and after several more abortive attempts the trials were called off for the day.

Slightly nonplussed, the critics from the Ministry of Supply then conceded that the men *might* escape the direct effects of the flame, but claimed that they would all have been killed in any case. The well of the boat would, they said, have been filled with the hot products of combustion, and the men would have died from breathing carbon dioxide. It was therefore decided to repeat the trials using cages of animals in the boat, and Byng, who had returned to London to report developments, was told to procure fourteen mice.

Finding mice in the West End of London proved surprisingly difficult. There seemed to be no recognized Admiralty procedure for

[1] Now Earl of Strafford.

D

indenting for them from Naval Stores, and when he suggested that he might buy some mice in the open market Richardson said, "Yes, but have you got a Mouse Licence?"

"No," said Byng.

"Well, then," said Richardson discouragingly, "no one's likely to sell you any mice. You'll have to get a permit. Mice can only be used according to regulations laid down by the Medical Research Council."

This opened up a promising line of attack, and Byng eventually arrived at the Gloucester Hotel, Weymouth, with his fourteen mice and several cages. Next morning he took six of the mice, distributed them among three cages, and placed them in the landing-craft. Once more, before a large gathering of senior officers, the boat was towed through the fiery furnace. The mice showed no ill effects whatever. Several times that day the trial was repeated. The topsides of the assault landing-craft became scorched and blistered, but when the proceedings were called off the mice were still completely unharmed.

Feeling that the department had proved their point, Byng returned to his hotel with the six mice, only to find that of the eight left in his bedroom one had died. In his opinion this was clear proof that the apprehension excited by the flame-thrower was more lethal than the flame-thrower itself—a conclusion which the department had great pleasure in incorporating in their official Admiralty report!

The troubles of Lieutenant Byng were not, however, quite over. He had to return to London early next morning—and he still had thirteen mice on his hands. Late that night he made a cautious reconnaissance of the corridors. And under the door of every bedroom which had a pair of lady's shoes outside it he liberated one mouse!

5

ARMOUR FOR THE BATTLE

By the late summer of 1940 the Wheezers and Dodgers had expanded their activities and their numbers. To the relief of the sorely tried Kite Balloon party, they moved into a large room overlooking Trafalgar Square, where they acquired a valued counsellor in Admiralty procedure—a cheerful and imperturbable Civil Servant named Jamieson; several more recruits from *King Alfred*; and a shorthand typist with golden-red hair named Miss Ottley. As sixteen people were now working in the one room, she had to do all her typing in the passage outside!

To every new recruit Goodeve said much the same thing: "You'll have no set hours and no official leave. You will often be required to work all night as well as all day—and seven days a week if necessary. You'll see many secret documents. Don't talk about what you see."

Many of the early recruits had a faintly piratical air about them. One had been a skipper of a South Sea island schooner; another, who had an impressive red beard, had flown aircraft for the Chinese Republican forces. Currie arrived, protesting, like Norway, that he had joined up to go to sea. Goodeve set him to work on camouflage problems, for he had found, to his astonishment, that in spite of the increasing threat of German air power no serious attention had been paid to camouflage in the Navy since the First World War. Two Staff Divisions in the Admiralty had already been pressing for the camouflage situation to be examined when Goodeve agreed to look into it, but his intervention led to a surprising incident. Into the department stamped an irate officer who introduced himself as Commander Pouter. Marching up to Goodeve, he said angrily, "What's this I hear about your section meddling with camouflage?"

"We're looking into it to see what can be done to make our ships less visible," said Goodeve. "The absence of any form of camouflage is presumably due to the failure, under modern conditions, of the dazzle painting of the Kaiser's war. If no one studies these new conditions nothing will ever get done. . . ."

"I'll have you know that *I* am entirely responsible for all Admiralty policy regarding camouflage," said the Commander, "and that policy is that there shall be *no* camouflage . . . and no experiments either!"

It took Goodeve a few seconds to recover from this. As he got up to open the door for his visitor he turned to Richardson and Currie.

"Our way is now perfectly clear. You're to go straight ahead with the experiments."

To Commander Pouter he said, a little brusquely, "Our report will go to the First Sea Lord. If you wish I will send you a copy."

This classic interview led to the coining in the department of a new term of measurement—the Unit of Obstruction. This unit first became known as the 'Pouter.' On further reflection, however, this seemed altogether too large to have any application inside the Admiralty, where obstruction, it was fervently hoped, would rarely reach such dimensions. So the term 'micro-pouter' was introduced forthwith. From that day it was used to assess all such absurdities. Happily for the war effort, they proved to be rare.

Aiding the Merchant Navy was Goodeve's most urgent task, for the defence of merchant ships was an Admiralty responsibility. Efficient camouflage might obviously help to hide convoys from the searching aircraft, particularly during the danger periods at dawn and dusk. So Currie was sent off on a series of reconnaissance flights from Oban to examine the appearance of ships in different light conditions. From his reports a standard shade of light grey paint was evolved for the side and top colouring of merchant ships.

Passive measures like camouflage, however, only touched the fringe of the problem. The crying need was for more weapons and some form of physical protection for the men who had to face a hail of cannon-gun fire on an open bridge whenever an aircraft attacked them. Before Dunkirk the sole armament of some ships was a Ross rifle; the only organized defence came from a shuttle service of 120 Lewis guns moved from ship to ship, and not until March 1941 was it possible to give each vessel even one machine-gun of her own.

As for protection against enemy fire, armour-plating was out of the question; because of the nearness to the compass it had to be of the non-magnetic type, and there was none of this to spare in the country. The only substitute was a structure of concrete blocks built round the bridge. These had presumably been sanctioned on the principle that some sort of shield against gunfire was better than none at all, but the concrete slabs were proving more dangerous than protective. They cracked and splintered. Often the entire structure would collapse, and once the bridge was out of action the ship was at the mercy of the bombers.

It was Lane who came upon the first slender clue. Lane was not a scientist, but he had a passion for things mechanical, an alert, inquiring mind, and great tenacity. When he first arrived in the department, Goodeve put him on to help Terrell with the analysis of Intelligence reports, and one morning, reading through an account of an air attack on a ship at Dunkirk, he came across a marginal note which intrigued him.

"I noticed that whenever machine-gun bullets struck the deck there were no ricochets," wrote the commanding officer. "The surface of the deck is covered with a cork-filled mastic substance to aid waterproofing."

Lane read this again, and took it over to Terrell.

"Do you think this is worth following up, sir?" he asked. "If the makers could produce thick slabs of this stuff it might give some sort of protection to ships' bridges and gun positions."

"Check on the makers and give them a ring," said Terrell. "It might be a good idea if I went and had a talk with them."

After that things moved fast. Lane found that the mastic—a bituminous cement rather like asphalt—was made by a London firm. Terrell interviewed them with Lane at the Admiralty, and he ordered four sample slabs, and on August 17, a sunny Saturday afternoon, when the Battle of Britain raged over Southern England, Terrell took a revolver and the four targets down to the Road Research Laboratories at Colnbrook. Setting them up on the range near the Laboratories, he fired at them, first with the revolver and then with special armour-piercing bullets. The trial was a hopeless failure. All the rounds went straight through the slabs.

Dr Glanville, head of the Laboratories, was watching.

"I'm sure this mastic stuff has possibilities," said Terrell as they re-examined the targets, "but we must find some way of strengthening it. . . . I've got it—we want two *different* layers for the bullet to penetrate. If we put a thin steel plate at the back of the slab that might do the trick."

They tried again with the same mastic slabs and a backing-plate. This time there was a slight, but quite definite, improvement. Greatly elated, he rang up Goodeve and told him what he had done.

"We've got the answer. If we order another lot of samples we can get them to mix in different types of stone instead of this cork filling. I'll get some one from the makers to come in to the Admiralty to-morrow; if he takes the specifications back with him we should be ready for another trial in forty-eight hours."

"You're an optimist," said Goodeve; "to-morrow's Sunday."

"They won't mind," said Terrell. "They're as keen on this as we are."

At the meeting in the Admiralty that Sunday afternoon Terrell had another idea. He had once been briefed to appear in a lawsuit for a Cornish quarrying company, and he recalled some figures showing the tremendous crushing strength of Penlee granite.

"Can you make me one extra sample this time?" he said. "In the fifth slab I'd like you to mix some Penlee granite chippings in with your mastic stuff."

When the trial was held two days later it was the fifth sample which showed spectacular results. Several armour-piercing rounds barely reached the steel backing-plate.

Terrell was certain now that the department was on the brink of its first major success. All that remained was to discover, by trial and error, an exact formula. He had to find the right size of granite chips; the right proportion for mixing the granite with the mastic; and they must ensure that the new armour would stand up to heat. The ships which fitted it might need its protection in the Red Sea just as much as in the North Atlantic.

The following morning he went to see Captain R. P. Selby, a senior officer of Trade Division, in the Admiralty. Trade Division looked after the convoys. It was their responsibility to find and fit what guns were available, and train the Merchant Navy gunners.

"Would you be interested in a new type of armour, sir?" he asked.

Selby stared at Terrell as if he was some kind of magician.

"Look at these," he said, pointing to a pile of papers on his desk. "All of them are complaints about the protection we've installed up to date. This concrete is splintering and causing heavy casualties. If you've got anything as an alternative it will be a godsend."

"We've discovered an alternative all right," said Terrell. "We're thinking of calling it Plastic Armour, and we're giving it another trial in four days' time. Already we *know* it won't splinter, and it will *stop* A.P. bullets. Would Trade Division like to see it tested?"

"I'll send one of my chaps along," said Selby. "I only hope it's as good as you say it is."

So far all had been plain sailing. With Trade Division interested, thought Terrell, there should be no difficulty in speeding development of the armour if it stood up to its next tests, and he was already wondering how the new department could tackle the problems of mass production when he got a message from Lane.

"Goodeve wants you to join him in Bath straight away," said Lane, when Terrell got back to the room where they worked. "I think there's going to be some trouble with D.N.C. over our armour."

Trouble there certainly was. D.N.C. was the Department of Naval Construction—one of a number of Admiralty bodies evacuated to Bath. Goodeve knew that before the new protection could be for-

mally tested and adopted by the Navy it would have to be approved
by D.N.C. as the Admiralty organization officially responsible for all
matters connected with armour. And the frigid atmosphere at the
meeting that afternoon made it plain that D.N.C. did not welcome
this encroachment on their territory. Unchallenged since the days of
the *Dreadnought*, they were a conservative body, and they viewed
the intervention of this newly formed research section with undis-
guised suspicion.

Goodeve explained how his team, directed by Admiral Somerville
to investigate anti-aircraft problems, had discovered the possibilities
of the new armour. Then Terrell described the successful tests
already made.

"We feel that things have now reached the stage where you may
wish to take over Plastic Armour and conduct firing trials of your
own," said Goodeve.

"As far as we are concerned there will be no firing trials," said
one of the men at the conference table. "It is not necessary to try
this so-called 'armour' of yours. There's nothing new in it. I have
had thirty years' experience in this subject, and I *know* it cannot be
any good."

On this uncompromising note the meeting ended. Although
D.N.C. had refused point-blank to co-operate in any way, their
attitude—as in the case of camouflage—at least gave Terrell a free
hand to carry on his own investigations. Working day and night,
Terrell and the Road Research Laboratory staff soon produced the
new samples, further strengthened by specially screened chippings of
granite from the Penlee quarries in Cornwall. By the end of the week
Plastic Armour had emerged triumphantly from another, stiffer test
on the range, and the critical observers from Trade Division reported
enthusiastically to Captain Selby.

With a success on his hands Goodeve was now in a quandary.
Terrell's energetic researches had produced a revolutionary discovery,
but it was equally obvious that Plastic Armour would be stillborn
unless a way could be found to force D.N.C.'s hand. The opportunity
came when H.M.S. *Excellent*, the gunnery establishment at Portsmouth, heard about the new armour and offered to let their experts
test it.

At Whale Island, the home of naval gunnery, they subjected the
tough black slabs of granite-filled mastic to the most exhaustive trials
they could devise.

"Shall we start with reduced charges?" said Lieutenant-Commander Smith, in charge of the firing party.

"No . . . that won't be necessary," said Terrell. "I think it will
stand up to anything you can do to it."

And it did. From varying angles and distances they fired round after round at it, and the hard cores of the bullets broke up in the mastic. In one series of eleven rounds ten never even made a bulge in the steel backing-plate. After trying in vain to ignite the armour with blow-lamps as a final experiment to test its resistance to fire H.M.S. *Excellent* reported in glowing terms:

> There is no doubt that Plastic Armour is very greatly superior to any other non-magnetic material, excluding non-magnetic bullet-proof steel, so far tried . . . it is most strongly recommended that the fitting of concrete protection should be discontinued and Plastic Armour fitted in its place.

As soon as the trials at H.M.S. *Excellent* were over Goodeve raised the whole matter officially in a docket to D.N.C., with a report of the trials as supporting evidence. The docket asked D.N.C. for their official approval of Plastic Armour so that action in fitting could begin.

Back came the docket with a strongly worded minute denouncing the project as a waste of time.

It was a strange and disturbing *impasse* at a time when war was raging at sea and in the air, and the situation became even more farcical when H.M.S. *Excellent's* report was circulated almost immediately by the Commander-in-Chief, Portsmouth, to many Admiralty departments, praising Plastic Armour and stressing the urgency of adopting it. Goodeve's only desire was to get the armour into service. He realized that D.N.C.'s minute made it doubly difficult for the latter department to change their attitude, so the whole docket was destroyed and D.N.C. were informed of this. After allowing a few days to elapse Goodeve sent to Bath a fresh docket in almost identical words.

By now, however, Plastic Armour was arousing much interest and curiosity in the Admiralty, and Terrell put some some slabs of it on display in the department for a party of very senior officers—among them the First Sea Lord—to inspect after lunch one day.

Examining it while Terrell was at lunch, Norway made the entertaining discovery that it was quite possible to insert a drawing-pin in the armour plate between the granite chippings.

When the V.I.P.'s arrived the largest slab had pinned to it a printed card bearing the startling legend:

PLASTIC ARMOUR—THE ONLY ARMOUR PLATE WHICH WILL TAKE A THUMB TACK!

Goodeve's conciliatory gesture to the inflexible opponents of Plastic Armour at Bath inspired no change of heart. Ignoring the

merits of the new protection, they denounced H.M.S. *Excellent* for
carrying out trials on anything armoured which had not come from
D.N.C.'s department itself. A few days later the controversy took an
even stranger turn when an official who had played the leading part
in obstructing the trials announced that he would be prepared to
withdraw his opposition to the use of the material if the word
'Armour' was dropped.

There could now be no doubt whatever as to the reason underlying the obstruction, and Terrell referred the issue to Captain
Selby, who firmly rejected the suggestion. He knew the title would
give confidence to merchant seamen, who were often mistrustful
of innovations; he knew also that H.M.S. *Excellent's* report
had brought him powerful enough backing from other quarters
in the Admiralty to defeat any further attempts to kill the new
invention.

With keen support from Captain Selby and Trade Division
Terrell went ahead. Road-manufacturing firms with plant lying
idle were recruited to mass-produce the armour. Factories were set
up, and at many ports special plant installed in the open enabled
ships to be fitted with the protection as soon as they came in.

Within a year the success story of Terrell's Plastic Armour could
be charted in impressive statistics. It was made in nearly every sea-
port in the United States, after one of Goodeve's team, Lieutenant-
Commander A. H. Laurie, R.N.V.R., had enterprisingly enlisted
the aid of the New York Police Department's Homicide Section to
experiment with different types of quartz on their range at Hakensack,
New Jersey. And U.S. Navy Department statisticians worked
out that the new protection saved over 44,000,000 dollars' worth
of special steel alone. In Egypt Plastic Armour was made, not
with granite or quartz, but with porphyry—hard purple rock hewn
from quarries which had yielded stone for the tombs of the
Pharaohs.

From Plastic Armour an even tougher protection was developed.
And since some one, with tact born of bitter experience, chose for
it the name of Plastic Protective Plating, peace was made at last with
D.N.C.! Most of the landing-craft which took part in the invasion
were armoured with the plating. In all some 10,000 ships were fitted
with Plastic Armour before the war ended.

Terrell, whose energy and persistence drove the project to success,
stayed with the new department until the production of the armour
was in full swing. Later, in another post, he did outstanding work in
U-boat warfare problems and produced a rocket-accelerated bomb
for attacking the vast enemy submarine pens. To-day exhibits of
Plastic Armour in the Imperial War Museum record the depart-

ment's first triumph, and Terrell's part in it was marked by an award to him of nearly £10,000 when the Royal Commission came to assess the value of war-time inventions.

In the big, gloomy room in Archway Block North there were many other projects afoot. The Department was still small enough for Goodeve to have a detailed knowledge of everybody's work. And as Lane, analysing interrogation reports and garnering a flow of useful information on enemy air tactics from other mysterious sources he would only hint at, drew attention to specific trends in the German offensive against our ships, Goodeve directed research to counter them.

Richardson was already working on improved methods of lighting the night sky so that guns could be aimed with reasonable accuracy. There were conferences on night camouflage and the development of rocket-propelled wire devices; and Lane was urging the importance of producing a workable acoustic warning equipment. He maintained that it should have a special direction-finding gadget incorporated so that guns could be trained more rapidly.

"I'm not convinced that you need this directional aid," said Goodeve. "After all, the acoustic warning itself will get the guns manned, and your ears will give you the direction in ten to thirty seconds after that. Anyway, a directional acoustic would be a complicated affair."

This was typical of his common-sense approach. Goodeve was all for cutting out the frills on the various projects they were examining. It gave the department more chance of rapid progress.

The Acoustic Warning Device was an early brain-child of Norway's. Without radar the merchant ships were at the mercy of aircraft when cloud covered the sky. The first warning they had was the swoop of the 'plane from the grey ceiling above the ship and the whistle of the bombs.

Thinking this problem over, Norway wondered if it was possible to put a device on the masthead which would react to the sound frequencies generated by an aircraft. Working with Sir Dennistoun Burney on the gliding torpedo, he had paid several visits to the research department of a large gramophone company at Hayes, and what he had learnt about acoustic problems there made him certain that something of the sort could be designed.

A search through D.S.R.'s files gave little encouragement. He found reports of extensive trials carried out in the past on board ships with Army listening devices. They had been a failure. Next Norway went to talk to the men who did research into all sound problems for the Services at an establishment in the New Forest; he also revisited his friends at Hayes, and soon experiments evolved an apparatus consisting of twin microphones ingeniously arranged to give a heart-shaped lobe of sensitivity. This helped to screen noises from the ship itself, but if an aircraft came within a range of two miles the listening microphones would pick it up. Immediately a warning bell would ring, and a red light would flash on the bridge.

To speed development of the device I.A.A.W. & D. took on another newcomer, Lieutenant Arthur Biddell, R.N.V.R., who had specialized in sound research for some years before the war. Biddell was no stranger to the sea. He had started his working life as a radio operator in ships of the Royal Mail Line, and soon after joining the Admiralty he found himself afloat again in an old Channel Islands passenger boat off the Firth of Forth, where the warning apparatus was given its trials. The first snag cropped up with the discovery that they would need some form of outer covering to shield the sensitive microphones from the sound of the wind—a teasing problem, for they would obviously have to find a material which did not blanket off the aircraft noises as well.

This led to one of the department's most unusual quests, and England was combed for bathroom loofahs. Like Byng's mice, it was difficult to find enough of them, and in the end 10,000 had to be shipped from abroad. Later on the loofah scarcity prompted further researches, and an even better substitute was discovered in the stuffing of ordinary domestic mattresses!

Biddell now set to work to filter out a variety of other irrelevant noises. In spite of the clever design of the microphones the early models tried at sea proved distinctly fallible. Masters of ships sailing down the Thames Estuary claimed that they always got an 'aircraft' warning from the trams on Southend Pier. Heavy bow waves, and even particularly raucous seagulls, also alerted the device, but gradually Norway and Biddell improved the equipment to such an extent that it would automatically filter out all noises lasting less than four seconds. This rid them of their greatest difficulty, for in the early stages any very loud, sharp noise on board, such as a hatch-cover being slammed down, was liable to set the alarm going, and the men on the bridge would frantically scan the sky for approaching bombers.

The device had one lasting drawback. It reacted just as violently whether an aircraft was friendly or hostile. On the high seas, however, where friendly 'planes were few and far between, it soon proved its value, and on one occasion, when a convoy was steaming slowly across the Atlantic in thick fog, the warning bell in a ship straggling astern rang all the afternoon. The microphones had unerringly picked up the engines of a U-boat stalking them on the surface.

The listening ear was fitted to the masthead of many hundred merchant ships, and it did much to relieve the nervous strain of hard-pressed watch-keeping sailors. It also allowed guns' crews to rest safe in the thought that they could man their guns in time after the warning sounded. Later, in the larger ships, the task of the Acoustic Warning Device was taken over by radar, but this, incidentally, was to encounter its own special problems over filtering out the inappropriate. At Dover in the following year radar operators got some most convincing echoes from gannets; at Gibraltar a 'large force of unidentified aircraft' detected at 5000 feet proved to be gulls wheeling over a passing ship; and a supicious object 'reconnoitring' Malta turned out to be nothing more hostile than a migrating stork![1]

While passive-defence measures like the development of Plastic Armour and the Warning Device were occupying some of Goodeve's team others were examining all manner of strange projects put up to the department.

The weapon shortage, highlighted by Lord Croft's clarion call to arm the Home Guard with pikes, even induced Currie to experiment with a monster catapult in a wood above Honiton, and in turn the department investigated the possibilities of a Dazzle Gun for blinding enemy pilots; a "Galvanized Scatter Gun" for destroying aircraft by delayed action of chemicals; and a high-pressure Water Gun. There was also a more innocuous apparatus called the "Dazzle Flash." This elaborate contraption of mirrors and flash-bulbs was designed to frighten enemy bomber crews by giving an impression that an area was more heavily defended than it really was. Although never brought into service in air attacks it was used by Royal Marine port-defence parties at Dover to simulate cross-Channel bombardment.

The Dazzle Gun, on which Terrell worked with his usual energy, acted on the same principle. It consisted of six gigantic flash-bulbs, mounted on a spindle which could be rotated by a trigger device. Behind the bulbs was a great curved mirror of metal, and it was thought that if by this means a sudden, searing blaze of light could be focused on a pilot coming in for a low-level attack it might temporarily blind him and spoil his aim.

The whole project involved a great deal of painstaking research, mostly carried out in the laboratories of the General Electric Company at Wembley. Special types of flash-lamp were evolved, and testing them in a darkened corridor of the laboratories produced unexpected hazards. The bulbs were liable to explode, showering glass over the assembled scientists and setting light to the heavy velvet curtains which surrounded the 'gun.' More than once the G.E.C.

[1] See *Science at War*.

staff, creeping round the district at night to carry out illumination tests, were pounced on by the local police.

Eventually they rigged up a model ship, armed with the proto-type Dazzle Gun, in the biggest room in the laboratories, and to simulate the attacking aircraft they procured a canteen tea-trolley. Terrell, who always liked to try things out for himself, spent most of one eventful afternoon lying prone on this while he was propelled violently down the laboratory floor and the Dazzle Gun flashed on and off at him.

The results were highly promising, but the experts were not yet satisfied. An additional mirror was introduced, and a rapid reload-ing gear was designed. This stepped up the rate of 'fire' to four flashes in each mirror at short intervals.

After checking calculations of the illumination through civil, nautical, and astronomical twilight, and measuring the reflection properties of ruffled water on a near-by canal, they took the Dazzle Gun to Worthy Down one day at the end of September for its first full-scale trials.

To Currie, diving from the night sky towards the darkened air-field, the Dazzle Gun's debut was distinctly unimpressive. All they saw from the aircraft was a flicker of light as though some one had lit a large match. So further experiments were made, and then the 'gun' was taken to sea in a Channel convoy.

There it was not long before Currie discovered that the success of this strange weapon depended on two irreconcilable factors. If the Dazzle Gun was to achieve any real effect it had to be aimed ex-tremely accurately at the approaching target, like a rifle. But since the operators of the contraption could not see to use their sights after dark the trials afloat ended in stalemate. Two Dazzle Guns were, in fact, manufactured for operational use, but they languished in a naval store until some one cast them on the scrap-heap.

This was a borderline project. Some of the knowledge gained was to prove useful in other, later experiments, but the department were not sorry to see the end of the Dazzle Gun. Goodeve was a shrewd psychologist. Once he had seen the unwieldy nature of the appara-tus he knew that the sailor would never take kindly to a piece of equipment the size of a small mizzen sail which had to be strapped to the shoulders of any unfortunate operator—and then fired nothing more lethal than rays of light! Still, the basic idea had been worth investigating.

6

THE GUN FROM SWITZERLAND

WHEN it became known that Admiral Somerville was not returning to the Admiralty his Research and Development Section gained a new temporary parent. The Signals Division relinquished their authority, and the Wheezers and Dodgers moved under the wing of D.T.S.D.—the Director of Training and Staff Duties. It was through one of the D.T.S.D.'s staff, Commander Stephen Roskill, that Goodeve became involved with the Oerlikon gun.

The story of the Navy's connexion with the Oerlikon had its beginnings several years before the war. In the late twenties study of anti-aircraft defence problems in the Admiralty led to the development of two specialized weapons—a 2-pounder gun with an eight-barrelled mounting which was to become known as the "Chicago Piano," and another gun with four barrels, made by Vickers.

Both had very definite drawbacks. The Chicago Piano was large, heavy, and expensive to build, and its range was relatively short. The Vickers gun also had a limited range, and since it fired shot of very light weight it was unlikely to cause much damage to an aircraft unless it hit a vital spot. In addition to these two weapons a development contract was placed in 1933 for a 4-inch twin mounting gun; but, although about a thousand eventually went into service, they too were large and heavy affairs, and they were not suitable for all classes of warship.

This latter gun did not come into service until 1937. By then it was alarmingly certain that if war broke out in the near future the Royal Navy would start at a serious disadvantage against any adversary with a powerful air arm.

One of the few naval officers to foresee clearly the danger from the air was Lord Louis Mountbatten. In January 1937 he was serving as a commander in the Naval Air Division of the Admiralty when an Austrian named Antoine Gazda was brought to see him.

Gazda produced the plans of a remarkable new weapon designed for use against dive-bombers. It had a very high rate of fire, spewing out cannon shells at 450 to the minute from its single barrel. This was the Oerlikon, and behind its development in a factory in Zürich lay an interesting story.

There had been an Oerlikon engineering firm in Zürich since 1876, but after a spell of great prosperity in the First World War business had slumped in the early twenties. In the autumn of 1923 control passed into the hands of a machine-tool company in Magdeburg, who sent one of their executives, an energetic young man named Buhrle, to take charge of the Zürich plant.

Buhrle quickly saw that the Oerlikon business would never recover its prosperity if its activities were restricted to building machine tools alone. Casting about for new outlets, he discovered that in Seebach, a neighbouring suburb, was an armament firm which had fallen on evil days. It had been making 2-cm. guns for the Germans, who were forbidden by the Treaty of Versailles to build armaments in their own country, but eventually subsidies had dwindled, and with the death of the manager the fortunes of the undertaking declined rapidly.

Buhrle suggested to his employers that they should take over this additional factory, together with the patents, designs, and manufacturing rights of the Seemag gun made there. By 1932 Oerlikon's new staff of designers and constructors had evolved the most up-to-date 2-cm. gun in the world.

It attracted wide attention, and after Lithuania had placed an order others quickly followed from Germany, Japan, and Yugoslavia.

One evening in 1935 Buhrle was dining in a Zürich restaurant, when a friend introduced him to Antoine Gazda, an Austrian who had been trained in Vienna as a mechanical engineer and was now working in Paris. Gazda mentioned that he was on his way to Japan, where he had many influential contacts, and Buhrle suggested that he should join forces there with the Oerlikon agents in that country, Mitsubishi. As a result the Oerlikon gained a large order from the Japanese Government for wing guns for aircraft.

On his return from this successful mission Gazda was sent to England to offer the gun to the British Government. He took with him an impressive film of the Oerlikon in action, and as soon as Lord Louis saw this he realized that here was the very weapon which the Royal Navy so desperately needed.

Within a week he had arranged for Gazda to lecture and show the film to a number of senior officers, including members of the Board of Admiralty, but when the day arrived Gazda found, to his dismay, that he had completely lost his voice. The situation was saved by Mountbatten, who gave a masterly running commentary on the film. In that short time he had studied the technicalities of the gun so thoroughly that even the problem of transposing all the figures in Gazda's notes from metres and millimetres into feet and inches came easily to him.

The lecture was a *tour de force*, but it produced no immediate results, and Mountbatten soon discovered that opinion was strongly ranged against any move to adopt the new gun. Possibly the naval ordnance authorities were loath to act because they had staked their reputations on the existing anti-aircraft weapons, and shrank from the inevitable dislocation and expense of introducing a radically different alternative. Certainly they could, and did, raise the technical objection that at least one feature of its design ran counter to the Navy's strict safety precautions—the Oerlikon breech did not lock and seal before firing. At any rate, the Oerlikon was not looked upon with favour, and all through 1937 and 1938 Lord Louis waged a lone campaign to secure an unprejudiced trial for the revolutionary new anti-aircraft cannon.

There were endless conferences, repeated demonstrations of the gun at naval proving grounds, and the unfortunate Gazda was summoned to no fewer than 238 meetings with Admiralty officials.

To Mountbatten, with his passionate interest in technical progress, this apparent obstruction of a weapon which would increase the fighting efficiency of the Fleet was incomprehensible and distressing. His courageous campaign brought him no popularity with the powers that be, and his opponents even put about ugly rumours that he had a financial interest in pushing the Oerlikon. Although his identity undoubtedly gave him more influence than others of his rank, many officers in similar circumstances would have shrugged their shoulders and done no more about the matter when they found opposition so obdurately aligned against them.

Not so Mountbatten. In a bid to force the hand of the Navy's ordnance advisers he got an Oerlikon fitted to a new type of M.T.B. undergoing trials at Portsmouth, and an officer from Whale Island, where the gun had already been under the microscope, came aboard to give it a further test. But it was not until Admiral Sir Roger Backhouse, the Commander-in-Chief of the Home Fleet, came to dine one evening with Mountbatten at his penthouse in Park Lane that the Oerlikon found a powerful and determined champion in high places.

Admiral Backhouse, a gunnery officer himself, was quick to see the importance of the new cannon, and when he became First Sea Lord the claims of the Oerlikon at last began to receive pressing attention. In 1939 a contract was placed for 1500 of the guns from Switzerland, but so much delay had occurred that we secured only 109 of these desperately needed quick-firing weapons before France fell.

ANTOINE
GAZDA
FIRING THE
OERLIKON
GUN ON THE
PROVING
GROUND AT
WAKEFIELD,
U.S.A.

GAZDA WITH ADMIRAL OF THE
FLEET EARL MOUNTBATTEN OF
BURMA

Mountbatten played a leading part in
persuading the Royal Navy to adopt
the Oerlikon.

COMMANDER F. D. RICHARDSON, R.N.V.R.

Richardson eventually succeeded Goodeve in scientific
control of D.M.W.D.

LIEUTENANT C. F. TOLMAN, R.N.V.R.,
TESTING THE F.B.B. BALLOON IN THE
REFRIGERATING CHAMBER AT WEST MALLING

Once they had made up their minds about the Oerlikon, however, the Admiralty sent to Zürich the best man they could have chosen to supervise and energize production. Steuart Mitchell[1] had had a brilliant record as a young gunnery specialist, but after gaining early promotion his health broke down and he was invalided from the Service. In April 1939, when he went to Switzerland, he was on the civilian staff of the Chief Inspector of Naval Ordnance.

Mitchell found that the Germans were taking a much greater interest than we were in the Oerlikon. The Luftwaffe had ordered an aircraft version as their answer to the Hispano, and a somewhat Gilbertian situation developed when war broke out. The factory at Zürich was busy turning out guns and ammunition for both sides— but all the steel for gun barrels and recoil springs came from Germany, who knew perfectly well that the Oerlikon firm were using some of it to make guns for the Royal Navy.

Strangely enough, the Germans made no attempt to hamper the British contract, but by the morning of June 7, 1940, it was plain to Mitchell that he would be able to get no more guns out of Switzerland. The fall of France was imminent, and Italy was on the brink of war. He arranged for his wife and two naval assistants to leave, and on June 16 he himself tried to escape by car to Spain.

It was a bright moonlight night, and for some hours they made good progress on their journey westward. Eventually, however, they reached the side of a great valley; below them, flowing swiftly towards Lyons, was the river Rhône. At this moment a strong premonition of danger made Mitchell stop the car, and, deciding to reconnoitre the river bank, he clambered down through the scrub at the side of the road. It was lucky he did, for he was still moving cautiously under cover when he saw a squad of German motor-cycle machine-gunners ride on to the bridge below him and dismount. His only escape route in that direction was blocked, and there was nothing for it but a return to Zürich.

With Italy in the war Mitchell's only chance was now to head east, and he set off alone through the Balkans for Turkey. He took with him information about Oerlikon production, drawings of the gun, and three bulky Foreign Office sacks, crammed with enough jewel centres for aircraft instruments to last the Allies several months —a priceless treasure trove, for we were now cut off from our main sources of supply in France and Italy.

Making his way through Turkey and Palestine, Mitchell reached Egypt, and there a 'plane was waiting to take him to England. In three weeks he was back at the Admiralty.

[1] Now Sir Steuart Mitchell, Controller of Guided Weapons and Electronics at the Ministry of Supply.

E

Although an agreement had been reached some months earlier to build the Oerlikon under licence in England, progress had not so far got beyond the planning stage. A factory had been ear-marked at Brighton, but when France fell this was considered too vulnerable, and a new prospective site was suggested at Bangor, in North Wales. The Navy's Director of Armament Supply (D.A.S.) had chosen a well-known civilian engineering firm in the Midlands to make the gun, but they had many other projects on their hands, and there the matter rested. June and July passed, and still no manager for Oerlikon production was appointed.

Normally the manufacture of an established and tested weapon like the Oerlikon would not have concerned Goodeve, but several Gunnery officers in the Admiralty who knew that the new depart-ment was working on 'anti-aircraft weapons and devices' voiced their opinion that more attention might profitably be paid to close-range guns and less to 'devices.' They were well aware that Goodeve could not conjure up guns like rabbits out of a hat, but Commander Roskill, for one, thought that Goodeve's drive and initiative might infuse some sense of urgency into the lagging Oerlikon negotiations.

Goodeve was therefore asked to look into the Oerlikon situation, and after he had talked things over with Mitchell they both went to Bath to confer with the Admiralty department officially responsible for the gun's production. As a scientist in his civilian days Goodeve had always known complete freedom to seek out the facts relevant to any problem on which he was working; in the commercial world competition was regarded as the natural, healthy corrective to in-efficiency. Government establishments, on the other hand, tended to regard competition in an entirely different light, condemning it as 'duplication' and trying to suppress it. The system encouraged resentment of any criticism. It provided for one expert in each sub-ject—and if that expert was rash enough to invite criticism he inevi-tably lost caste. Reflecting on this new environment, Goodeve came to the conclusion that his intervention over the Oerlikon was unlikely to gain him any popularity.

So it proved, and the opening broadside fired at him at the meet-ing took precisely the line expected.

"The fact that you have come down here at all implies quite unjustifiable criticism of us," he heard—and the speaker went on to deliver a homily on the ethics of Government service. Everything was going according to plan. Interference from 'outside' would only slow up the project, he declared. There was no special urgency in building a factory, because they had no machine tools, and if any help *was* needed it could only come from some one with gun-production experience. The meeting broke up on the complacent note that the first Oerlikon might be produced from the British factory in two years' time.

Soon after he got back to London Goodeve was summoned to see the First Sea Lord, Admiral of the Fleet Sir Dudley Pound.

"We seem to be getting no farther with the Oerlikon," said Pound. "What's the reason for all this delay?"

Goodeve explained the incongruous situation—there was no factory because there were no machine tools, and yet the Admiralty were not entitled to any machine tools unless they had a factory to put them in!

Mitchell had actually located a large number of machine tools which would have enabled them to start working on the Oerlikon, but he had been told that these were already earmarked for the Ministry of Aircraft Production. Lord Beaverbrook was the last person to sit back and wait for factories to fall into his lap; he had made sure of getting his factory buildings first, and characteristically he was first in the queue for any machine tools that were going.

Pound listened intently.

"You have my full backing in anything you can do to get the guns," he said.

With this *carte blanche* Goodeve went ahead.

On the way back from a profitless three-day search for a suitable building in the Midlands he noticed from the train some new railway running sheds at Ruislip. These looked ideal for conversion to the factory they needed, but there seemed little chance of persuading the Ministry of Supply to hand them over to the Admiralty unless he resorted to bluff.

He took his courage in his hands. When he appeared before the Chairman of the Allocation Board next morning to state his claim he explained the vital need for the Oerlikon, and then announced boldly that he had 250 machine tools but no factory to put them in. A few moments later he walked out of the meeting with a requisition notice for the Ruislip sheds in his pocket and went to see Sir Percy Mills, the Controller-General of Machine Tools. After waving the requisition note in front of him Goodeve got an initial allocation of tools within a week. At long last the Oerlikon project seemed to be moving ahead.

The next step was to persuade D.A.S. and the firm they had chosen to make the gun that the Ruislip sheds now in their hands provided a sensible alternative to a non-existent factory at Bangor. In addition, a target time for production had to be fixed. This produced a battle royal round the Controller's conference table, with Admiral Fraser acting as a firm referee.

Goodeve's opponents, prophesying prompt destruction of any

project at Ruislip by enemy bombing, lost their case for Bangor; the saving in time by using a ready-made building justified the risk of bomb damage. Argument then switched to the target date for producing the first gun.

Having gone into the design of the Oerlikon with Mitchell and studied the production problems as closely as he could, Goodeve was sure the first gun could be finished in six months. "Ridiculous," said the manufacturer. "Nonsense," said the representative of D.A.S. The discussion raged for three and a half hours before Admiral Fraser rapped on the table.

"Gentlemen, I have to make a decision," he said, "and that decision is that the Oerlikon is to be produced six months from now." Then, turning to the losers of this argument, he added with a mischievous smile, "If you don't know how to do it, ask Goodeve."

At tea after the meeting Goodeve backed his opinion with two wagers. To the Manufacturer he offered a bottle of brandy if a bomb fell on Ruislip before the first Oerlikon was finished; to the Director of Naval Ordnance he promised another if the first Oerlikon took longer than six months.

For a short time there was furious activity. The makers of the gun rushed their architects to Ruislip; London Passenger Transport Board moved their Underground railway coaches out of the sheds; and machine tools began to arrive. It was the machine tools, however, that caused the first serious hitch. There were not enough of them, and it took several pitched battles between Engineer Rear-Admiral Harold Perring, the Admiralty machine-tool controller, and the Ministry of Aircraft Production, who wanted all available tools for making the Hispano gun for their fighters, before Perring, a very forceful character, got what he needed. Goodeve, who had been dealing with personnel problems, also ran up against a snag which threatened to slow up production. There were not enough executives to supervise the work at Ruislip, and by the end of October things looked black. Only thirty of the machine tools had been wired up; the architects and builders were weeks behind schedule, and Goodeve often found himself in sole control at the sheds issuing and approving plans because the manufacturers had no one on the spot to take decisions.

The firm under contract to build the gun had many other projects on their hands for the Services, and they had been used to dealing with the influential M.A.P., whose organization steam-rollered over all supply difficulties for them. Accustomed to every priority, they were unwilling to improvise with the trickle of equipment which the Admiralty could secure now that convoy losses were cutting down supplies of everything from machinery to food. They took the attitude that they could do nothing to hasten the job, and Goodeve, worried at the lack of drive which left the existing resources of the factory idle, was finally forced to report to Admiral Fraser.

The Admiral descended on Ruislip, toured the silent factory, and gave the contracting firm a piece of his mind. As he stamped out he said to Goodeve, "You're in charge from now on. And I want a progress report handed to me personally once a week."

His visit galvanized the manufacturers. Whatever further complications Ruislip might produce, they wanted no more salvos from the Admiral, and every one got down to work. Within a few months the factory was a hive of industry, and Goodeve, who was spending half his time there and half at the Admiralty directing the labours of his research team, began to feel that his somewhat thankless task with the gun was almost at an end. Before he could return to his own department, however, he was involved in two memorable incidents.

When work on the gun began at Ruislip Russia was still an ally of Germany, and Communist agents lost no time in stirring up trouble in the factory. With Ruislip not getting under way until the end of 1940, the Oerlikon management could not pick and choose their workers; they had to take on a very mixed bag, among them a number of undesirables already dismissed from other factories. Here was fertile ground for Communist propaganda.

Agents were infiltrated into key positions, and for some time the shop stewards were able to discover in advance the gist of many decisions taken by the management. Whenever these related to welfare problems a violent agitation would promptly be launched to secure precisely the concessions which were about to be announced. This tactic won the Communists much support as champions of their workmates, until a dummy resolution was deliberately fed into the minutes of the Management Committee, and thus the leakage was traced to a clerk in the drawing-office. He had been passing copies of all confidential memoranda straight to the shop stewards!

The spirit in the factory worried Goodeve. With the country fighting for survival, here were British workmen doing their level best to sabotage the war effort. To bring home to the bulk of the men the importance of the Oerlikon he got permission for a sailor who had fired the gun in action to come down to Ruislip and give a talk one day during the lunch break. The ideal ambassador arrived from one of the home ports—a great, burly Able Seaman who gave a vivid description of the fighting at Narvik, where he had manned an Oerlikon mounted on a railway truck, and his gun had been heavily engaged against the German dive-bombers. In his breezy, natural way he was the best possible advocate for the new gun, and he got a tremendous reception, which made the sequel to his visit all the more bizarre. On the following morning the shop stewards demanded to see the management. "We realize now how important this gun is," said their spokesman, "and we think it's a damned disgrace what you're paying us." With that he thrust forward a claim for higher wages for the whole factory staff, and threatened an immediate strike if this was not granted. The sabotage campaign was stepped up, with more demands, more strikes and threats of strikes—and finally the ringleader and two others overreached themselves.

With the shortage of manpower it was not easy to deal with indiscipline, and permission to dismiss workers had to be secured from the Ministry of Labour. "You'll have to fire them," Goodeve told the works manager, and, to his relief, the permit was given. Two hours after the trouble-makers were sacked the inevitable deputation of shop stewards arrived with an ultimatum. "Either the men are reinstated or we call out the whole works," they said.

Goodeve walked down into the factory and, calling the men round him, he said to the ringleaders hanging on the fringe of the crowd, "Tell your brother-workmen what your complaints are!"

The malcontents had their say, and then Goodeve's turn came. He told the men of the ultimatum which had followed the Able Seaman's talk; he told them about the leakage from confidential meetings, and how in every case the agitators had taken the credit for decisions already made by the management. He then suspended work for the day. "Make up your minds by nine o'clock to-morrow if you want to go on working here," he said bluntly.

That same afternoon another group of workers called on the management, and presented a different ultimatum. *They* threatened a counter-strike if the agitators were re-engaged! By nightfall the story of the real issues behind the dispute had spread through the whole district, and there was a great deal of frank talking in the local pubs. Next day every man in the Oerlikon factory, with the exception of the three who had been dismissed, was back at his job. The workers held a fresh election of shop stewards, and from that time there was no trouble.

The last major problem for Goodeve to tackle before he returned to the Admiralty developed through an unexpected failure in the supply of gun barrels. The elaborate machinery needed to bore the channel through the immensely tough steel they were using failed to arrive. It was a serious bottleneck, threatening a delay of three to four months in the production of the gun. Searching for some way out of the impasse, Goodeve suddenly thought of William Dennis Kendall.

At his engineering works at Grantham Kendall was turning out hundreds of barrels every day for a gun very similar to the Oerlikon —the 20-mm. Hispano which he was making for the R.A.F. Whereas the Oerlikon had to stand up to very rigorous use—it had to be completely waterproof and be capable of instant use after months of idleness and exposure to rough weather—the Hispano was a lighter and much more intricate weapon. But Goodeve knew that Kendall's machines could make barrels for the Oerlikon, and the idea of enlisting the aid of an M.A.P. factory to turn out parts for a naval gun particularly appealed to him. It offered, too, a chance of success at a particularly difficult sport—the game of Beating the Beaver. In the priorities battle Lord Beaverbrook was already one round up, thanks to his astute cornering of the machine tools which the Admiralty had coveted for the Oerlikon.

To Lincolnshire, therefore, went Goodeve and Admiral Perring. They found Kendall a willing ally, and as soon as the predicament of the Oerlikon factory was explained to him he made an immediate offer of fifty barrels within a month, to be followed by a second fifty. "All I want from you is the steel to make them with," he said. "I can't very well use M.A.P.'s steel."

"How are we going to pay your firm for this?" asked Goodeve.

"Oh, don't worry about that," said Kendall cheerfully. "The Beaver will pay the bill; he won't mind a bit."

To Goodeve it seemed distinctly doubtful whether M.A.P.'s boss would, in fact, support this illicit naval co-operation quite so readily if he ever came to hear about it, but Kendall was as good as his word. Within a month fifty barrels had quietly arrived at Ruislip, and this tided the naval factory over its crisis.

With the teething troubles of the Oerlikon now at an end, Goodeve was free to grapple once more with other 'weapons and devices.' From the Admiralty in February and March 1941 he continued to follow reports of the Oerlikon's progress with keen interest. No bomb ever dropped on Ruislip, and although he lost one of his wagered bottles of brandy his estimate was not far wide of the mark. The first gun was finished and sucessfully tested in seven months. Within a year Ruislip was turning out 750 Oerlikons every month, and by the autumn of 1942 this output had risen to 1000. Shadow factories in the West of England were turning out half as many again.

To tell the full story of the gun which played such a vital part in the war at sea would be out of place here, for Charles Goodeve and the members of his team who helped in the birth of the Ruislip factory only appeared in this first phase. But the American venture which had its beginnings in Mitchell's genius for organization and improvisation calls for special mention.

To insure against the destruction of the Ruislip factory by enemy bombing Mitchell had been sent to America in October 1940 to set up an organization for making the gun there. The difficulties he had to contend with from the start were enough to dismay anyone less determined, for he found a nation still at peace, and, with all production geared to peace-time needs, no large firm would look at the Oerlikon contract. Mitchell turned to the small jobbing firms in New England. He had an Admiralty credit for 40,000,000 dollars and soon he had persuaded over a hundred of the little firms to turn out parts for the Oerlikon in driblets of twenty and thirty. A small mill was leased in Providence, Rhode Island, and equipped with thousands of second-hand machine tools. Mitchell set to work to convert all his Swiss drawings of the gun; every calculation had to be transposed from millimetres to inches. The works at Zürich had shipped a gun for America to act as a prototype, but it fell into the hands of the Germans at Bordeaux. Another was then sent by destroyer from England.

In spite of all these early setbacks Mitchell felt confident enough to cable the Admiralty a month after he arrived, giving an estimate of seven months for production of the first gun, but before they could go ahead there was an all-important hurdle to clear.

No war material could be made in the United States unless it was considered suitable for use by the American forces. The fate of the Oerlikon therefore hinged on the opinion of the U.S. Navy, and to their proving ground at Dahlgren one day came Captain William Blandy, then serving in the Bureau of Ordnance as an anti-aircraft specialist. Manning the gun himself, Mitchell fired bursts at a strip of armour plate, at an aircraft wing, and at a self-sealing tank. The Captain said little, and Mitchell could not make out whether he was impressed or not.

After some minutes Mitchell sat him in the seat behind the gun and strapped up the harness. "Just write B for Blandy in the sky. . . . That'll show you how easily the gun handles," he said. Captain Blandy began a little gingerly, but he quickly warmed to his work as he neared the lower half of the letter B. When he unbuttoned his harness he was grinning broadly. "Well, Commander," he said, "I guess we'll buy that!" And that was all. In precisely twenty minutes one man, acting on his own judgment, had reached a decision which had taken the Admiralty eighteen months of trials and bitter argument.[1] Admittedly the U.S. Navy by then had the benefit of a report from the Admiralty on the performance of the gun in action, and on a visit to Washington Mountbatten himself had confirmed the Oerli-

[1] Captain Blandy was later to become one of the great naval figures of the war, and he was Commander-in-Chief of the first atom trials at Bikini Atoll.

kon's potentialities—but the speed with which the American Navy acted was impressive.

For their country too the war clouds were gathering now, and on the afternoon of Pearl Harbour Mitchell had a 'phone call. "We're commandeering everything you've got," said the voice at the other end of the line. The quick-firing cannon gun from Switzerland was a vital factor in getting the U.S. Navy back into the fight which had begun so disastrously for them, and before long they were fitting as many as 90 Oerlikons into one ship.

Mitchell worked on in the States for two more years, and he never ceased to marvel at the flexibility of American industry. There *was* no ammunition industry there at the start. It simply did not exist, and the Americans had to be shown every move—how to make cartridge cases and filling plant, how to develop propellant which matched the ballistics of the gun, and how to develop the filling of primer caps and shells with new types of explosives. But in the end they were turning out 30,000,000 rounds every month and making as many Oerlikon guns every eighteen hours as the Admiralty had ordered altogether when they handed out the first contract to the factory in Zürich.

Cold statistics reveal that the United States alone spent 2,000,800,000,000 dollars on the cannon which Earl Mountbatten, now Britain's First Sea Lord, had had to fight so hard and so long to introduce into the Royal Navy—and they employed over 460,000 men and women to make it.

7

COUNTERBLAST! THE ROCKET WAR

ALTHOUGH the invasion threat passed, the closing months of 1940 were anxious ones for the Admiralty. Between May and December 745 British, Allied, and neutral ships were sunk, and, writing to President Roosevelt in December, the Prime Minister described the situation as almost comparable to the worst year of the last war.

In the five weeks ending November 3 losses reached a total of 420,000 tons. Our estimate of annual tonnage which ought to be imported in order to maintain our effort at full strength is 43 million. The tonnage entering in September was only at the rate of 37 million, and in October at 38 million. Were this diminution to continue at this rate it would be fatal.[1]

Although the Wheezers and Dodgers had been chiefly concerned with anti-aircraft problems at the start, their readiness to tackle anything soon involved them in every sphere of the war at sea. In the early stages they had had to 'sell' their wares to other departments in a stronger position for pushing them through official channels, but as they became better known various naval Staff Divisions brought problems to *them*. By the time Goodeve became involved at Ruislip his team were hard at work on all kinds of counter-measures to the enemy shipping blockade. Dove was exploring radar deception problems with Dr R. H. Purcell[2] and a tall young South African R.N.V.R. lieutenant named Harris; new anti-aircraft wire devices brought frequent conferences with a Sapper major, Millis Jefferis,[3] who had taken over the headquarters of Radio Normandie, in Portland Place, where he was conducting strange researches with high explosives; and Norway was now engrossed in experiments with rockets.

[1] Sir Winston Churchill, *The Second World War*, Vol. II, p. 495.
[2] Now Chief Scientific Adviser to the Home Office.
[3] Later the Sapper major became Major-General Sir Millis Jefferis, K.B.E., M.C.

With the shortage of guns the rocket seemed the only substitute. It was simple to make, and it needed no elaborate barrel or mounting. Professor Lindemann,[1] the Prime Minister's scientific adviser, fore-saw the rocket supplanting the gun altogether, and intensive research into the development of 2-inch and 3-inch rockets was launched by a team headed by Sir Alwyn Crow, first at Fort Halstead and later at Aberporth, on the Welsh coast.

Goodeve did not share Lindemann's enthusiasm for the rocket as a substitute for the gun, but considered that its peculiar characteris-tics might prove useful. It was a highly capricious missile in these early days, and its tendency to do the unexpected was destined to give several members of his team some hair-raising experiences. But he realized that rocket weapons offered the only immediate hope for the merchant ships, and the Inspectorate began its own programme of research and development to apply Crow's rockets to ships.

The first outcome of this was a fearsome device called the "Pig Trough," which Norway designed to shoot down dive-bombers. To keep it pointing vertically while the ship rolled it had a swinging mounting which looked like a large umbrella-stand, and into this were crammed fourteen rockets (then known as U.P.'s[2]), each carry-ing a 2-pounder shell. The German dive-bombers attacking a ship had to pass immediately over the vessel as they pulled out of their dive, and the Pig Trough gave the effect of a monster shotgun, laying a vertical barrage in the path of the attacking 'plane. The inaccuracy of the individual rockets was a blessing, as it gave a good spread to the shots.

The first sea trials of the Pig Trough were held in H.M.S. *Conqueror*, a 900-ton yacht which in peace-time had been owned by Gordon Selfridge. She was now an experimental vessel, and, armed with a wide variety of unorthodox devices, she used to trail her coat off the French coast. Her ship's company took the Pig Trough in their stride, but early acquaintance with the explosive umbrella-stand showed that the weapon had to be treated with marked respect. The fuse was operated by vanes which revolved to bring it to the striking position, but unfortunately its designers had not provided an effective method of stopping these vanes turning prematurely. As a result the rounds were often on the verge of explosion when they were lifted into position in the mounting.

Working under Norway was an able engineer named Goodfellow, who was to do a good deal of experimenting with rockets in his first

---

[1] Professor Lindemann was in 1941 created first Baron Cherwell. He was made a Privy Councillor in the following year, and a Companion of Honour in 1953.
[2] Abbreviation of 'Unrotating Projectiles.'

year in the department. A phlegmatic man, not given to superstition, even Goodfellow regarded Friday the 13th as a singularly ill-chosen date for the initial sea trials of the Pig Trough, and his misgivings increased when one of the early salvos brought down a seagull. After that everything went wrong. Before the rocket shells fired the vanes on the fuse were supposed to do four and a half turns, but one of the early rounds he handled had plainly been ill-treated in transit. Its fuse had reached its last half-turn as he picked it up, and he was holding the round in his arms, when he saw a sudden puff of smoke. All he could do was to hurl it into the scuppers and dive for the deck. In the resulting explosion one of the *Conqueror's* crew was wounded painfully but not seriously in the posterior! Worse was to follow, for a cascade of Pig Trough rockets from one salvo fell back on the ship, several rounds penetrating two decks and exploding in the engine-room.

The fuse continued to give trouble, and Goodfellow spent much of his time dumping live rounds over the side into deep water before the Admiralty called for the withdrawal of the initial supply altogether and redesigned the fuse with an efficient safety-pin. In due course the Pig Trough became the first rocket weapon to be installed in merchant ships. Its success was limited, for the slung mounting was not steady enough to give the required accuracy, but it was undeniably impressive to see in action, and it did at least give the hard-pressed merchant seamen something to hit back with.

Norway's next venture was a shore-based rocket projector called the "Radiator." Although, now that winter had set in, there was no likelihood of a major invasion attempt, it was thought that the enemy might well try again in the spring, and the Admiralty called for a weapon which could be mounted at the mouths of rivers, to fire on approaching landing-craft. Once again speed was the essence of the problem; Norway had to find a simple contrivance which could be easily mass-produced at a time when the country was desperately short of steel. The Radiator was simple enough; it fired salvos of ten 2-inch rockets horizontally, and it did not have to be elevated or trained. Again, the inaccuracy of the rocket was useful.

For its trials a secluded stretch of water west of Aldeburgh, in Suffolk, was chosen, and Tolman, who by then had finished his abstruse gunnery calculations in the office in Archway Block North, went down to Suffolk with Brinsmead, another new recruit to the department. When they arrived and unpacked their gear they found they had not brought a firing switch with them, so an ordinary cheap tumbler switch was bought at a shop in the nearest village. Rocket weapons have one particularly unpleasant trait; at the moment of firing a searing tongue of flame belches from the rear of the mounting. Mindful of this, Tolman and Brinsmead followed a set safety routine, and two switches—a safety switch and a firing switch—had to be brought into operation before each salvo was loosed off across the marshes.

When the Radiator was wired up they fired several rounds successfully, and they were both standing behind the rocket gun, when Brinsmead said, "Let's try one more salvo, and then pack up." He flicked over the safety switch, and Tolman had just started to walk across to operate the firing switch when there was a tremendous explosion. The tumbler switch had short-circuited, everything was enveloped in flame, and Brinsmead, standing right in the path of the blast, was instantly scorched brown from head to foot. Several discs of thick millboard from the base of the rockets struck Tolman, hurling him flat on his face, but he got off lightly, his only substantial wound being caused by a most unlikely projectile—a spirit-level, which the blast had swept from a bench at the rear of the mounting. The arrival back at the Admiralty of the Radiator trial team caused quite a stir, for the unfortunate Brinsmead had lost his eyebrows, his eyelashes, and most of his hair—and he was deaf for several weeks afterwards. It was a salutary lesson in safety precautions!

Radiator passed its trials with no other mishaps, and many of these anti-invasion rocket guns were installed on the East Coast. By this time Goodeve's team had learnt a good deal about rockets and their possibilities, and Goodfellow, studying the shortcomings of the unloved Pig Trough, evolved a much more ingenious and advanced rocket weapon for ships.

Christened the "Strength through Joy," it consisted of two large projectors connected by hydraulic pipes to a remote-control cabin rather like a squirrel's cage which contained a sight and a joy-stick. When the layer of the gun had strapped himself into a sort of cradle beneath the sight and grasped the joy-stick he could swing the rockets to any angle he wanted by moving up or down steps inside his circular steel pillbox. By this means he could engage an enemy aircraft coming in low over the water, follow its course right over the ship, and continue to attack it as it flew away.

On the drawing-board the Strength through Joy looked an ingenious and formidable weapon, and since there were only forty component parts in the whole device it had the added merit of simplicity.

The first demonstration model was soon completed in the works of a famous car company in the Midlands, but a heavy air raid destroyed the factory. No trace could be found of the Strength through Joy, and only one of Goodfellow's drawings survived the raid. Working night and day with another engineering firm a few miles away, he made an entirely new set of drawings in three days, and three weeks later a new prototype was loaded on to a lorry and sent south for trials at Portsmouth.

On its way through London the lorry halted on the Horse Guards Parade so that Goodeve and some of the senior officers from the D.E.M.S.[1] organization could inspect it. One or two admirals, filled with curiosity, also emerged, and examined the Strength through Joy with much interest, and the High Brass became thicker and thicker round the parked truck, until one of the Board of Admiralty went into Number 10 Downing Street and brought out Winston Churchill himself.

The Prime Minister climbed into the control cabin and swung himself on the sight for a minute or two, doing gymnastics and watching the rocket projector follow his movements at a distance. "A very impressive weapon," he said when he emerged. "Order a thousand of them!"

Some one hesitantly remarked that the Strength through Joy had not done any trials. The Prime Minister reddened.

"I said, order a thousand of them."

So a thousand were ordered—and then the new rocket weapon developed a ghastly snag. The hydraulic follow-up mechanism which guided the movement of the projector from the sight by remote control was supposed to be accurate to within a quarter of a degree—a margin which would have been more than satisfactory for a shotgun weapon of this sort. But, although the mechanism attained this degree of accuracy in the hands of the makers, it was an alarmingly different story at sea.

By the time the Strength through Joy was ready for its trials on board ship Norway's rocket-development team had been strengthened by the redoubtable Menhinick, last heard of as an Army officer at Portsmouth. Alec Menhinick's arrival at Archway Block North came about in a way unusual even for recruits to the unorthodox circle of the Wheezers and Dodgers; it was mainly due to an ancient tank which for twenty-two years had sat, embedded in concrete, on a plinth overlooking the jetty at Whale Island. When the invasion scare was at its height Second-Lieutenant Menhinick had taken his four naval guns and twenty-six soldiers to Suffolk to repel the enemy. After three weeks of inactivity he was ordered to hand over his guns and some of his men to an Army unit at Wickham Market and return to Portsmouth to await further orders.

[1] Defensively Equipped Merchant Ships, a branch of Trade Division responsible for the arming of the Merchant Navy.

This suited Menhinick down to the ground. It meant that, for the time being at least, he was still attached to the Navy.

"What are you going to do now?" asked Captain Brind, who was commanding H.M.S. *Excellent*.

"I'll find something," said Menhinick. He was certain of one thing only. He had no desire to be summoned back to the R.A.S.C., and, casting round for something to occupy his attention, he thought of the Whale Island tank.

This proved on closer inspection to be a 105-horse-power Daimler Mark II, presented by the Army to *Excellent* in 1918. To Menhinick it seemed a pity it should be lying idle on its concrete slab at a time like this. Even if it *was* a quarter of a century old it might still make a useful addition to the defences of Portsmouth if it could be persuaded to function.

Captain Brind warmly agreed, and Menhinick set to work. A number of parts had been removed from the engine: the external oil-pipes had rusted away; and some of the controls were missing. The engine itself was thick with rust.

Daimler's had no spare parts, but a call on the Lord Mayor of Portsmouth produced permission to strip another presentation tank which reposed on Southsea Common. The naval dockyard made some oil-pipes, and after spraying the tracks every day for a month with a mixture of paraffin and oil Menhinick started the clattering engines and drove the veteran gingerly off its plinth. Watched by an admiring crowd of naval officers, he and a corporal then set off on their first trial run, with a large White Ensign fluttering proudly from the tank's stern.

They safely negotiated the river-bed crossing from Whale Island to the mainland, and headed for a hostelry in Copnor Road, Portsmouth. The tank proved difficult to steer, for neither Menhinick nor the corporal could see out to either side, and the sharp camber of the road added to their problems.

To their surprise and relief they reached the Traveller's Rest without mishap, and there the giant was refreshed with forty gallons of water while Menhinick and his companion—hot, exhausted, and covered in oil—dispatched several pints of beer. They then began the return journey.

With their field of vision limited by the giant tracks, and both of them deafened by the shattering noise inside the tank, they thundered towards Whale Island blissfully unaware of the disaster about to befall them. Suddenly Menhinick sighted a policeman dancing up and down in the centre of the road and waving his arms. He braked as hard as he dared, and the 27-ton tank came to a grinding halt. When they clambered out they found, to their consternation, the total wreckage of a commercial traveller's saloon car pinned under the tank's left sponson. The sponson had literally sliced the car in half as it stood parked and, fortunately, empty at the side of the road.

"The owner was very good about it," said Menhinick afterwards, "but we were not insured, and the outlook seemed pretty black as we disentangled ourselves from the crushed remains of the car and crawled back to *Excellent*." The Navy, however, came to the rescue, half the bill for damages being appropriately passed through the Gunnery Improvement Fund.

They were still wondering how to meet the rest of the bill, when the Corporal had a brainwave and volunteered to call on the Lord Mayor, who had taken a great interest in their activities with the tank. He emerged with a generous grant from the Lord Mayor's War Fund.

With the recommissioning of the tank, H.M.S. *Excellent* now had a powerful mobile fortress of their own, and Captain Brind, impressed with Menhinick's initiative, said, "I'm putting in a commendation to your Commanding Officer for your work on the tank."

"I'd much rather you didn't, sir," said Menhinick, aghast. "Once they're reminded where I am they're bound to post me away from *Excellent*. I suppose there's no chance of a transfer to the Navy?"

"There might be," said Brind. "I'll see what I can do." With the backing of Brind's recommendation, the Admiralty took a more friendly view of Second-Lieutenant Menhinick when he applied for the second time to join the R.N.V.R., and the transfer went through. Meanwhile Goodeve had just sent a request to *King Alfred* for another officer with some mechanical aptitude to be appointed to his section, and, still in his Army uniform, Alec Menhinick went up to London for an interview.

His posting to what seemed a highly scientific department of the Admiralty filled him with misgivings, and he voiced these to Goodeve.

"You know I'm not a scientist, sir. . . . I can hardly add or subtract."

Goodeve rose from his desk and led him to the door of his room. "Look, Menhinick," he said. "Out there are all sorts of clever chaps with slide-rules who spend all day adding and subtracting. If you ever have any adding or subtracting to do just give it to them!"

Alec Menhinick soon found his fears were groundless. He had wanted excitement, and in the next four years he found it in full measure. Goodeve had engaged him for war trials. Within a few weeks of his arrival in the Admiralty Lieutenant Menhinick, R.N.V.R., was wounded and swimming for his life in the North Sea

A SWORDFISH AIRCRAFT LANDS ON THE LILY FLOATING AIRFIELD
ASSEMBLED OFF LAMLASH, ISLE OF ARRAN

RONALD HAMILTON AND HIS SON PETER
Peter assisted his father in the trials of Swiss Roll.

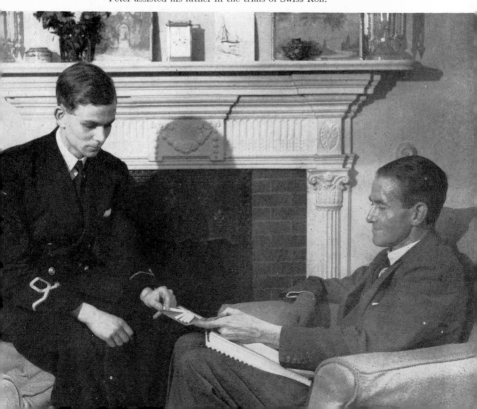

AN ARTIST'S IMPRESSION, BY CLIVE UPTTON, OF AN ARMY TRUCK NEGOTIATING RONALD HAMILTON'S SWISS ROLL, WHILE

when the ship in which he was testing the latest rocket weapon was bombed and sunk under him.

With the Prime Minister's interest aroused, the first Strength through Joy was soon ready for sea trials, and it had its first unhappy baptism in the Kilbrennan Sound, south of Arran Island.

Menhinick checked over the equipment. Everything seemed in order, and he watched the gunlayer strap himself into the harness below the sight in his revolving cabin and test the controls, the two batteries of rockets swivelling easily and obediently as he moved the joy-stick. Then the aircraft came in sight, heading towards the ship with its towed target.

Just as the initial firing order was given from the bridge something made Menhinick glance over his shoulder at the projectors. To his horror, he saw them gradually begin to sag towards the deck; there was a fault in the hydraulic system, and they were no longer answering to the controls.

Watching the target through his glasses, the Commander R.N. in charge of the trials was unaware of anything amiss, and at this instant he shouted, "Fire!"

"Stop everything!" bellowed the Captain of the ship, who had heard Menhinick's startled exclamation and saw the projectors still drooping towards the deck. It was too late. The firing key was pressed just as the rockets sagged to their limit, and the full salvo went screaming low over the deck into the sea just off the port side, throwing up a towering column of black foam.

For a moment there was an awestruck silence, and then the Captain spoke.

"A fantastic weapon, Menhinick," he observed dryly, "a really fantastic weapon!"

Hard though they tried, Norway's rocket team and the makers of the Strength through Joy were unable to eliminate this fatal flaw. However well it performed at the works, and on trials ashore, it went wrong with unfailing regularity at sea. Perhaps people were too busy to give it the careful attention it needed; at any rate, the connexion between the sight and the projectors was frequently so erratic that an error of ten degrees was common. Only a few of the thousand were ever made, and these were installed in merchant ships, where they proved highly unpopular. It was not until the department turned their attention to two new devices, the Pillar Box and the Harvey Projector, that real progress was made,

The Pillar Box, so called because it looked just like one, was operated by a man who shut himself inside a circular, swivelling cabin with a bank of 2-inch rockets on either hand of him outside

F

the casing. There were fourteen rockets, and he could train or elevate them by moving levers mounted on a contraption resembling the handlebars of a bicycle.

Designed by a certain Lieutenant Hinton, on D.N.O.'s staff at Bath, it was a much more refined affair than its predecessors, and more expensive to make, but by the time it went into production the pressure on the factories was easing and the Oerlikon was coming along. Norway's team helped with its development, but the rocket weapon which occupied most of their time was the Harvey Projector.

With Professor Lindemann's backing, the Harvey had been made in large numbers for the Army, who disliked it intensely, and it had no refinements whatever when Norway saw it first. In appearance it was starkly functional, several pieces of gas-piping being mounted on a pedestal composed mainly of other pieces of gas-piping. It had tin shields on either side, and into each of these was built a glass window with crossed lines to provide a rough-and-ready sight.

Down the centre of this ugly contraption ran two rails, and on these lay a single rocket shell. If the mounting of the Harvey was unimpressive to look at, the projectile itself was a very different matter. Over nine feet long, it had an aerodynamic brass fuse in its nose, carried nearly a stone of high explosive and cordite, and was capable of travelling at least seven miles. Heath Robinson himself would have been proud of the firing mechanism, which was actuated by a small Ever Ready torch battery and a household bell-push!

At first sight the Harvey was an unpromising weapon for sea service, but the Navy were in no position to pick and choose, and Norway went to work on it at the Ministry of Supply's rocket-testing range at Aberporth, a remote place on the Welsh coast near Cardigan. His team included Menhinick, Cooke, and another R.N.V.R. lieutenant, Ian Hassall, son of the famous cartoonist.

Even in the unconventional setting of Goodeve's band of experimentalists Hassall was a notable character. Older than most R.N.V.R. recruits to the department, he had travelled the world and been many things in his time—a welterweight boxer of some ability, an artist, cow-puncher, and sailor as well. He had great physical strength, and could smash wooden planks with his bare fists without any apparent discomfort! And he was something of a rebel—a highly engaging rebel, who delighted in drawing brilliantly mischievous cartoons of his senior officers. Hassall had not been long in the department when he drew an instructional picture of the Harvey Projector to warn gun crews against the danger of flame blast. This was most necessary, for when each Harvey round left its guide rails a roaring tongue of fire 15 feet long rushed back from the mounting. The illustration was just what Norway wanted, but in the background, minus his trousers, which had been removed by the blast, was an unmistakable caricature of Admiral Sir Frederick Dreyer, whose wrath was only appeased when Hassall asked him to accept the original of his sketch.

Norway's team had almost completed their modifications to the Harvey Projector when a large party of senior Army officers and civilians, among them Professor Lawrence, President Roosevelt's scientific adviser, descended on Aberporth for a demonstration of various weapons undergoing trials there.

As the Navy's sole representatives, Hassall and Cooke were allotted a star rôle with Harvey, and as they stood to attention in their concrete emplacement high on the cliff-head the generals gathered round and gazed with awe at the huge rocket lying on its rails.

"I suppose you can't get much accuracy with these contrivances, eh?" queried one of them.

"Oh, I don't know about that, sir," said Hassall airily. "It all depends how they're handled, you know." Glancing out to sea, where the guns had been firing all morning at a glider target suspended below a balloon, he added, out of sheer bravado, "Would you like us to see if we can do something really difficult? How about cutting the balloon cable away from the ship, for instance?"

The generals looked astonished, as well they might. At a range of one and a half miles they could barely see the cable. In point of fact the Harvey had no precise accuracy at all, and no one knew this better than Hassall. But he would have to go through with it now.

On the previous evening he and Cooke had rehearsed an entirely meaningless jargon of shouted commands to impress their visitors, and as they began bellowing at each other the generals backed away from the projector. With a belch of flame the rocket left the rails, and it was Hassall's turn for astonishment. Suddenly the balloon jerked and rose slowly away from the ship, its cable dangling. With one single, incredibly lucky shot the Harvey had cut it from its moorings, and the resulting hue and cry only ended when the balloon was located and shot down over Somerset by a Spitfire!

The first Harveys to go to sea were fitted to some large banana ships converted to carry out independent patrols in the North and South Atlantic. Their task was to intercept blockade runners, and, already quite heavily armed, their ships' companies at first regarded the new rocket device with no great enthusiasm. It was not always easy to give exhaustive training to Merchant Navy crews in handling and maintaining the Harveys. Some took the attitude that too much fuss was being made, and they ignored safety precautions altogether; others thought up new methods of keeping the rockets dry, and in one ship the locker in which they were stored was carefully moved to a new home just abaft the funnel. This effectively cooked all the rounds to a turn, and when the crew went to Action Stations one morning off Milford Haven the first rocket to be lifted from the locker ignited instantly, blowing all the gunlayer's clothing from his back!

The really spectacular career of the Harvey did not begin, however, until a group of scientists who had been working at the University at Exeter with all encouragement from Lindemann and the Prime Minister produced a remarkable new fuse.

One of the most difficult problems which the dive-bomber set the gunnery experts was the great speed of the aircraft and the angle at which it approached its target. A *contact* fuse would only detonate an anti-aircraft shell if it scored a direct hit. And designing a *time* fuse which would cause the shell to explode at the precise moment when it passed near to the aircraft was beyond even the scientists.

The Harvey's 3-inch rocket, however, gave them room to experiment with more ambitious mechanism, and the outcome was an uncanny robot which itself determined the right moment to explode by responding to the changes in the intensity of light near to an aircraft in the sky.

This 'proximity fuse' was the forerunner of an American fuse, based on a principle akin to radar, which was used so successfully later in the war to destroy enemy flying bombs.

The new fuse was Top Secret. So Top Secret, in fact, that when Cooke arrived to install three Harvey Projectors in the steamship *Alleghany*, refitting at Belfast, and prised open the packing-cases containing their ammunition he stared in amazement. Instead of the normal bronze A.D. fuse they had been using ever since their first experiments at Aberporth he saw a sinister black object, some 18 inches long, with what looked like a lens forming a ring right round the upper part of the nose.

While he was staring at it an R.N. Commander came into the naval store.

"We've had a signal that you're not to fit any Harvey fuses or even touch them yet. Your people are sending some alleged expert over by 'plane, and you're to wait for him before you do anything. Have you brought an ammeter?"

"Ammeter?" said Cooke blankly. "What for, sir?"

"I imagine it might be for measuring electric current," said the Commander, with heavy sarcasm. "Don't you know anything about these fuses at all?"

"No, sir. I've never seen one before."

"Nor have I—and I don't want them lying about here. As soon

as this expert arrives you're to get them out of this store. Why your people can't send properly qualified officers who know what they're doing I can't imagine."

The Commander was in a thoroughly bad humour, and the arrival of a civilian named Horsley later that afternoon made matters worse.

"So you've turned up at last," barked the Commander. "How long will it take you to fit these fuses?"

"It's rather difficult to say till I've had a look at them."

"What!" roared the Commander. "You're an expert on the damned things—and you don't know?"

"As a matter of fact, sir," said Horsley apologetically, "I think there must be some mistake. I do know a little about this fuse, but it's got a top security grading. The only two people in our section who are fully in the picture are Commander Goodeve and Lieutenant-Commander Norway, and they were both away on duty when this job came through."

"Well," said the Commander grimly, "you'd better find out more about it pretty quickly. We can't keep the *Alleghany* here any later than to-morrow, and you've got seventy-five rounds to fuse before she sails. And get these boxes out of this store first. I'm not having any explosions here through young idiots playing with crack-brained devices they don't understand, see?"

Cooke and Horsley had an equally chilly reception when they went on board the *Alleghany* with their cases of rockets. Another banana ship flying the White Ensign, she had just finished fitting out as an anti-aircraft vessel, and she was bound for the Red Sea.

Her R.N.R. Captain disliked new-fangled scientific devices on principle, and, having already heard an alarming report from the Commander of their alleged incompetence, he disliked Cooke and Horsley even more.

"We shall be leaving harbour at 0800 to-morrow and going a few miles up the coast. I'm not wasting any time on these stunt weapons of yours. The sooner you fuse these rounds and get off my ship, the better—understand?"

Cooke and Horsley understood, and when they went ashore they held anxious conference.

"What *do* you know about these confounded things?" asked Cooke.

"Not much. They've got this selenium cell and a small radio set in the nose. There's an electronic triggering device worked by a small H.T. battery, and that sets off the priming charge."

"Yes, but what is it that actually starts the whole process?"

"A change in the light," said Horsley. "It's a pretty tricky job, because so far no one's found a way of rendering the thing safe. And there's no means of telling when it's started functioning."

"Well," said Cooke. "We seem to be in for an interesting day."

The following morning the *Alleghany* steamed fifteen miles up the coast of Northern Ireland, the lifeboats were secured, and the Captain, who was in a worse humour than ever, ordered all hands off the upper deck. Cooke and Horsley were left in splendid isolation, and, working without a break, they soon fitted the new fuses to all seventy-five rounds. Then came the task of firing a trial round from all three projectors. They walked over to the Harvey on the poop.

"It's no use just firing the rocket," said Cooke. "We've got to try the fuse out as well. What are we going to fire it at?"

Horsley scratched his head. "It's supposed to go off when any shadow falls across the lens. Why not try it out on that cloud over there?"

Cooke elevated the projector, they counted "One, two . . . three," and he flicked over the switch. The rocket left the rails with a rush and a roar, and, to their delight, they saw a white puff of smoke in the far distance. They were still congratulating themselves on this satisfactory performance when a bellow of anger came from the bridge.

"What the hell do you think you two damned young fools are up to? Look at my ship!"

They turned and looked. To their horror, everything—the bridge, the mast, the funnels—was smothered in mashed potato. In their anxiety over the fuse they had completely forgotten the Harvey's terrific flame blast, and behind them when they fired the first round was a lazaret—one of those latticed lockers for storing vegetables. Through this the blast had swept, pulping the entire contents and distributing them impartially over the upper deck!

Dejected at this anticlimax, Cooke and Horsley prepared to test the second projector, amidships on the port side. This increased their unpopularity, a huge balk of timber being hurled right across the deck and through one of the lifeboats! But it was not until they tried the third and last projector that they struck really serious trouble. When Cooke pressed the firing switch the rocket remained inert on the rails. A hang-fire was what they had dreaded all along, and, as nothing was known about rendering the fuse safe once the complicated mechanism had become alive, the next step baffled them. At any moment the shell might explode, causing casualties and damage to every one and everything in the vicinity.

While they stood over the Harvey, wondering what the first move was, a cheerful voice boomed, "Can I give you an 'and, sir?" and an immense Chief Gunner's Mate appeared.

"We've got a hang-fire," said Cooke.

"You don't want to go worrying abaht that, sir," said the C.G.M. with massive assurance. "I'm a bit of an expert on 'ang-fires. 'Ad two of them in the *Nelson*. If she 'asn't gone off thirty minutes from now we'll pitch 'er over the side."

The round was eventually ditched without further mishap, but by this time the Captain had had more than enough of the Harvey Projector and its luckless operators. Ordering a boat to be lowered, he roared, "Put those two officers ashore," and with that Cooke and Horsley, unceremoniously dumped on the nearest beach, were left to find their way back to Belfast. It certainly had been an interesting day!

The spring of 1941 brought a sharp increase in shipping losses. Enemy aircraft alone sank more than half a million tons—mostly in coastal waters—and the Harvey did not have to wait long for its baptism in action. Menhinick had fitted the Projector into an ocean boarding vessel, H.M.S. *Patia*, and on the evening of Sunday, April 27, he sailed in her on her maiden voyage in naval service.

When she left South Shields *Patia* headed north, and by dusk she was approaching the Farne Islands. There had been no warning of enemy air activity, and Menhinick was in the wardroom when he heard a sudden stampede on the deck above and, almost simultaneously, a loud roar of engines and the whistle of bombs. In the gathering darkness no one saw the Heinkel as it came in at wave-top height, and *Patia* shuddered as one bomb scored a near-miss on the port bow.

Patia's gunners were waiting for it when the second attack came, but the aircraft, flying well below mast-head height, offered a difficult target. Until it was almost on the ship they could not depress their weapons sufficiently to engage the 'plane. The barrage from the ship appeared to disconcert the bomb-aimer, however, and Menhinick, manning his Harvey on the starboard side, saw two more bombs fall harmlessly.

The Heinkel then went away in a wide circle and came back, much more slowly, from dead astern, raking the decks with machine- and cannon-gun fire, and causing heavy casualties. Among them were several of Menhinick's seamen gunners, and their places for the fourth and final attack were taken by cooks and stewards.

Circling again, the Heinkel made its run in from the port quarter, and dropped a stick of three bombs very close together. One fell right under *Patia's* stern; one hit amidships; and the third was a near-miss level with the bridge on the starboard side. The Heinkel's machine-gun fire had already smashed the sights from the Harvey, but when the 'plane was only a hundred yards or so away Menhinick got a direct hit on its tail with one of his rocket shells. The bomber yawed violently, a bright flash of light blazed out from under the fuselage, and the 'plane came down on the water off *Patia's* starboard bow.

By now, however, the ship herself was a shambles, and sinking fast. Weak from loss of blood—he had been shot in the neck—Menhinick crawled to a Carley Float, which was launched a shade too late, and was sucked down the funnel as the ship dived. The float bobbed free, but as it rose it struck the searchlight platform and the half-drowned men clinging to it were dragged under again. Miraculously enough, they were all still gripping it when the float finally surfaced, and they paddled away from the centre of the débris.

Not far from them they saw the vast shape of the Heinkel, lying on the water. The Germans were busy launching a rubber dinghy, and, noticing this, an elderly pensioner, Chief Petty Officer Prior, dropped off the float and swam towards them. The only weapon he had was a large pocket-knife, but when he reached them he brandished this fiercely, threatening to rip the rubber dinghy to shreds unless they let him climb in. He then ordered the wet and frightened Germans to throw their revolvers overboard, and informed them in lurid and unmistakable English that they were his prisoners!

In the bitter cold and darkness of the North Sea the hours that followed were a nightmare. On one Carley Float *Patia's* captain and first-lieutenant died of exposure. Of the 18 men clinging to Menhinick's float 12 froze to death, and when the French trawler *Chassiron* picked them up after six hours in the icy water another seaman died before they reached port. In all, 119 men of *Patia's* complement lost their lives. The Harvey had accounted for its first enemy aircraft, but the bitter cost of this lone action in the North Sea was yet another reminder of the 'price of Admiralty.'

8

CABLES IN THE SKY

SINCE the departure of Admiral Somerville the Wheezers and Dodgers had been working virtually on their own, without any powerful advocate to help them in their battles. Considering their lowly status, they had already achieved a surprising amount, but Goodeve was well aware that they had roused opposition in certain quarters.

Hardly had the team been formed before moves were afoot to restrict its activities, and between the new, unorthodox, and rapidly expanding research section on the one hand and various permanent bodies connected with gunnery, naval construction, and the electrical side of the Navy on the other there was continual friction.

This was not altogether surprising. The machine, rather than any individual, was to blame.

As in any other large organization, the smooth running of the Admiralty depended on detailed delegation of responsibility, but whereas in a big commercial undertaking the efficiency of each self-contained unit is kept at a high pitch by the competition from rival firms there is not the same vital corrective factor in the life of a Service ministry. Indeed, one obvious safeguard which could easily be applied is actually suppressed by the insistence of the Treasury that there shall be no overlapping of responsibilities. Each department has its carefully circumscribed and jealously guarded sphere of influence. In that realm it is supreme.

The drawbacks of this system are plain. In commerce competition rapidly exposes the incorrect decision; a Service ministry, on the other hand, has not the same ready criteria by which decisions can be evaluated.

In such a carefully compartmented world the apparent freedom of the Wheezers and Dodgers to trespass on the preserves of all and sundry cut right across tradition. The very existence of the new research section was a potential irritant; if one of the permanent departments condemned an idea and it was subsequently taken up successfully by Goodeve's team *amour-propre* was offended.

Quite unwittingly some of the hustling young Reserve officers made matters worse by their initial ignorance of 'Admiralty procedure.' Haste was rarely appreciated if it entailed any short-circuiting of established routine, but in their anxiety to get on with the job in hand some of the newcomers barged straight ahead on what seemed to them the most logical course. All too often they ran full tilt into difficulties which longer experience of the working of the machine would have enabled them to avoid.

The chief source of friction lay with the Admiralty departments dwelling in inconvenient isolation at Bath. Partly for geographical reasons they often found themselves left right out of the picture until they were presented with a *fait accompli* in the shape of a new weapon or device suggested by the Wheezers and Dodgers at some hurriedly convened meeting in London where none of the Bath departments had been represented. The latter would then either have to accept it or instantly put forward alternative plans of their own. Not unnaturally they often felt that acceptance of a suggestion as it stood might well condemn them for not having thought of it earlier themselves. In other instances they might genuinely disagree with the proposed weapon or device from a technical point of view. If, however, they rejected the proposal altogether, and set to work to design a weapon of their own, much valuable time and money were liable to be needlessly wasted.

Early in 1941 several attempts were made to get the Inspectorate of Anti-aircraft Weapons and Devices abolished altogether, but Wright, the Director of Scientific Research, whose opinion naturally carried much weight, refused to support these moves. He realized that the need for getting things done at high speed almost inevitably meant offending some people.

Admiral Fraser, too, had good reason to know what Goodeve was achieving. It was suggested to him that the new organization should be disbanded and its officers distributed among other existing departments, but he stoutly resisted this plan. He valued Goodeve's team as a separate entity, but he saw they needed greater authority. He therefore proposed to the First Sea Lord that the Wheezers and Dodgers—hitherto, in football parlance, little more than a side on the fringe of the Third Division in the Admiralty League trying daily to compete with the big guns of the departments in Division I—should themselves be raised to the status of a full-blown Admiralty department. After several attempts to find a suitable title for a party whose interests covered the whole field of naval warfare some one suggested D.M.W.D., and they became the Department of Miscellaneous Weapon Development, with Captain G.O.C. Davies, R.N., a Gunnery specialist, as Director.

This was the happiest of choices. "Jock" Davies, a natural leader with an engaging personality and a flair for getting the best out of every one, had much sea experience behind him—he had fought at Jutland as a midshipman, and had been commander of the *Nelson* —and he knew the Admiralty organization backwards. He came to the new department from a short spell at the Ordnance Board, where he had been concerned with some of Lindemann's rocket experiments, and he had taken a keen interest in Goodeve's work on the anti-aircraft problems of the Merchant Navy.

Admiral Fraser knew this, and realized that Davies was just the man to smooth over many of the difficulties which had arisen in the Wheezers and Dodgers' dealings with other Admiralty departments. When he took over his new duties in March 1941 Goodeve was formally appointed Deputy Director, and D.M.W.D. settled down, happy in the knowledge that they could now go ahead with their status fully recognized.

A few days later the Prime Minister's concern over casualties to merchant ships led him to issue a special directive. "The Admiralty will have the first claim on all the short-range A.A. guns and other weapons they can mount upon suitable merchant ships plying in the danger area," he ruled.[1] In addition to the rocket weapons already undergoing trials, D.M.W.D. had for some time been working to adapt for sea service an ingenious Royal Air Force device called the Parachute and Cable—or P.A.C.—and soon their efforts brought forth success.

The name of Schermuly had been familiar to seamen for more than half a century. Old William Schermuly had invented the lifesaving rocket apparatus adopted by navies and merchant fleets throughout the world, and when the war came the firm's long experience of explosives was put to full use by the Services. To their factory, hidden in a Surrey wood, came demands for all manner of devices, and one urgent need—explained to the three Schermuly sons now directing the destinies of this unusual family business—was for a form of airfield defence against low-flying aircraft.

The brothers quickly designed a powerful rocket which could carry a steel cable up to a height of 500 feet; on the end of the cable was a parachute.

By this means an aerodrome ringed with P.A.C.'s could provide its own emergency 'balloon barrage' at the touch of a switch, and enemy pilots soon found that low-level raids brought a new hazard. At the height of the Battle of Britain one Dornier blew up over Kenley after its port wing had been torn clean off by a P.A.C.

[1] Sir Winston Churchill, *The Second World War*, Vol. III, *The Grand Alliance* (Cassell, 1950), p. 108.

In the Admiralty it was soon realized that the device might be a valuable deterrent at sea. Aircraft attacking a ship at masthead height could drop their bombs with deadly accuracy, but if they were forced to bomb from a greater height the results might be very different. Although the P.A.C. had never been tried out at sea, it seemed doubtful whether a pilot would be keen to hold on his course if he knew that at any moment he might become entangled with a mass of wire and the dragging deadweight of an open parachute. So it proved, but first D.M.W.D. had to tackle several interesting problems.

Two parachutes were used, one at each end of the cable, and in early trials on a Devon moor it was found that the bottom parachute often failed to open at the critical moment. This difficulty was overcome by the insertion of a special explosive link. The rocket had to be made completely waterproof, and some means had to be found of preventing the wire from kinking. A kink in the wire sometimes led to the cable breaking under sudden stress, but patient research showed that this could be cured if the shape of the canisters in which the wire lay coiled was altered.

It was a fascinating apparatus. To make the parachutes D.M.W.D. enlisted the aid of the soft-furnishing department of a well-known Oxford Street store, and, using linen and nylon cord, the firm produced a tremendously strong canopy. One of the parachutes pulled the wing right off an old Wellington which was lent to D.M.W.D. for trials, and later on a German aircraft which had the misfortune to pick up several P.A.C.'s at once was literally dragged to a standstill in mid-air.

At first Richardson took charge of the naval experiments, but after a while he handed over the work to James Close, a tall, genial young R.N.V.R. lieutenant with a Cambridge engineering degree. Close wore spectacles, but in spite of his indifferent eyesight he had somehow managed to wangle his way into the Navy as engineer of an ancient armed yacht which eventually fell to pieces off the coast of Scotland. Development of the P.A.C. was his first task when he joined the department. His duties often took him to the Schermuly factory, and there he learnt something of the art of filling (or 'stemming') the rockets. This highly skilled job was carried out by men working in separate cubicles with shields of armour plate between the rocket and the stemmer. Peering through a thick glass slit above the armour, they would pour in the black powder, cupful by cupful, and tamp it down with small boxwood mallets. Occasionally there were moments of high drama. A rocket would catch fire, and the stemmers would dart from their armour-plated cubicles like greyhounds from a trap!

When the first P.A.C.'s were fitted to merchant ships there was the inevitable tussle before the Admiralty could persuade anyone to give them a proper trial in action. Perhaps it was not surprising that in the sudden moment of attack first thoughts went to manning whatever guns the ship had; the mysterious rocket apparatus was only remembered when it was too late.

By the spring of 1941, however, encouraging reports began to come in. The mate of one small ship in convoy, the *Fireglow*, was standing near the windward P.A.C. when a heavy air attack developed. Seeing one German bomber diving at the *Fireglow* from dead ahead, he pulled the lanyard, and up soared the cable. A large section of the 'plane's wing was dragged off by the wire, and the aircraft came down in the sea.

Skipper Soames, of the *Milford Queen*, had another successful encounter, with a Dornier 17. His guns had hit the bomber on its approach run, and when the P.A.C. was fired it wrapped itself firmly round the Dornier's wing. Losing height rapidly, the aircraft disappeared into the haze, and a few seconds later the *Milford Queen's* crew heard a loud explosion. Skipper Soames was certain that his P.A.C. had destroyed the attacker.

The success of the device depended largely on the operator's judgment. It was no use waiting until the aircraft was right over the ship. When the s.s. *Stanlake* was attacked by a Heinkel her captain was able to estimate its distance very accurately in the bright moonlight, and, putting his helm hard over, he fired a P.A.C. when the 'plane was still several hundred yards off.

By the time the parachute opened the Heinkel was right on to the cable. "I had seen our bullets hitting the forepart of the bomber with little effect," he said, when he was interrogated later, "but after I fired my P.A.C. the Heinkel sheered violently, and I thought he was going to carry my bridge away. For a moment the pilot seemed to regain control, but when he was about 900 yards from us, and hidden in the darkness, we heard his engines suddenly stop dead."

Soon significant evidence began to filter from the German side. An enemy bomber pilot on leave was overheard by one of our agents discussing the hazards he had to face. "It's no joke, I can tell you," he complained. "The English are shooting up these spirals from their ships, and you're lucky to get home at all with a thing like that wound round your airscrew." The captured crew of a Junkers 88 were interrogated. They had been carrying out regular shipping reconnaissance flights, and from one of these, off the East Coast, they struggled back to their base with a huge gash in one wing, between the engine nacelle and the fuselage. "We could not understand it. It looked as if it had been caused by a wire attached to a rocket," said their captain.

Greatly encouraged, the department went to work on larger and more lethal versions of the Parachute and Cable. One, ominously entitled the "Fast Aerial Mine," had an explosive charge attached to the wire, and Dove, experimenting with an early model of this formidable contraption on Haldon Moor, in Devon, had a memorable misadventure. The parachute failed to open, and the mine, which was filled with a special coloured liquid, fell through the roof of a cottage, smothering the whole interior with a vivid pink dye.

Close also had some eventful experiences with an apparatus called "Type J," which had a bigger parachute, a larger rocket than the standard P.A.C., and a 5-ton cable which the rocket could haul up to 600 feet. The trials of this device were carried out in a desolate area on the Somerset coast, but there was farmland near by. Type J fired with a brilliant flash, accompanied by a noise like vast sheets of calico being ripped apart, and this invariably stampeded horses and cattle for miles around. On one occasion it so startled two horses pulling a reaper that they broke into a full gallop with the cumbersome machine and charged a bank bordering the field. In due course the Director of Naval Accounts received a stiff bill for broken cutter blades, and this agricultural item was duly charged to scientific research!

At sea, too, the P.A.C. occasionally provided light relief. A certain coaster on passage from Dover to Hull had two of the rockets installed, and the firing lanyards straggled somewhat untidily from the mounting into the wheelhouse. Off the Essex coast the ship was suddenly attacked by a dive-bomber, and her master, hearing the roar of the 'plane, rushed from his cabin to the bridge. As he entered the wheelhouse he tripped over the lanyard of the starboard P.A.C. and fell flat on his face, knocking out several front teeth. There was wild cheering, and he picked himself up angrily; he objected to being made a laughing-stock by his crew. The uproar on deck, however, was for a very different reason. A million-to-one chance had come off! In falling he had fired the P.A.C. with his foot, and the German 'plane, flying straight into the trailing wire, had plunged headlong into the water!

Equally remarkable but less satisfactory was the sequence of events on board another merchant ship in coastal convoy. She was flying from her main topmast the usual barrage balloon. A gust of wind blew the cover off the spare binnacle, and this fell on the lanyard connected to the P.A.C. projector. The rocket fired, and the P.A.C. scored a direct hit on the balloon, which burst into flames. Its cable, falling over the stern, became wound round the propeller, and this immediately acted as a winch. Before the master realized what had happened the topmast was pulled out of the ship!

The threat of the P.A.C. led to a radical change in enemy tactics. For a time the German pilots, learning that the rocket devices were mounted on the bridge, switched the direction of their low-level attacks, coming in across the stern. To counter this additional P.A.C.'s were placed on the poop, and before long the old attacks at masthead height were abandoned altogether.

Early in 1943 the apparatus came off the Secret List, and D.M.W.D. were able to tell the workers in the Surrey factory something of what the device had achieved. Nine enemy aircraft were known to have been destroyed, and at least thirty-five ships claimed that they had been saved from destruction by the 'spirals' which the German air crews feared so much.

9

THE POTATO-THROWER

IN the department's new title, 'M' stood for Miscellaneous. Goodeve interpreted this in the widest sense, and although his team naturally concentrated on their own research and development programme they lent a willing hand with many projects on which they were consulted by other naval departments and, indeed, by the Army and R.A.F. as well, for there was no exact counterpart of D.M.W.D. in the sister-Services.

Training men in the use of new weapons and devices became an important part of their activities. Already D.M.W.D. had set up a range for rocket weapons on the southern arm of the breakwater at Portland, and Merchant Navy gunners were sent there from the ports for instruction. While hundreds of ratings were going through the Portland course Cooke—his experiments with flame-throwers now at an end—was dispatched to Tyneside to start a similar school for men from the trawlers and other coastal craft in which "Holman Projectors" had been fitted.

As unorthodox in its way as any of D.M.W.D.'s own rocket weapons, the Holman was probably the first and only steam-gun to be used in modern warfare. It was conceived and built by private enterprise in the grey, windswept town of Camborne, which for generations had sent mining machinery to all parts of the world. The Holman family had been associated with that great engineer Richard Trevithick, maker of the first steam locomotive, and their engineering works, flourishing with the prosperity of the Cornish tin-mining industry, continued to prosper when prosperity left the mines of Cornwall. They made compressors and drills which helped to hew out the network of London's Underground Railway; their equipment was used for the salvage of the German Fleet from the sea-bed at Scapa Flow. And in September 1939 Treve Holman, great-grandson of Trevithick's partner, pondered how the resources of the Camborne works could play their part in the war effort. The firm specialized in compressed-air plant, and as he recalled the Stokes mortar of the First World War an idea suddenly came to him for a compressed-air *gun*.

Within a fortnight of the start of the war the first experiments proved that the plan was feasible. A tube connected to a compressed-air supply hurled a short steel bar twenty feet into the air. Modifications were made, and an 18-pound weight was thrown nearly a hundred yards. At this stage the Director of Naval Ordnance, Captain John Leach, R.N., heard of the new weapon taking shape in Cornwall, and he encouraged Treve Holman to go ahead, suggesting that the Projector should be developed to fire Mills grenades fitted in metal containers with open tops. In point of fact, this unusual gun could fire almost anything, for the barrel was not rifled, and early on some very successful results were achieved with loaded cigarette tins! When the Projector was taken out on to the bleak Victory Inn Moor at Porthtowan one of these tins was fired to a height of 650 feet.

In February 1940 the Holman Projector went to Whale Island for an official trial. Six other new weapons were lined up before a critical gathering of gunnery experts, and the nervous Holman team were relieved when one of the rival devices showed signs of temperament, a rocket shell disappearing on an entirely unpredicted course over Portsmouth. The Holman Projector's own début was, however, far more humiliating. Commander R. T. Young, Whale Island's chief experimental officer, dropped the container holding the Mills grenade down the barrel, but instead of it being instantly ejected to a height of 600 feet there was a faint click and the grenade rolled gently out of the barrel, falling to the ground ten yards in front of the serried ranks of distinguished visitors. With one accord they all flung themselves flat on their faces and waited for the explosion.

When, after an agonizing pause, nothing happened Young leapt to his feet. Bravely snatching up the grenade, he threw it into a bucket of water. No one quite fathomed why a bucket of water should discourage a Mills grenade from exploding, and when the bomb was examined later it was, in fact, found to be a dummy. Only half the weight of a live bomb, it had not been heavy enough to actuate the main air-valve at the base of the barrel.

For the rest of that morning the new Projector behaved perfectly, and as a result the Admiralty immediately placed an order for a thousand. The Holmans were to be made entirely of material in ready supply—cast iron and mild steel—and the ammunition was to be the standard type of Mills grenade with a 3·5-seconds fuse. High-pressure air bottles could each supply the power for about fifty rounds, and the weapon would fire thirty rounds a minute. A month later the initial batch was sent to Aberdeen, and the compressed-air guns had only been in service three weeks when a trawler claimed the first success, damaging a Heinkel. By this time Treve Holman and his technicians at Camborne had made some interesting experiments in a new direction.

G

Leach rang him up one day from Bath.

"We want to fit a lot more of your Projectors to steam trawlers. Can you adapt the thing to use steam instead of compressed air?"

Treve Holman thought for a moment. "I don't see why not. How soon do you want a report?" he asked.

"This week if possible," said Leach. "The skippers are howling for them. And I'll tell you something interesting. Some of them have been loosing off three or four of your bombs in quick succession whenever they've sighted a German 'plane—and every time the aircraft has made off immediately. We think it's that puff of smoke that scares them."

The Holman bombs had one strange idiosyncrasy. They exploded in the air with a large puff of black smoke—a peculiarity absent in any detonation of similar grenades on the ground. Seeing these heavy bursts, the German bomber pilots evidently concluded that the trawlers were armed with some much more powerful quick-firing automatic weapon, and they were giving them a wide berth. So far, so good. Now the problem was to make the gun work by steam. Obviously it was a sensible development, for the trawlers had great reserves of steam immediately available, but Treve Holman and his chief assistants, Maurice Oram and Richard Gilbert, were none too sure that the heat of the steam would not explode the bomb while it was still in the barrel.

A 'phone call to the Cornwall County Council secured the loan of a steamroller and its driver, and when this reached the moor at Porthtowan they ran a pipe from its boiler to the base of the Projector. The driver of the roller then raised his steam-pressure to 200 pounds, and after a bomb had been placed in position the party of experimentalists all retired to a safe distance while the escaping steam eddied round it. They allowed the bomb to 'cook' for twenty minutes, and then, concluding that fears of a premature explosion were groundless, they carried out firing trials. Tested under 80 pounds' pressure from the steamroller, the Holman Projector threw a heavy metal weight a distance of 90 feet, and as soon as they reported successful progress in this direction the resourceful Captain Leach suggested another alteration in the design of the gun. On board the trawlers, often at sea for long periods in wild weather, it was difficult to give enough attention to any sort of weapon. He saw that, with the new type of Holman, valves were likely to rust, and steam would condense in the pipes so that just a dribble of water emerged instead of the pressure needed to hurl the grenade into the air. The principle of the Stokes Mortar was therefore abandoned, and, instead of the bomb being dropped down the barrel and ejected instantaneously, a firing trigger was devised. This removed the danger of the bomb, in its tin container, firing prematurely and hanging up in the barrel through rust.

By the late spring of 1941 the Projector was beginning to make quite a name for itself. A training school was opened at Camborne, and from as far as Stornoway ratings were sent there for a week's course. They spent two days firing on the range and three days at the works attending lectures on maintenance and learning how to strip and reassemble the gun which the trawler men had christened the "Potato Thrower." When two ships met at sea it became a regular practice to fight mock battles, each crew bombarding the other with potatoes fired from their Holmans, and this game was taken up with great enthusiasm by the craft of Coastal Forces on their way back to base from sweeps along the enemy coast.

Soon the Projector was fitted to destroyers, minesweepers, and motor-gunboats, as well as hundreds of small coastal vessels, and one of the compressed-air guns was even mounted on the top of Admiralty Arch. Eventually the Prime Minister asked for a demonstration at Aldershot. For this the team from Camborne took no ammunition. With its smooth bore the Holman Projector could be fed with almost anything, and already it had been tested with anti-tank grenades and Molotov cocktails—the glass-bottle bombs containing phosphorus and petrol. Treve Holman assumed that some form of ammunition would be provided for them on this occasion, but when they arrived at the range they found that the Army had overlooked this altogether. *153/55*

With Mr Churchill waiting somewhat impatiently, the situation was only saved when somebody remembered the half-dozen bottles of beer they had brought with them for a picnic lunch. The first one exploded in the barrel but, to the delight of the Prime Minister— always fascinated by new devices— the remainder scored direct hits on the target, amid a flurry of froth. "A very good idea, this weapon of yours," he said approvingly; "it will save our cordite." After praise from such a quarter the small party from Cornwall felt the loss of their lunch-time ale well worth while!

A few days after the Aldershot demonstration news reached Camborne of a spectacular action at sea in which the Holman Projector proved its worth. Armed with only a Lewis and one of the compressed-air guns, a small merchantman, the s.s. *Highlander*, was attacked at night off the East Coast of England by two Dornier bombers. The first 'plane was shot down almost immediately, and when the second Dornier came in the *Highlander's* gunners got further hits, a Holman bomb bursting in the root of the wing. The big bomber lurched on towards them, losing height, and after a wing-tip had hit one of the lifeboats the aircraft slewed round and crashed on the little steamer's poop. In his story of the Merchant Navy at war[1] Sir Archibald Hurd has told how next morning the gallant little *Highlander* steamed into harbour with the wreckage of the Dornier still strewn all over the after part of the ship. Her total casualties in this successful action were two wounded.

Out in the Atlantic a much bigger ship, the s.s. *Thirlby*, bound from Halifax, Nova Scotia, to Britain with 8000 tons of wheat, also used the new weapon with great effect. Her Holman Projector, bravely manned throughout by the Chief Officer in spite of a hail of cannon shells, eventually drove off a giant Focke-Wulf which had used cloud cover to carry out a surprise attack. Although badly damaged, with one hold flooded and open to the sea, the *Thirlby* limped into Loch Ewe with her precious cargo.

In its first year the Projector claimed at least a dozen enemy aircraft destroyed. Mark III was then introduced—a semi-automatic and much more powerful version which fired two or three grenades simultaneously to a height of 1000 feet—and the Admiralty ordered another thousand of these.

No one was more delighted at the success of this unconventional weapon than the Admiralty's Director of Naval Ordnance, Captain Leach, a tall, good-looking man with an engaging sense of humour. From the start he had taken a keen interest in the Projector, and throughout the early stages of development lengthy letters in his small, clear handwriting arrived almost weekly, offering suggestions which he embellished with his own neat sketches. He had never regarded the Holman as anything more pretentious than a stop-gap until the Oerlikon became widely available, but it had exceeded his expectations, and the progress of the gun owed much to his encouragement and advice. When the time came for him to go to sea again he was given command of the *Prince of Wales*. And from the Admiralty came a message that the battleship's new captain had asked for one of the Mark III Projectors to be fitted in his personal barge.

On October 23, 1941, Leach sailed from the Clyde as Flag Captain to Admiral Sir Tom Phillips, Commander-in-Chief designate in the Far East. The Camborne firm felt they were losing a friend as well as a wise counsellor. Before the end of the year came news of the disaster which overtook the *Prince of Wales* and *Repulse* off the coast of Malaya. John Leach, one of 839 men to lose their lives, went down with his ship.

Another of the Navy's outstanding figures who played no small part in the development of the Camborne gun was Lieutenant-Commander Robert Hichens, R.N.V.R. A solicitor in Falmouth,

[1] *Britain's Merchant Navy*, edited by Sir Archibald Hurd (Odhams, 1944).

only a few miles away from the Holman works, Hichens had earned a great reputation before the war as an international 14-foot-dinghy sailor. Joining the R.N.V.R., he became the master tactician of Coastal Forces and commanded the first flotilla of motor-gunboats on the East Coast, harrying enemy shipping off Ijmuiden and the Hook. The Holman Projector was particularly suitable for the lightly built, high-speed Coastal Force craft, for it had very little deck thrust, and Hichens developed a new technique for using it against E-boats. Going in to attack, he would split his flotilla into two sections, and when the enemy were sighted one section would menace the E-boats by firing flares over them with the Holmans at a certain angle. Turning away, as they invariably did, the enemy force would run head-long into the second section of M.G.B.'s, powerfully armed with Oerlikons, which Hichens had disposed on their flank.

The gallantry of this quiet, self-effacing young officer, who won the D.S.O. twice and three D.S.C.'s, was matched by his tactical leadership. He took a lively interest in gunnery problems, and while the Projector was undergoing its gradual development he had many discussions with Treve Holman. On one of his leaves in London early in 1943 they were dining together when he reached for the menu card. On the back of this he sketched out the design of a Mark IV "Potato-thrower" which he wanted for Coastal Forces. His drawing outlined a simpler, lighter, and smaller version, with a short barrel and a swivel mounting.

Treve Holman took the menu card back to Camborne, and the works produced a prototype which was sent to Hichens at Dover. It was then April, and on the night of Friday the 16th in that month, before he had had time to try out the new Projector, Hichens led his forces to sea. They joined action with a pack of E-boats, and in a running battle Hichens himself was killed by the last random shot fired by the enemy at extreme range as they broke off the engagement.

With his death the plans for the fourth and most advanced of the Holman guns was abandoned. The tide had turned, and more advanced weapons superseded the little mortar which had given such valiant service. In various other rôles, however, the Holman Projectors continued to play a useful part. They were used at Gibraltar to discourage raids by midget submarines; they were adapted to fire grapnels for the Commandos in cliff assaults; and D.M.W.D. carried out tests with them for attacking enemy Charioteers.

In all 4500 of these unusual guns powered by compressed air or steam saw active service in the war at sea, and to-day one of them has a place of honour in the museum attached to the Holman works at Camborne. Scarred and dented, it is the weapon which brought the Dornier crashing on to the poop of the little *Highlander*.

IO

THE WIRE BARRAGE

Other methods of striking down the hostile bomber were sought
tirelessly, and for many months to come these efforts were spurred by
repeated, costly, and bloody raids upon our ports and cities.

Sir Winston Churchill, *The Second World War*,
Vol. II, p. 346

PERHAPS the strangest and most spectacular of all the projects
which D.M.W.D. undertook in the early days was the "Free
Balloon Barrage."

From September 7 to November 3, 1940, an average of 200 German bombers pounded London every night, and at the height of the
Blitz the Prime Minister called a midnight meeting at Number 10
Downing Street. On the agenda was a remarkable proposal—to
strike at the raiders by firing into the sky a curtain of wire supported
by parachutes.

Among the naval officers summoned to the meeting was Captain
Davies, who had not yet been appointed to D.M.W.D. He was still
serving at the Ordnance Board, whose job it was to examine all
weapons and ammunition before they passed into use in the three
fighting Services, and he had recently been called into consultation
over a scheme of Professor Lindemann's for carrying wires into the
air in 6-inch shells. Trials showed this to be impracticable, but the
Downing Street meeting, with the Prime Minister in the chair, soon
revealed that the essence of the plan had not been abandoned. It
was now suggested that, in place of the shells, huge rockets should
be used to lay an aerial minefield.

The idea of wires in the sky was by no means new. The P.A.C.
was already proving its value at sea, and on board some warships
was mounted a multiple projector—later used with some success
ashore at Tobruk—which threw up bombs and masses of wire in
greater profusion. The Prime Minister had taken a personal interest
in this latter device, and, noticing one of them mounted on top of
H.M.S. *Nelson's* 'B' turret when he paid a visit to the battleship at
Scapa Flow, he had called for it to be fired.

The result on that occasion was unfortunate, for not enough allowance was made for the wind, and one of the wires drifted back on to the ship, where it became entangled with the wireless spur on the mainmast and exploded violently. Mr Churchill was quite unperturbed. His cigar remained clenched tightly between his teeth, and, staring up at the mast, he observed drily, "I think there's something not quite right about the way you are using this new weapon of mine." On his return to London he had sent for Davies and dispatched him immediately to Scapa Flow to explain to Admiral Sir John Tovey, in the *Nelson*, how the rocket device should be operated.

At the midnight meeting it was obvious that the idea of a whole minefield, laid in the sky by somewhat similar means, had captured the Prime Minister's imagination. He listened impatiently as the technical difficulties were argued backward and forward, and then said firmly, "I want a square of wire in the sky as big as the Horse Guards Parade, with parachutes holding it in place. We need four hundred projectors and four million rounds of ammunition. . . . Just think of the difficulty for an aircraft trying at the last minute to avoid a thing the size of the Horse Guards, gentlemen!"

The experts were sent away to cogitate on the many problems involved, and while they were wrestling with the suspension method and the rockets the idea of a minefield in the sky was put up to Goodeve and his team from a different source altogether.

A Commander Fraser, serving in the Admiralty Boom Defence organization, which handled the supply of wire rope for the Navy, brought to D.M.W.D. a plan of his own for hanging wires from balloons. He suggested that if a cloud of these balloons was released in an area through which the bombers were flying tremendous toll could be taken, and Richardson was detailed to look into the matter.

When he first thought about Fraser's plan he recalled a strange and formidable device he had come across in a store at Exeter some months before while carrying out some of his early rocket experiments. Called the "Long Aerial Mine," it consisted of a network of bombs and wire, and had been designed for the R.A.F. as a lethal surprise packet, to be dropped from bombers in the path of unwary attackers. Obviously it would be an advantage to embody this ready-made device in the new scheme if a compromise was possible, and he went to Exeter to examine it more closely. The Long Aerial Mine obstinately refused, however, to fit into the picture. After some days of further experiment in the West Country, Richardson transferred his researches to the Balloon establishment at Cardington, and gradually a novel and ingenious device took shape which demanded neither aircraft to launch it from the sky nor rockets—at that stage unreliable as carriers of equipment—to lift it from the ground.

The Free Balloon Barrage, as it was eventually known, consisted of hundreds of separate units. Each had its own large rubber balloon filled with hydrogen, and suspended from this was a yellow metal container, shaped like a biscuit tin; a large wooden spool carrying 2000 feet of thin piano wire; and a parachute.

The theory of operating the F.B.B. was simple enough. When the balloon reached a certain height a special mechanism came into play. This released the vast length of trailing wire, which had a parachute to anchor the lower end. At the same time the yellow container—a small but powerful bomb swinging on a board beneath the balloon —became alive.

From this moment any moving object which came into contact with the wire set in motion a swift train of unpleasant events. When the air billowed into the parachute, the wire tautened, and the bomb was dragged down towards the target. As it struck, a spring rim which surrounded the outside of the container was tilted out of its normal position, and the bomb exploded instantaneously.

As the design of the new infernal machine took shape it seemed brilliantly free from complications, but in early trials the behaviour of the F.B.B. proved quite unpredictable. After a certain time in the air the apparatus was supposed to destroy itself, but if there was a leak in the balloon it would float gently to earth in a highly dangerous state, and it was never easy, even for the experts, to determine precisely what stage the intricate mechanism had reached at any given moment.

This would not have mattered so much if the public could have been warned to leave these strange objects severely alone—but the F.B.B. was Top Secret. A.R.P. wardens in the London district had to be let into this secret to a certain extent, but the mechanism of the device could not be explained to them. They were merely told that on certain nights, "when weather and other conditions are suitable," a new form of night defence might be operated. The apprehensive wardens were further counselled that if they sighted one of these mysterious contrivances during the hours of darkness, and "a light appears to be burning underneath the hood, an explosion may be imminent." In such circumstances they were advised to take cover for thirty minutes after the light was extinguished; if they felt they must attack the apparatus without delay the authorities could only suggest that they attempted to subdue it with fierce jets of water "from behind some substantial cover such as a brick wall."

If the exploding mechanism of the F.B.B. was somewhat erratic at the start the antics of the balloons on their trial voyages across the

night sky were even more eccentric. They were only sent up when
the wind was blowing at a certain strength and direction, but however painstakingly the meteorologists prepared their forecasts for
D.M.W.D. the weather rarely developed according to plan.

In ideal conditions the F.B.B. units were supposed to operate over
a limited area, but if a high wind sprang up unexpectedly the balloons were blown far and wide, and the next morning astonished
householders as far away as Dorset and Devon would awake to find
their homes and gardens festooned with wire. Seizing the 'phone,
some would ring up the nearest military headquarters to report that
paratroops had landed; others would get through to the Air Ministry
or Home Office to announce that they had been attacked by a new
secret weapon, and were barricading themselves in until help arrived!

The balloons, wires, and bombs fell across railway lines, stopping
trains; they landed on high-tension cables and fused all the power
for miles around; they came down in open fields, and farmers complained that they could not get their cows in for milking. In the
department the aftermath of the early launchings was chaotic, and
a special Flying Squad was formed to hare round the country in
small plain vans recovering the apparatus before reckless civilians
blew themselves to pieces.

Two of the leading 'retrievers' were Tolman and Midshipman
J. R. D. Francis, R.N.V.R., the youngest member of the department, who had made a name for himself by his ability to take to
pieces F.B.B. bombs which had already armed themselves and were
liable to explode at any moment. Like Norway and several others,
Francis had never expected to find himself in a shore job. He had
volunteered for sea service, but the fact that he had come out top of
the University of London's examination list for a B.Sc.(Engineering)
attracted the immediate—and, for him, unwelcome—attention of
the Admiralty's C.W. Branch. Being many years younger than Norway and nearly every one else in the department, he could not pro-
test so outspokenly, but nevertheless he managed to extract from
Goodeve a promise that he should be released to go to sea at the
first moment he could be spared. In the meantime he was establish-
ing quite a reputation for energy and versatility—and he was entirely
unimpressed by any hazards he encountered.

Tolman too had made something of a name in the Admiralty,
where his demonstrations of "How to render an F.B.B. bomb safe"
were delivered with a fearless confidence not always fully shared by
his audience. Like Lane, who was always dismantling German
booby-traps with a nail-file and a hammer, and scaring the life out
of every one in the big room in which most of D.M.W.D.'s officers
worked, Tolman genuinely enjoyed handling explosives, but even

he was startled when he answered an SOS from the Dorset village of Piddletrenthide. A police constable reported that he had some strange objects in his back garden, and when Tolman arrived there in the Admiralty van he discovered, lying side by side in the yard, two of the familiar yellow containers with only two feet of wire still attached to each.

"What an extraordinary thing! Did they fall together just there?" he asked.

"No!" said the policeman proudly. "I put them there myself."

"But where is the rest of the wire?"

"Well, you see . . . it was like this," explained the constable cheerfully. "These things came down in a field about a mile from here, so I cut off the wire and brought them back with me. I reckoned they'd be safer."

Tolman stared at him in amazement. "How on earth did you move them here without blowing yourself up?"

The constable peered at the two containers with a new interest. "You reckon these things are some sort of bomb, then?" he said, obviously impressed. "I just tied 'em on the handlebars of my bike and rode back here."

It seemed almost unbelievable, but he had severed the wire without mishap, and had then cycled over a mile home with the bombs swinging freely against the frame of his bicycle. Miraculously, not once had the firing rim been disturbed!

Midshipman Francis had another experience of this 'beginner's luck.' Calling at a Hampshire farm, he said to the owner, "I hear you have a bomb somewhere on your land?"

"That's right," said the farmer, "but it's safe enough now. I've taken her to pieces. You'll find the bits on the kitchen table."

The little yellow tins looked so unpretentious that finders had few scruples about appropriating them as souvenirs. After one of the early launchings a recovery team was sent to Epping Forest. One of D.M.W.D.'s officers had some difficulty with an F.B.B. unit wedged in the upper branches of an oak-tree. He eventually cut it free, and was lowering it gingerly to the ground when a stranger who had been watching the operation with some interest called out sarcastically, "I reckon you chaps are making a lot of fuss about nothing. You're not telling me a little tin like that can do much harm!" This was too much for the young sub-lieutenant, who had already ruined an almost new uniform in his struggles in the tree-top, and, picking up the container, he hurled it into the undergrowth, where it exploded deafeningly. The uninvited critic, blown flat on his back, was much impressed!

On December 29, 1940, while the department were still working at high pressure to overcome the teething troubles of the apparatus, word came that the Free Balloon Barrage was to be given its first large-scale trial. It was the night of the big fire raid on London, and for some hours after dusk furious activity centred on Hatfield. The launching arrangements were on a prodigious scale, for to transport the hydrogen and other equipment to the windward side of London in the time available some 800 lorries and trailers were needed. Several hundred men of the R.A.F. handled the balloons; big tents, 12 feet high, were erected at the launching point, which covered an arc of some two miles; and inside these tents the balloons were inflated.

D.M.W.D.'s officers had their misgivings over such an early test. There had not been time to give proper trial to all the different components of the Barrage, and Richardson, for one, feared a débâcle.

That night, at the height of the terrific raid on the capital, nearly 2000 of the lethal balloons were dispatched skyward in two and a half hours, and as the D.M.W.D. party waited at the control centre at Hatfield the reports which flowed in confirmed their fears. The area over which the balloons were expected to drift had been mapped out in three zones. Some 30 per cent. of the units failed in Zone A, nearest to the launching site, because the wire had not run out smoothly or the balloons themselves had developed leaks. A further 15 per cent. came down over London itself because the height-keeping mechanism—an ingenious arrangement of small bags filled with sand—failed to function, and the balloons, climbing far beyond their operational height, burst with the pressure. In Zone C another 30 per cent. came to grief. One F.B.B. unit landed in the grounds of Buckingham Palace, some reached the South Coast, and several crossed the Channel to France.

Messages reporting the discovery of straying F.B.B. bombs poured in from far and near, and to retrieve them all before they caused casualties or damage set D.M.W.D. a major problem. Dozens of Boy Scouts were roped in to help, and Francis, commandeering a fire-engine and several firemen, scoured the immediate district. Soon the police station nearest to the control point was crammed with wire and unexploded bombs.

All the yellow containers sent up that night had, plainly painted on them, the legend "Danger—Do Not Touch!" This, however, seemed to have a magnetic attraction for any civilians who came upon the tangles of bombs and wires. The fire-engine and its busy crew met one shopkeeper cycling along with four of the deadly yellow containers dangling from his handlebars. One bomb had lifted the roof off a house. Others were found hanging in trees; and, completely disregarding the warning, a farmer who had come across no fewer than fourteen of them, had dragged them all together in a corner of a field. Then, as the strangest of afterthoughts, he had piled dung on to them—"to stop them blowing up."

When all the reports came in the final analysis was depressing to the team who had worked so hard to get the apparatus ready, but before any radical alterations were made it was decided to stage a special test in Bedfordshire, and there, a few days later, 200 of the balloons were sent aloft. The fuses were set to ensure that on this occasion the bombs and wires would all fall in a relatively small area. Even so an unexpected snag occurred.

Fifty sailors had been loaned to D.M.W.D. to help with the recovery of the units for examination, but although—marching in orderly lines through field after field and gazing intently to right and left—they combed the countryside, their total bag was a meagre half-dozen. To men searching on foot the thin piano wire and yellow containers were almost invisible unless they stumbled right upon them. In desperation Richardson dismissed the sailors and drove to the nearest riding school, where he hired every horse in the place for the afternoon.

It was a successful and unforgettable experiment. Few of his team of R.N.V.R. officers had ever ridden before, and as hedges and ditches had to be jumped most of the volunteer horsemen fell off with painful regularity. Between them, however, they tracked down almost every bomb. When they got back to the Admiralty, aching in every limb, Richardson laid the bill from the riding school on Goodeve's desk and asked how payment should be made. Even *his* limited experience suggested that the Director of Naval Accounts would look askance at an account for the hire of fourteen horses! Like newspaper reporters, who acquire an uncanny skill in making out convincing expense sheets, any naval officer hoping to extract payment for expenses incurred on duty had first to study the art of presentation. In this connexion there was the well-known story of the junior officer, journeying on official duty with heavy baggage, who put in a modest claim for "Porters 1s." When this was disallowed a shipmate of greater experience advised him to submit the charge again, this time ascribing it to "Porterage," and it was passed without demur. Encouraged to more picturesque efforts, he later secured payment for several taxi fares itemized as "Cabbage"!

Sure enough, Richardson's account for the "hire of fourteen horses for the use of officers engaged on F.B.B. trials" was swiftly returned with a request for more information, and although he wrote across it "No alternative form of transport available" (the standard excuse given by naval officers for hiring taxis) the Navy

Accountants next demanded to know why Admiralty vans had not been used. To this Richardson tersely replied, "Journey made over ploughed fields and hedges," and the correspondence ended abruptly.

When the gear launched near Bedford was examined in the department two main causes of failure were discovered. The wire was not unreeling smoothly when the balloons reached their operational height, and the balloons themselves were misbehaving. The very thin, springy wire in use was wound round a big wooden spool. To stop it uncoiling prematurely, rubber tyres were fitted round the outside of the spool, but it still tended to kink up. This was a serious problem, for if the wire became tangled on release the vital parachute at the lower end would fail to open. In addition, if an aircraft hit a kinked wire this would snap instantly, and the bomb would never come into action. By patient research the source of the trouble was finally located. As it unreeled the wire had to pass through a narrow hole in the board which held the bomb in place—and the edges of these holes were not smooth enough. Lane, who could draw on a fund of unusual information, declared that the only instrument guaranteed to bore really smooth holes was a red-hot poker, so an emergency squad of fifteen R.N.V.R. lieutenants set to work in an attic in the Admiralty, heating pokers and thrusting them through the thin bomb platforms. Cooke, looking in to deliver a message, found them all weeping copiously as they toiled in a dense haze of acrid smoke from the singeing woodwork.

The F.B.B. team then turned their attention to Failure Number Two. It seemed fairly evident that the safety-valve which was supposed to prevent the balloons from rising too high was not functioning consistently. The balloons were meant to operate between 14,000 and 18,000 feet, but many were climbing far above this. And when they burst under pressure the whole equipment came crashing to earth.

Intense cold might be causing the safety-valve to jam, so another D.M.W.D. team, consisting of Harris, Tolman, Lieutenant Duncan Bruce, R.N.V.R., and Lieutenant Tom Swan, R.N.V.R., were told to test this theory at a fruit research station in Kent, where there was a vast refrigerating chamber. A supply of hydrogen cylinders and four outfits of Arctic clothing were issued to them, and they set off for West Malling.

Bruce and Swan had only just joined D.M.W.D. Like Tolman, Swan had been a schoolmaster, teaching science, when war broke out, and, noting his name on the Central Scientific Register, the Admiralty had called him up. To his surprise, he then found himself posted to the Signal School at Portsmouth, who were in no need of a scientist and could not think what to do with him. So he was sent on a Divisional Officer's course, and it was some time before D.M.W.D. were able to track him down. For him the memorable experiments at West Malling were a prelude to intensive research on radar and anti-submarine devices for the department. Duncan Bruce, a young physicist who tackled many unusual jobs for D.M.W.D., was an engaging companion in any enterprise. He had a keen sense of humour, and his first assignment, at West Malling, certainly provided plenty of unexpected entertainment for him.

The task of the quartet was to observe the changes of buoy-ancy in the balloon when exposed to rapidly lowering tempera-ture. One by one they crawled into the refrigerating chamber, which was sealed after them, and sat shivering in front of a huge dial while the balloon floated above them. Isolated as they were from the outer world they found the silence oppressive, and the atmosphere made them so drowsy that they had increasing difficulty in jotting down the data they were collecting.

Although on the first day they each spent only half an hour at a time in the chamber, they felt decidedly queer as they walked back to the guest-house. At tea Bruce set fire to his trousers without notic-ing it, and all of them retired to bed early, suffering from severe headaches. On the second day the after-effects were even more pro-nounced, and in some concern the proprietress rang up the nearest doctor.

"I wonder if you could come and have a look at four of our guests," she said. "They're naval officers, and I think they're all mad."

When he arrived he was shown into the garden. Although rain was falling in torrents, Harris, Bruce, Tolman, and Swan were all sitting in deck-chairs on the lawn. Two of them were reading even-ing newspapers upside down, and all were howling with laughter! For two days, without realizing the gradual effect, they had been inhaling some mysterious gas from the fruit, and although they subsequently cut down the time spent in the chamber, and drew lots for their spells of duty, they were glad when the experiments were over.

When some of the major alterations had been made to the appara-tus practice launchings were resumed in the London area. On nights when the Free Balloon Barrage was to be tried out Jamieson would hang a large white rabbit on the notice-board in the department and announce, "Albino to-night, everybody!" Harris, the tall young South African, who was a leading spirit in most of these trials, would then tour the room, extending invitations with the air of a man offering his guests a day's shooting. "Doing anything to-night?" he

would ask. "I wonder whether you'd care to join me . . . Hendon,
about 2230 hours. Should be good sport!" There was no shortage of
volunteers.

The task of moving the equipment from place to place, and
launching the units, was taken over by the Balloon Barrage organization of the R.A.F., and headquarters were set up at North Weald,
Stanmore, and two other centres. Life at the launching point had its
hazards, for, as the fuse burnt through on the ascending bomb
boards, out of the night sky came a shower of wooden spools on
which the wire was wound. As these were 18 inches across and
weighed 3 pounds they were liable to make a distinct impression
when dropped from a height of several thousand feet! The apparatus was much more consistent now, but on nights when the weather
worsened occasional balloons still travelled immense distances. Those
which strayed as far as France caused some confusion, and the
Underground movement was soon reporting the arrival of

> mysterious objects of unknown origin in the sky over Ariège. They
> seem to have been brought to our district by the high wind of the
> last few days. The balloons are white, with a steel wire hanging from
> them. They carry a board armed with a bomb which explodes
> immediately on contact. The police sent a brigadier and a gendarme
> to the spot, and when they pulled the wire to bring one balloon to
> the ground the engine exploded at a height of ten metres. The gen-
> darme received a wound in the stomach. Another of these engines
> exploded over a farm at Calles, breaking some windows.

A French newspaper, reporting the explosion of an F.B.B. unit in
the canton of Mas d'Azil, announced that "the balloon, which was
deposited with the police, has been sent to the military authorities
at Toulouse, who have passed it on to technical experts." The newspaper added omnisciently:

> In spite of the fantastic stories which have been circulating it seems
> that the balloons are really nothing but English barrage balloons
> which have broken adrift in the high wind. The same thing, it will
> be remembered, has happened in Sweden, and some have crossed the
> Pyrenees into Spain.

The F.B.B.'s next operational launching was carried out near
Liverpool, the target of several heavy bombing raids in the spring.
It was on a fairly small scale, less than 150 units being sent up,
and though these few wires failed to ensnare any aircraft—the
device depended for material success on the release of many hundreds at a time—the modifications to the balloons and wire-release
gear cut down the failures substantially. Nevertheless, it proved an
eventful night for people living in the area between Warrington and

Tarporley, F.B.B. bombs breaking eighteen windows in one house, and a herd of cattle became quite remarkably entangled in some of the descending wire. A telephone exchange was put out of action, and two of the main electric grid cables on farmland near Sandiway were brought down by a violent short circuit.

These were, however, minor disadvantages compared with the incidents in the earlier trials, and the final design of the Free Balloon Barrage reached an efficiency of 80 per cent. Fate decreed, however, that this spectacular method of defence was never to be given a full-scale test in its final, improved form. The mass air raids on England ceased as suddenly as they had begun, and for nearly three years the Luftwaffe turned their main attentions to other battle fronts. Stressing this fact in his summing up of the brilliant research work carried out on the F.B.B., the Proximity Fuse, and other anti-aircraft devices, the Prime Minister expressed the opinion that "the value of these efforts, which could only be proved by major trial," should not be underrated.[1]

The Free Balloon Barrage might well have launched a shattering attack on the morale of the German bomber pilots, and, viewing this strange, ingenious apparatus against the background of later events, Mr Churchill, for one, considered it a formidable invention. "It was surprising and fortunate," he declared, "that the Germans did not develop this counter to our mass bombing raids in the last three years years of the war."[1]

[1] Sir Winston Churchill, *The Second World War*, Vol. II, pp. 346–350.

II

HIGHLY EXPLOSIVE!

By the spring of 1941 the fledgelings were spreading their wings. In rapid succession they acquired not only a new Director, but a new home in the West End of London and, strange to record, a seaside pier in Somerset.

For a non-scientist the task of controlling and co-ordinating the activities of the Wheezers and Dodgers called for qualities unusual in a practical seaman. Captain Davies took the new appointment in his stride. Like Admiral Fraser, he realized that the usefulness of D.M.W.D. largely depended on their freedom to tackle a wide variety of projects in their own way. For one thing, as a temporary, war-time organization, they felt themselves under no obligation to defer to the views of established 'authorities' whenever they considered these incorrect; they had no post-war repercussions to fear if friction arose with other departments.

Their energy and novelty of outlook were a powerful stimulus to some of the Staff Divisions which tended to rely overmuch on past experience, but as they ventured into wider fields Goodeve's team felt the need of some one at the helm who knew the ways of the Admiralty from long experience.

Often it was far easier to evolve a new weapon than it was to pilot it through a maze of officialdom, and with any new idea no progress could be made until it had been put up in a 'docket'—a report of the project which was sent round in an Admiralty folder for the comments of all other departments which might be concerned, and which finally went to the Board of Admiralty for approval. The docket system was sensible enough. Almost every naval project called for some degree of co-ordination or co-operative action between many Admiralty departments, and the machinery which initiated and circulated these informative files had been built up to ensure that every one was kept in the picture over current suggestions and developments. A ship is a self-contained unit, and nothing can be done in one part without others being affected.

This was particularly true in the case of a new weapon. After the

H

initial research, design and development brought in their train problems of production, inspection, storing, transport, and fitting. Then men had to be trained to maintain the weapon, and fight with it. Right from the start of that weapon's evolution, therefore, a host of different Admiralty bodies had to be considered and consulted.

In some ways the docket system served its purpose admirably, but since the whole of the Admiralty was flooded with dockets on every conceivable subject some took an unconscionable time to complete their journey. Ignorance of Admiralty procedure could increase this delay by weeks.

To steer a proposal rapidly and successfully round its predestined course one needed to be something of a psychologist, and here Jock Davies proved a tower of strength. He had an uncanny ability to size up in advance the likely attitudes of the established Admiralty departments to any proposition which D.M.W.D. wanted to make, and, while quite ready to explore unorthodox ways of overcoming opposition, he was generally able to suggest the constitutional solution to the department's problems. His tact and sound common sense smoothed over D.M.W.D.'s difficulties, and he was the ideal foil for Goodeve, who had a somewhat impetuous approach to the restrictions of the Civil Service machine.

Goodeve was always anxious to speed the course of events. Impatient with meticulous precision in design and trial work, he chafed, too, at the more intangible human factors which could hold up an urgent project. He was reluctant to wait for a day, or even an hour, in order to see the right man or the right group of people about some plan which he wanted to push through, and by this over-anxiety to rush things to a conclusion he occasionally forfeited both time and sympathetic co-operation. The arrival of Davies freed him of much irksome administrative responsibility, and the two men— the scientist and the sailor—worked in complete harmony. Goodeve was still the guiding genius, stamping his strong personality on every man and every project in the department, but firmly and unobtrusively Davies made his own very positive contribution. A regular observer of all major trials of weapons and devices, he soon became the able spokesman at Admiralty conferences on any scheme in which D.M.W.D. were involved.

For an Admiralty department the atmosphere of D.M.W.D. could be described as distinctly informal, and the new Director must have been somewhat startled by the un-naval appearance of some of his charges.

Many of them, urgently needed for their scientific qualifications, had been pitchforked into uniform at a moment's notice, their initial training in the customs and traditions of the Service confined to one afternoon's lecture from a petty officer. Having rattled off some irrelevant information about Lord Nelson—still referred to by some members of the lower deck as though he was the current First Sea Lord—their mentor would tell the surprised scientists how to sling a hammock, and what would happen to them if they failed to salute the Quarter-deck! This confusing indoctrination at an end, they were let loose in the Admiralty. To their relief they found no hammocks to sling and no Quarter-decks to salute, and if Lord Nelson seemed at times to survey them rather severely from his plinth in the Admiralty's main entrance the atmosphere of their earlier quarters in Archway Block North was reassuringly reminiscent of their normal, peace-time environment.

D.M.W.D.'s rooms were like no others in the dignified precincts of Whitehall. Most Admiralty offices had a stark simplicity—a few hard chairs, large desks smothered with papers which overflowed from the In and Out trays, and, on a small table in the corner, the inevitable paraphernalia of tea-making. That was all. No adornment, no visible clue to the work in hand. In sharp contrast D.M.W.D.'s quarters resembled some monstrous Wellsian workshop. Parts of aircraft wings rested nonchalantly against the walls; there were piles of parachutes and balloons of various colours, empty projectile cases, bundles of ignitors, and coils of wire. Every drawer seemed to be crammed with explosives, and several Free Balloon Barrage bomb-containers were in use as soap-tins or ash-trays. The main room was always alive with comings and goings. Distinguished professors in plain clothes would wander in to confer on some abstruse problem of ballistics or aerodynamics; officers would set off for distant trial grounds laden with bomb-cases or electrical gear. Some one, probably Lane, would be busy in one corner of the room sawing a new type of German fuse in half to see how it worked. Near by, and oblivious to the noise and the possibility of imminent explosion, others would be working at their drawing-boards.

At lunch-time, blissfully unconscious of their dishevelled appearance, the officer-scientists would wander towards their favourite hostelries, trying to detach their minds from the problems of the morning and remember who it was that they had to salute in the street. Ranks in the other services were only slightly more confusing to some of the lesser trained of the party than the Royal Navy's own distinctive order of precedence. As a result they invariably guessed wrong, saluting American top sergeants and their own petty officers punctiliously while they completely ignored admirals and major-generals with startling results. The Naval Provost Marshal and his lynx-eyed staff, always on the look-out for unshorn locks and caps awry, rarely failed to bag at least one scientist in the early days!

D.M.W.D.'s erudite recruits were not the only scientists at war to run into sartorial difficulties. A world-famous physicist who was advising one of the other services rang up Goodeve one day.

"I'm attending the trials of this airfield-protection device of yours this afternoon," he announced. "Can you give me a lift in your car?"

"Certainly," said Goodeve. "I'm leaving the 'Senior' at two o'clock. Meet me there, and I'll drive you down."

The chosen rendezvous, the United Service Club, was the favoured haunt of senior naval officers. King Haakon of Norway had his own special corner of the coffee-room, and most of the Board of Admiralty lunched at the club. Nothing normally disturbed the cloistered calm of the "Senior," but as Goodeve hurried down the corridor after lunch that day to collect his cap and greatcoat he saw a vigorous scuffle in progress in the entrance hall. A visitor, who was putting up a spirited resistance, was being propelled towards the door by the Head Porter, and, to his dismay, Goodeve saw that the unwelcome intruder was his colleague, the Professor.

Always a spectacularly untidy man, he had excelled himself that day. He was wearing a particularly filthy old raincoat and a pair of tattered trousers. His hair straggled in a tangled mass over his eyes, and his face was streaked like a coalheaver's. It was small wonder that his attempt to gain admittance had been energetically repulsed!

Diving into the fray, Goodeve separated the combatants, and with profuse apologies he led the angry scientist to the Admiralty car waiting outside. Throughout the whole of their journey to that afternoon's trials the Professor remained speechless with rage. It was, in fact, several months before they were on speaking terms again!

Just before Easter the Wheezers and Dodgers moved to new quarters in Lower Regent Street, where they took over a whole suite of offices above the Hungaria Restaurant. In next to no time the large, airy room where most of the staff worked was crammed with the impedimenta of their varied experiments, and the floor round Lane's desk was knee-deep in fuse wire, batteries, miscellaneous tools, and pieces of equipment from German aircraft.

For a man who had spent much of his life in the peaceful, contemplative study of tree culture Lane had a surprising passion for things explosive. He loved dismantling infernal machines, and his pockets were always crammed with bullets, fuses, and detonators. Hurrying into the office, he would beckon every one to gather round, and with an air of a magician he would produce a cannon shell or a piece of one.

"Now this is very interesting," he would say. "You won't know what this is. *You* think it's just an ordinary shell, don't you?"

Playing up, his audience would agree.

"Well, it's nothing of the kind. It's probably the first one of these things to fall in England. Can't tell you how I got hold of it, but I'm pretty certain this shell is actuated by the new Flugelspitz XIK self-determining mechanism. Pass me that hammer!"

Some one would always pass Lane a hammer, and the rest would stand there, rooted to the ground and wishing they had the moral courage to tell him that they thought he ought to treat the new projectile with proper respect. Warming to his demonstration, Lane would strike the nose of the shell several resounding blows and hold it intently to his ear.

"Did anyone hear anything then?" he would ask. "I thought I heard a faint tick."

At this juncture his audience would generally begin to melt away, inventing other urgent appointments, preferably outside the office! Oblivious by then to the loss of his audience, Lane would spend the rest of the morning happily hammering, sawing, and tormenting the shell until he had reduced it to a mass of small fragments. Although several minor explosions occurred in his house in St John's Wood, he never blew up any Admiralty property. And his researches, despite the scarifying manner in which they were conducted, yielded many valuable results.

Menhinick, fascinated by Tolman's "Safe Bomb" demonstrations, always maintained pessimistically that D.M.W.D. had a high accident potential, and it was not long before a delightfully spectacular incident enlivened Lower Regent Street. Richardson was one of the least reckless of the department's officers, but he had an uncontrollable habit of doodling on his blotter or fiddling with anything that came to hand whenever he was talking on the telephone.

One morning in May he was waiting for the Admiralty switchboard to take his call when he picked up his ebony ruler, and in an absent-minded way administered several playful blows to a 2-pounder shell which he was using as a paperweight. To his intense surprise the shell exploded, ejecting a flare and a parachute, and the whole department was filled with choking clouds of bluey-green vapour.

Some officers fought their way to the emergency fire-escape. Enthralled crowds in Lower Regent Street watched others, silhouetted against a baleful glare from the stricken room, hang gasping for breath out of the windows over the Hungaria Restaurant while the green fog swirled around them. Noting the uniforms of the distressed victims, knowing bystanders concluded with satisfaction that the Royal Navy had invented a new secret weapon!

To some people mishaps never come singly. Shells vanished from the desk of Commander Richardson, but in their place arrived two Free Balloon Barrage detonators. Richardson soon forgot his unnerving experience, and a month later he was again speaking on the 'phone—this time to Captain Long at the Ordnance Board—when he prodded one of the detonators with his pen-nib. There was a deafening explosion, and as Richardson staggered into the outer room clutching a wounded hand the phlegmatic Swan picked up the receiver.

"Would you mind calling back a little later, sir?" he said. "Commander Richardson has just shot himself, but I don't think it's anything more serious than usual."

For all these lighter interludes D.M.W.D. was no playground. The department was hard at work on an astonishingly wide range of projects, and the need for a trial ground became increasingly pressing. So far development had been carried out by any means available, small teams of officers working at the universities, in civilian factories, or at the various experimental establishments run by the other Services. The wire devices took some to Exeter, many of the Free Balloon Barrage problems were examined at Cardington. Other officers under Richardson were developing powerful anti-U-boat flares at Newdigate, in Surrey; and research into underwater explosions went on in the grounds of a country house in Berkshire requisitioned by the Ministry of Supply. Much useful work throughout D.M.W.D.'s career was carried out in the Engineering Laboratories of King's College, where the laboratory mechanic, John Shoesmith, gave yeoman assistance with the development of the Pig Trough and freshwater stills.

This need to bat on other people's wickets caused frequent difficulties, and when the department began work on one of its most important projects of all—a weapon which was to revolutionize Allied tactics against the U-boats—Goodeve cast around for a site which would allow them to carry out their own trials with complete freedom. To develop this weapon, the "Hedgehog"—of which more anon—he needed somewhere with a high rise and fall of tide over sand or mud; experimental projectiles had to be fired into deep water and then recovered, undamaged, when the sea receded. The resourceful Francis, now promoted to sub-lieutenant, was therefore dispatched on a tour of the West Country, and it was not long before he found the ideal spot—seventy-five-year-old Birnbeck Pier, at Weston-super-Mare, where in peace-time holiday crowds embarked for steamer trips to Cardiff and Bristol, Clovelly and lonely Lundy Island. For more than a year now no steamers had used the Birnbeck landing stage, and few visitors tramped along the desolate planked roadway to the little island at the Pier's far end, where the amusement booths stood shuttered and deserted.

Noting plenty of buildings on the end of the pier which could be easily adapted as workshops, Francis also saw that the place had advantages from a security angle. It lay well away from the main part of the town. The pier master, much intrigued, allowed him to set up his mortar and fire a few Hedgehog rounds into the sea, and not long afterwards the Admiralty descended on Weston-super-Mare. The pier became H.M.S. *Birnbeck*. For the rest of the war it was destined to play a memorable part in the Navy's scientific researches.

With trials facilities greatly increased, Captain Davies made a number of changes in the organization of the department, and a special section was formed to handle the supply of all the materials needed for D.M.W.D.'s many experiments. The Engineering Section, too, became a separate entity under Norway, who about this time unpatriotically contracted German measles. Bored with his enforced idleness in the sick bay, he occupied the time in writing a novel which, later on, Goodeve used to refer to as one of D.M.W.D.'s most successful 'by-products.' It was *The Pied Piper*.

As the spring of 1941 merged into summer the weight of the enemy air attack on shipping shifted from the narrow waters far out into the Atlantic, where the huge Focke-Wulf Condors took heavy toll. Between February and June we lost nearly 70,000 tons of shipping from air attack alone; there were losses, too, nearer home, and during May the Blitz on Liverpool cost 91,000 tons in ships sunk or damaged in two days.

D.M.W.D. examined the possibilities of camouflaging both the dock area at Liverpool and the prominent landmarks which gave the German pilots their position on the run in to the target. The department also asked to look into the feasibility of designing movable blast-screens to protect ships lying alongside during an air raid. Proposals for wider use of smoke, suggestions for covering the surface of the water in the docks with coal-dust, and the provision of elaborate nets over the reservoirs which lay between Manchester and the Trent Valley were all investigated, but happily the major attacks on the port died away. By midsummer, too, the Prime Minister was able to announce a decisive decline in the losses from air attack in the North Atlantic.

The U-boat situation, however, became increasingly grave, and in twelve weeks enemy torpedoes accounted for no less than 818,000 tons of Allied shipping. D.M.W.D.'s main efforts were henceforward to be directed more and more against the enemy beneath the water, and if they needed any spur to their endeavours they had only to study the reports of the interrogations carried out in the Admiralty's Trade Division by Commander Norman Holbrook, V.C., R.N.

Every master of a merchantman which had undergone attack by aircraft, submarine, or surface raider, or had become a victim of an enemy mine, was sent to Holbrook to tell his story. From these interrogations emerged a picture of enemy tactics which was invaluable in the planning of counter-measures. And, day after day, Holbrook and his small committee of experts from various departments in the Admiralty listened to stories of almost incredible heroism and self-sacrifice, all the more moving for the simple, matter-of-fact way they were told. One master of a little Boston steam trawler described how his ship had been mercilessly shelled by a U-boat. Their only lifeboat had been holed in the attack, but a wounded seaman thrust his leg into the cavity, and for twenty-two hours he kept it there while his shipmates pulled the boat forty miles to the Irish coast.

Occasionally the drama of the survivors' stories was lightened by touches of unexpected humour. Holbrook once asked the master of a ship what weapons he had fired and who had manned the guns in a successful action against a Heinkel bomber.

"We got off 600 rounds from our two Lewis guns and six bombs from the Holman Projector. The mate was at the Holman, and the boatswain and a fireman handled the machine-guns," he replied.

"Half a minute," said Holbrook. "You said earlier on that you had a military gunner. What was *he* doing all this time?"

"Oh . . . he didn't take much part in the action," said the Master. "When we first sighted the bomber he flung his arms round my neck and burst into tears. I think he was a bit nervous, like."

Commander Holbrook readily gained the confidence of the most diffident and reserved men. He had a complete understanding of the tasks facing the Merchant Navy, and his cheerful, sympathetic personality put every one instantly at their ease. In the First War he had won the Victoria Cross for a supremely gallant submarine venture, taking his small boat beneath the elaborate underwater defences of the Dardanelles and torpedoing a Turkish battleship. Many of the Merchant Navy officers—he interviewed over 3000 survivors—came somewhat reluctantly to the Admiralty, thinking they were going to be cross-examined and criticized for their handling of their ships, but Holbrook won them all over. The stories he drew from them played a vital part in improving life-saving equipment, increasing the efficiency of convoy protection by sea and air, and providing the right weapons.

Although they had started their existence as an anti-aircraft organization, it was not long before the Wheezers and Dodgers became concerned with U-boat warfare.

Not, perhaps, surprisingly, their intervention in yet another sphere was soon to involve them in conflict once again—this time with various bodies which had long regarded submarine-warfare problems as their own special responsibility. Goodeve was, however, becoming resigned to this kind of opposition. It was at least more understandable than some of the minor frustrations which the department encountered.

Two prime examples of the latter occurred soon after the Wheezers and Dodgers moved to Lower Regent Street, and the first of these centred, strange to relate, on the complete absence of clocks in the new offices. As D.M.W.D. now had a staff of sixty Goodeve felt that the department might reasonably be entitled to two clocks, and he asked Jamieson to indent for these from naval stores. Soon afterwards he was rung up by a Civil Servant, who said abruptly, "No clocks are available. I'm afraid you will have to do without any."

Goodeve thought no more about the matter until, one day when he was in the laboratories of University College, he came by accident upon a whole room crammed with clocks. There were nearly a a hundred of them lying unused, and they were identical in pattern and make to those in Whitehall.

The University authorities said they had no objection to the Admiralty buying all they wanted, so Goodeve rang up the official again.

"I've just found a hundred clocks," he said. "I've been told we can have two—or more, if they're any use to you. What is the procedure for purchasing any we want?"

The official sounded annoyed. "There are no funds available for purchasing clocks except through this department," he said tersely —and hung up.

A few days later Goodeve invited the official to have a drink with him. Meeting him in the offices over the Hungaria, he led him to the two clocks he had, after all, acquired from the University College.

"Do you know what those really are?" he asked. "I'll tell you. They may look like clocks, but actually they're Experimental Chronometers, and the Admiralty has paid for them."

After a few drinks the official went away in quite a genial frame of mind. He even agreed that an official Admiralty Clock-winder could henceforth 'maintain' the two Experimental Chronometers. So, for the rest of the war, the official clock-winder appeared once a week and wound up the two 'chronometers.' They were, the latter was heard to observe more than once, so like ordinary clocks that a lot of people wouldn't have known the difference!

Another brush with officialdom had its origins in the days when air raids on London were at their height. So much working time was liable to be wasted that a system of graded warnings was introduced, and alarm bells sounded only when enemy aircraft came within a certain radius. This never worried the Wheezers and Dodgers, because they had no alarm bell anyway, but a year after the raids on London had ceased altogether a swarm of workmen descended on the office in Lower Regent Street, and with great labour installed a huge electric bell.

For several months nothing happened, and then, one day when Goodeve was holding an important conference—it was one of the earliest discussions on problems connected with the invasion of Europe—the bell, hitherto silent, began to ring furiously. All work stopped. The bell's deafening clangour made conversation impossible. After enduring this for ten minutes Goodeve went out into the corridor where the bell was hanging. Returning with the bell itself in his hand, he placed it on his desk, and for several weeks it rendered useful service as an ashtray. Three or four times a day the mechanism on the wall in the corridor whirred quietly at the moments of routine testing, but it disturbed no one, and Goodeve had forgotten all about it when an inspector suddenly arrived in the department.

To his astonishment he saw the bell itself no longer in position, and, entering Goodeve's room, he was just about to report the theft when he noticed the missing object lying upturned on the conference table, filled with cigarette-ends.

The inspector fairly bristled with indignation. "This is a serious matter," he declared importantly. "You'll hear more of this."

And Goodeve certainly did. Almost immediately he was summoned to the main Admiralty building by quite a senior Civil Servant, and a heated interview took place. The official, becoming angrier and angrier, finally thumped the desk and said, "The bell goes back within twenty-four hours, or I will see that this very serious breach of regulations is reported to higher authority."

Since there was nothing to be gained by fanning the flames of this trivial dispute Goodeve returned to Lower Regent Street, emptied the cigarette-ends out of the bell, and had it screwed back in position on the wall.

Next day a Chief Inspector appeared. Looking at the bell with evident satisfaction, he remarked to the room at large that he was glad D.M.W.D.'s Deputy Director had seen sense at last.

Officialdom was satisfied, but from that day until the end of the war the bell never, in point of fact, uttered a sound louder than a pleasant purr. Before replacing it Goodeve had taken the precaution of lining the inside with Plasticine!

12

THE BIRTH OF THE HEDGEHOG

WHEN Doenitz unleashed his Wolf Packs the war at sea took a serious turn for the Allies. The new type of 770-ton Atlantic U-boat could travel faster on the surface than many of the convoy escorts, and during the long winter nights they wrought terrible execution, one convoy alone losing twenty ships out of thirty-four.

Submerged, these modern U-boats set just as difficult a problem, for although the Royal Navy, thanks to the efforts of its permanent scientists before the war, were far ahead of other nations in their ability to detect a submarine under the surface, it was quite a different matter to ensure its destruction. In this one field science had not kept abreast of technical development, and the only weapon available, the depth-charge, had not been substantially improved since the First World War. A large round canister, it contained 300 pounds of explosive, and was dropped from the stern of the hunting ship, sinking slowly enough to give the ship herself time to escape the effects of the explosion.

This method of attack had worked well enough two decades earlier, when submarines could only crawl along under water and their hulls were not sufficiently strong to allow them to dive to great depths. Now it was a different story altogether. They could travel at more than eight knots when submerged; they were easily manoeuvrable; and their hulls could stand much greater pressure. If they were picked up by the Asdics of the convoy escorts they still had a good chance of escaping unscathed, for there was an appreciable period of 'blind time' in which they could take evasive action. The escort vessel which got a 'contact' on her anti-submarine detecting gear had first to steam to the spot where she estimated the U-boat to be, and then release the slow-falling canister, which might take a further half-minute or more to reach its intended depth.

When they examined the whole problem before the war two possible methods of cutting down the 'blind time' suggested themselves to the naval scientists. First they could redesign the depth-charge so that it fell faster through the water—but the faster it fell, the greater likelihood there was of damage to the hunting ship before it could steam out of range.

The alternative was to invent a new type of weapon altogether, which could hurl explosive charges far *ahead* of the ship. When this idea was first conceived its sponsors were still thinking along the lines of using depth-charges as missiles, but it was soon found that the effort of throwing these huge projectiles any considerable distance would set up a terrific thrust on the deck of the ship. The normal charge was designed to explode at a certain depth whether it struck an obstacle or not, and therefore had to be large enough to cause damage over a wide area. It now occurred to the scientists that if they used a missile which exploded only when it hit the target they could afford to cut down its weight very substantially. If, also, they could devise a species of gun which hurled a whole pattern of these smaller charges in a circle they would enormously increase the chances of success. Charges which detonated only on contact had a further advantage. If the pattern of bombs missed the target altogether there would be no violent underwater explosions to put the hunting ship's Asdic gear temporarily out of action.

This 'ring attack' method was evolved in the Royal Navy's Anti-Submarine Experimental Establishment before the war started, but little headway was made with the design of a satisfactory weapon, simply because the rigidity of the allocation of duties prevented this establishment from carrying out any experiments, except secretly.[1]

Goodeve first heard about the new 'ahead-throwing mortar' from Dr Bullard in the spring of 1940, when he was clearing up his work on the magnetic mine. Like many others, Bullard realized that the U-boat threat was only in its infancy. Soon the losses from enemy submarine attack would increase, and he was worried at the slow progress of the new weapon. Goodeve had no opportunity to examine the project there and then, for he was on the verge of joining Admiral Somerville's staff, and for a long time afterwards he was busy with anti-aircraft research. Some months later, however, a talk with Richardson about a new type of wire device suddenly suggested a solution to the problem of killing U-boats.

Richardson had been to Portland Place, where a small staff of soldiers and civilians under Major Jefferis was working on various secret projects for disrupting the lives of the Germans. Millis Jefferis, a short, dynamic man with sandy hair, was a sabotage expert who had recently commanded the 1st Field Squadron of the Royal

---

The A/S Experimental Establishment was evacuated to Fairlie, on the Clyde Estuary, after the fall of France.

Engineers at Aldershot. Then the War Office had sent for him. There were many plans afoot for sabotage on the Continent, including a scheme for blowing up oilfields in Rumania; Jefferis, who had brought destruction to a fine art, was put to work in a hush-hush department handling all manner of intelligence and research problems.

In matters of sabotage his interest ranged wide, and a plan of his for sowing fluvial mines in the Rhine attracted the attention of the First Lord of the Admiralty. Mr Churchill was much impressed, and when he became Prime Minister he took steps to discover whether Jefferis' drive and initiative were being used to full advantage. To General Ismay he minuted:

> Report to me on the position of Major Jefferis. By whom is he employed? Who is he under? I regard this officer as a singularly capable and forceful man who should be brought forward to a higher position. He ought certainly to be promoted Lieutenant-Colonel as it will give him more authority.[1]

It was not long before the Sapper major found himself raised in rank and given a department of his own. He took over some offices and workshops in the old headquarters of Radio Normandie, and from time to time he would wander into the Admiralty to exchange information and ideas with Goodeve and Richardson. One morning in the autumn of 1940 he arrived with some rough drawings of a new weapon. This was the spigot mortar—an unusual device which completely reversed the normal process by which a missile was discharged into the air. The base of the bomb itself fitted round an ingenious electrically actuated peg—the spigot—and it was this which fired the projectile. The spigot was the brainchild of Lieutenant-Colonel Stewart Blacker, and Jefferis was using it to develop an anti-tank gun—the "Blacker Bombard"—in his workshops in the Radio Normandie building.

Blacker, a whimsical Irishman in his early fifties, had been inventing things ever since his schooldays at Bedford at the turn of the century. As a boy in the Lower Fifth Form he had been highly intrigued by reports of the successful use of mortars in the Sino-Japanese war, and, procuring some black powder, a stock of cigarette papers, and a croquet ball to act as a projectile, he built his first mortar there and then. With it he carried out a spectacular bombardment of the headmaster's greenhouse at a range of 300 yards!

This resounding success fostered an interest in mortar weapons throughout his military career. Not long before the war he had writ-

---

[1] Sir Winston Churchill, *The Second World War*, Vol. II, p. 583.

ten to the Admiralty suggesting a type of spigot weapon for attacking submarines, only to be informed that there was "no naval requirement" for this idea. By then, with the help of the village clockmaker at Petworth, he had built the first trial model of the Bombard, and it was a variant of this weapon which Jefferis suggested to Goodeve for use in the U-boat war. He thought it might be developed to fire single projectiles, but Goodeve already had another idea. "I've heard something about this from Richardson," he said. "Do you think we could use this spigot mortar of yours to fire a whole ring of bombs?" He outlined the kind of weapon that was needed, and Jefferis went back to his drawing-board. A few days later he returned with a design which seemed distinctly promising. His bomb-thrower looked much lighter and simpler than the Fairlie Mortar, and it promised to be a lot more seaworthy.

Goodeve now had to find an organization in the Admiralty willing to sponsor the new weapon. The Wheezers and Dodgers were still primarily an anti-aircraft body, with neither the authority nor the facilities for developing an underwater weapon singlehanded. Normally this was the special province of D.T.M.—the Directorate of Torpedoes and Mining—but when D.T.M. were approached they said the new bomb-thrower was really a gun and, as such, was the responsibility of the Directorate of Naval Ordnance.

D.N.O., however, were equally reluctant to act as the foster-parents. Inspecting the drawings, they said it was really an underwater weapon, but in the end they agreed to take a benevolent interest in it provided that the Wheezers and Dodgers made themselves responsible for most of the development work.

This was just what Goodeve wanted. It gave him the authority to go ahead on his own; at the same time the backing of D.N.O. would be invaluable in any dealings with the Ordnance Board—the joint-Service body which sat in judgment on every new weapon devised for the Navy, the Army, or the Air Force.

It was a sound principle that the designer should never do the testing of his own productions. An independent and unbiased examination was necessary, and the Ordnance Board thus filled an important rôle. By any standards, however, it was a cumbersome and unwieldy organization, ill-fitted to discharge its heavy responsibilities in time of war. To cope with the task of inspecting a vast range of guns, shells, and fuses a younger and more energetic staff was needed. Instead, the heavy programme was carried out largely by elderly, retired officers or civilians set in their ways and possessing little zest or novelty of outlook. Anything which emerged with their seal of approval was, admittedly, one hundred per cent. safe, but they seemed unable to strike a happy mean between cautious conservatism and enterprise. When a project came before them there were conferences by the dozen and actual trials by the hundred before the smallest piece of equipment was sanctioned.

Many of the Ordnance Board staff seemed a little confused by the impact of war. On one of his early visits to the establishment Richardson had tried to explain to one elderly Army officer the urgency of pushing forward a certain weapon for use against dive-bombers, which for weeks past had been harrying our coastal shipping and attacking the Channel ports.

"I don't quite understand what you're driving at, Commander," said the expert. "What precisely *is* this dive-bombing you keep talking about?"

Not surprisingly, the Wheezers and Dodgers had some misgivings about the Ordnance Board!

Soon after the plans for the new anti-U-boat weapon were presented to this House of Lords of the gunnery world Goodeve rang up a very senior officer on its staff to seek his support and secure some priority for certain trials. To his astonishment, the very mention of the spigot mortar produced a violent diatribe against the device and all its advocates.

"This idea was put up by Major X in 1910, and it was turned down by the Ordnance Board then. The spigot mortar was put up by Colonel Blacker in 1930, and it was turned down again. It was put up by Major Jefferis in 1939, and the Ordnance Board turned it down for the third time. If God Almighty Himself sponsored the spigot mortar, I tell you it would still be turned down by the Ordnance Board!"

To Goodeve, listening to the outburst, it seemed fairly evident that the Wheezers and Dodgers could count on little support from this quarter. They would have to go ahead, trusting that the bomb-thrower would argue its own merits.

From the start many different people and organizations took a hand in the development of the new weapon. Bombed out of his headquarters in Portland Place, Jefferis and his staff moved to a country house near Aylesbury, and Sub-Lieutenant Francis, still protesting that he wanted to go to sea, was sent there to work on the electrical mechanism of the weapon. C.I.G.M.,[1] a sub-department of Naval Ordnance, tackled the design of the mounting, which was to be built by a large firm of boilermakers in Bristol, and Boosey and Hawkes, the famous musical instrument makers, said that the machines they normally used for turning out trumpets for dance bands could construct the projectile.

So far the bomb-thrower had no name. Goodeve offered a bottle

[1] C.I.G.M. was the department of the Chief Inspector of Gun Mountings.

of sherry for the best title, and, though several of his staff laboured enthusiastically to drag in a musical allusion, the prize went to Hassall, with his "Hedgehog." It had a splendid suggestion of prickly hostility, and in the weapon taking shape the rows of spigots which bristled from the mounting bore a striking resemblance to the quills on a hedgehog's defiant back.

When work began on the Hedgehog three other ahead-throwing weapons were under consideration. One, rudely entitled the "Bell-mouthed Bastard," was designed to fire quite large projectiles from a huge mounting sunk in the deck. Another, similar to the Hedgehog, was powered by rockets. The third, an even more massive contraption than the Bell-mouthed Bastard, had five projectors for hurling full-sized depth-charges, but development of this languished when some one discovered that any ship fitting it was liable to overtake its own projectiles!

The only serious rival was the Fairlie Mortar, which had been progressing slowly and somewhat uncertainly since the start of the war. Having cleverly devised the principle of throwing a ring of bombs ahead of a ship, its designers had become firmly bogged down in their efforts to produce a suitable projectile. To make the bombs stable in their flight through the air they had hit on the idea of fitting a heavy cast-iron nose, but this straightaway cut down the space available for the explosive. In addition they had placed the fuse in the tail.

Now the fuse was the critical factor. It had to stand a sudden terrific shock at the moment of firing; it had to strike the water at high speed without setting off the explosive; and yet, when it hit any solid, underwater object even a glancing blow, it needed to react instantly.

For the Hedgehog Goodeve planned to have the fuse in the nose, and 30 pounds of high explosive immediately behind it. In the Fairlie projectile not only was too much space taken up by the iron nose, which limited them to 20 pounds of explosive, but with the fuse placed in the tail their bomb was unlikely to explode at all unless it struck the target at a certain angle.

The opening rounds of the controversy over the competing weapons were fought out on the drawing-board and at innumerable meetings. Maintaining that their own mortar, with its 20-pound charge, would be fully equal to its task, the sponsors of the Fairlie claimed that work on the Hedgehog was a waste of the Admiralty's time. To refute this Goodeve had to prove that his own Hedgehog bomb would be stable in its flight without the weighted nose which was handicapping his rivals.

He proposed to give stability to his projectile by fitting a tubular

THE PANJANDRUM
ON THE BEACH AT
INSTOW AFTER BEING
LAUNCHED FROM ITS
LANDING-CRAFT

WESTWARD HO!
NOVEMBER 12, 1943:
THE FIRST STEERING
TRIALS

Nevil Shute Norway is at the
controls as the Panjandrum
gathers speed. By his side
is Williamson.

THE DEATH THROES
OF THE GREAT
PANJANDRUM, AT
WESTWARD HO!
JANUARY 1944

A PATTERN OF HEDGEHOG
BOMBS SEEN (LEFT) AS THEY
CLIMB THE SKY AND (ABOVE)
AFTER THE EXPLOSION UNDER
WATER

A HEDGEHOG MOUNTING
WITH THE BOMBS IN POSITION
The ingenious propeller fuse can
be clearly seen.

tail, and Francis was sent off to Birnbeck with several dummy bombs
of different shapes and sizes. Setting up his spigot mortar on the end
of the pier, he fired them into the sea. Most of them tended to slide
on hitting the water, but eventually the observers discovered that if
the projectile was designed with a flat nose the skidding action
ceased altogether.

Next they carried out tests with submarine plating. Against this
they exploded various-sized charges, and the results convinced Goodeve that 20 pounds of explosive was certainly not enough to do the
required damage to a submarine's hull. Until he knew the answer
to one vital question, however, he was still not sure that even his own
estimate of 30 pounds was sufficient. Somehow he had to discover
the exact distance between the deck and the pressure hull of the new
German U-boats; it was no good producing a bomb which would
explode on the deck and fail to burst open the main casing of the
submarine.

The Wheezers and Dodgers took their problem to every conceivable intelligence source, but the only reports and drawings available
were all out of date. Short of capturing a U-boat intact, there seemed
no way of securing this one, all-important measurement, and Goodeve was wondering what to do next, when a recent issue of a popular
Italian weekly magazine came into the hands of the Naval Intelligence Department.

It contained an illustrated feature article on the Italian Navy, and
one large picture showed a dockyard worker repairing a U-boat. The
Italian censors had gone to considerable trouble to black out almost
everything which might have given any hint of the U-boat's design
and special equipment—but they had not been quite careful enough.
Examining the picture, Goodeve noticed that one of the workmen
was obviously standing on the pressure hull itself as he hammered at
something on the deck below his waist.

Taking into consideration the probable length of the man's legs,
he could work out quite simply the distance he had been seeking.
His calculation showed that either the Italian workman was a
midget or the estimate put forward by the sponsors of the Fairlie
to justify their smaller explosive charge was wrong by over a
foot.

It was now obvious, too, that secrecy was vital on the British side.
If the enemy got wind of the new weapon, and raised the height of
the duck-boarding on top of their U-boats' hulls, the mortar bombs
would explode harmlessly. Realizing this, the Admiralty shipbuilding
experts added fresh fuel to the argument. To insure against any constructional changes by the enemy they claimed that a larger mortar
bomb was an absolute necessity. In the Fairlie camp this ultimatum

I

caused something like consternation, for their projectile was already as heavy as they dared to make it, it had substantially less explosive than the Hedgehog's bomb, and, to make matters worse, this was in the tail instead of the nose.

While the Fairlie team were still trying to find a way out of this difficulty Goodeve tackled the next stage in the Hedgehog's evolution. He had to calculate the exact bomb pattern which, in size and shape, would give a hunted U-boat the smallest chance of escape.

In the big room in Lower Regent Street Dr Guggenheim rigged up an apparatus resembling a roulette wheel, and for hour after hour and day after day he and an assistant spun the wheel, throwing tiny missiles at a scale model of a submarine. From these experiments they worked out the correct elevation for the spigots, and were able to estimate the significance of any accidental deviations from the pattern of bombs eventually chosen.

When the answer emerged Guggenheim's ideal pattern had to be reproduced on the range with actual projectiles, and experiments switched to Whitchurch, where Jefferis and his staff were now established.

A Secret Service research station, Whitchurch was the ideal place for developing the new weapon. There Jefferis had his own facilities for filling projectiles, detonators, and fuses; a special electronic apparatus was available for measuring velocity; and there were large water-tanks where Hedgehog rounds could be tested against submarine hulls.

All manner of remarkable projects—bombs which jumped about on the ground, bombs which leapt in and out of the sea, and rockets which fired bridges over rivers—were given their first secret trials there. Professor Lindemann, a frequent visitor, was once present when Jefferis decided to test the thrust of one of his new projectiles by firing it down a stretch of railway track specially laid in the park. The missile in question was a homing bomb, fitted with air fins and propelled by a monster rocket.

The bomb was first anchored to a huge steel plate, and then strapped to the floor of the truck by powerful metal clamps. In spite of these precautions the terrific stress set up when the rocket began its journey—the thrust was over a thousand tons—wrenched the vast missile free from its moorings. Taking off from the rails, the runaway bomb forced the startled spectators to take swift avoiding action. On another memorable occasion a workshop filled with mortar rounds and carboys containing some lethal liquid caught fire, and the whole corner of the building blew out. Probably the least concerned observer present when things went wrong was the impresario of this unusual establishment; Jefferis, whose habit of walking about with his pockets crammed with detonators, small batteries, and pieces of wire greatly impressed the Wheezers and Dodgers, never allowed minor mishaps to worry him!

The new Hedgehog problem he tackled with characteristic energy, but for some time little headway was made. No matter how many rounds were fired from the spigots the bombs refused to land in the prescribed formation.

The Ordnance Board then decided to take a hand. Under their supervision a further hundred rounds were prepared with different sizes of cordite charge. For most of one day these were fired off and the results were carefully analysed. But the distribution of the bombs still remained obstinately inaccurate. When they adjourned to Jefferis' room for tea that day the Hedgehog party held an anxious post-mortem.

"There are still two ideas we haven't tried," said Goodeve. "We need fifty more rounds with two different types of sealing gland."[1]

A commander from the Ordnance Board immediately objected. "That's all very well," he remarked, "but it'll take us another six weeks, you know. We can't possibly prepare you fifty more rounds in a shorter time than that."

It was Jefferis' turn to look astonished, and he pressed the bell on his desk. In came his senior N.C.O., Sergeant Tilsley, who had done much skilled work on the Hedgehog projectile. Jefferis made a couple of quick sketches on the back of an envelope and passed it to him. "I want you to make up another fifty rounds with these changes incorporated—and I want them by six o'clock, an hour from now," he said.

At 6 P.M. they walked back to the range. The new rounds were ready for them, and one batch of twenty-five gave the exact pattern they were seeking. When they hit the ground the space between the charges was a little smaller than the diameter of a U-boat; the distance across the circle was shorter than a U-boat's length. Any enemy submarine trapped in this ring of Hedgehog bombs could not escape serious damage. At long last the dispersion problem was solved.

By now the mounting of the Hedgehog was under construction. In the early stages this had given a lot of trouble, for although the design put forward by C.I.G.M. had its ingenious features they had estimated a recoil far greater than Goodeve or Jefferis anticipated. Assuming that their figures were accurate, Jefferis spent most of one train journey between Bath and London sketching furiously on empty

---

[1] The sealing gland prevented the explosive gases from escaping prematurely round the spigot from which the bombs were fired.

cigarette packets. There and then he found a way of altering the mounting so that most of the thrust was not taken on the deck, but carried down into the bottom of the ship. Even so, the safety margin proved to be still insufficient. Poring over the designer's calculations, and trying to reconcile them with his own, Jefferis eventually made a surprising discovery. All C.I.G.M.'s figures were based on a cordite reference table published in 1899! And, working with this out-of-date manual, they had allowed for four times the thrust exerted by modern cordite. It was small wonder that the problems of the mounting had seemed so intractable.

The vital feature in the whole development of the weapon, however, was the fuse. Goodeve found that fuse design was outside the province of the Director of Naval Ordnance; the task had to be passed through the Ordnance Board to the Chief Superintendent of Armament Design, who specialized in such matters. Instead of forwarding it to his latter organization, however, a senior officer in the Ordnance Board to whom the request for the new fuse was sent decided to use his own initiative, and, sitting down at the drawing-board, he himself designed a fuse of almost unbelievable complexity. It had no fewer than 127 different parts, and, like the fuse in the tail of the Fairlie bomb, it had a 'dead' angle; in certain circumstances it could strike the target and fail to function at all.

Goodeve, who had already had a somewhat heated altercation with C.I.G.M.'s staff over the Hedgehog mounting, blew up at this further needless delay. Taking over responsibility for the development of the fuse himself, he sent an SOS to half a dozen different technical bodies for "ideas by Tuesday next." It went to recognized Admiralty sections specializing in ordnance problems; to the Navy's mine-design experts; to the underwater-weapon branch at Fairlie; and even to the rocket-research station at Aberporth, the Royal Aircraft Establishment at Farnborough, and the chemical-warfare scientists at Porton. On the following Tuesday the suggestions which had come in were carefully examined, and three promising designs were placed on the short list. One of them, put forward by a Captain Hawes, greatly attracted Goodeve. This fuse armed itself by hydrostatic pressure through holes in the nose, the rush of water as the projectile dived into the sea setting the mechanism in operation.

Another worked by metal feelers protruding from the bomb like the antennæ of an insect. And the third fuse on the short list, designed by Dr Lindley, a scientist working at the rocket range in Wales, had a mechanism set in motion by a propeller which began to turn as the projectile hit the water.

Among those present at this meeting, held at the headquarters of the Chief Superintendent of Armament Design, was a retired Commander named Lucas, who had only joined the staff of C.S.A.D. on the previous day. A resourceful and energetic man, he had few illusions about the tempo at which the Ordnance Board normally carried out their researches, and, recognizing the urgency of getting the Hedgehog into service, he volunteered to make the prototypes of the fuses himself. Borrowing a lathe, he turned the corner of his garage into a workshop, and although he had no proper drawings to guide him he produced beautifully finished working models of the three chosen fuses in a matter of days. This cut out the need to secure a priority in the Ordnance Board's drawing-office, and saved months of delay.

The fuses were then taken to the Surrey Docks, where steel plates resembling the saddle tanks of a U-boat, and a wooden lattice-work contraption to simulate the submarine's deck, were rigged up. On to this target dummy Hedgehog bombs fitted with the different fuses were dropped from a gallows. Having passed this test, they were taken to Birnbeck, and exhaustive firing trials were carried out from the end of the pier.

At first none of the fuses would arm on striking the sea, Lindley's propeller mechanism repeatedly jamming, but this fault soon cleared. To Goodeve's regret the hydrostatic fuse, which had looked the scientist's dream at first inspection, never came up to his high hopes. It persistently fired prematurely just below the surface. On the other hand, once it had come through its initial teething troubles, Lindley's propeller was apparently proof against every stress and strain imposed upon it. On entering the water it revolved slowly and surely until the right depth was reached, and then, just as surely, was ready for action. Before the Birnbeck trials were over the Lindley-Lucas fuse had established itself as the logical choice, and thus, in a surprisingly short time, all the main problems in the design of the weapon had now been conquered.

The work on the fuse development was a good example of scientific research in a hurry, for the requirement was first explained to a widely varied group of technical specialists, which made for healthy competition; all the chosen fuses reached the prototype stage where they could be compared; and finally there was concentration on the best.

With the explosive side, in the charge of Lieutenant-Commander R. F. Strickland-Constable, R.N.V.R., producing no troubles, the stage was now set for 'selling' the Hedgehog to higher authority. So far the mainspring of the Hedgehog's development had been Goodeve's drive and persistence. Having paved the way for Jefferis to introduce the spigot mortar, he had compèred every stage of its construction, finding the right people to carry out the many different technical tasks, and visiting the factories to spur on their efforts. Closely following every phase in the Hedgehog's evolution, he had always been in a position to supply the authoritative answer to any question which cropped up, and his own complete confidence in the capabilities of the new weapon had won for it increasing support in the Admiralty.

The speed with which a new weapon could be put into service, depended, however, on the priority allocated to its full-scale production, and here Goodeve knew he would have to secure influential backing. No matter how much he and his department believed in the new U-boat weapon, they had no say in the matter of priorities; these were decided on a much higher joint-Service level.

He and Jock Davies were still considering ways and means of boosting the Hedgehog's claims when they learnt that the Prime Minister was to be present at the trials of a new type of anti-tank bomb which Jefferis was staging in a chalk quarry not far from Chequers. If they could capture Mr Churchill's interest in their own new weapon the battle was as good as won, and as Chequers was quite close to Whitchurch this seemed the ideal opportunity. The trial was taking place at ten o'clock one Sunday morning, and Lord Cherwell readily agreed to suggest to the Prime Minister that he should drive over to Whitchurch after watching the anti-tank demonstration. The Hedgehog could then be put through its paces before lunch. When the day came, however, Davies and Goodeve, deciding to leave nothing to chance, set off for the scene of the first trial. The area near the chalk pit swarmed with military police checking the identity of every visitor, but although neither of the interlopers from D.M.W.D. had passes with them Davies waved some entirely irrelevant documents out of the car window and they were allowed through the cordon.

On a grassy slope in front of the targets they found a distinguished gathering of Service leaders and civilians, and Jefferis put on a spectacular show for them with his anti-tank bomb—a glass container filled with nitroglycerine, which exploded with an impressive flash and a crack. The young officer chosen to demonstrate it had rehearsed an act requiring split-second timing. Standing in front of the tank, he saluted, and then, turning smartly about, he hurled the bomb at the target and saluted again as he threw himself flat on his face before the explosion. Mr Churchill was delighted, and when the demonstration was over he led the way down the slope to inspect the damage. He then decided on a little target practice himself.

Taking a tommy-gun, he fired a long burst at the tyres of a derelict Army lorry. The spectators began to edge back out of harm's way, and Mr Churchill next turned his attention to the lorry's Triplex screen, on which he cut his initials with bullets. More ammunition was sent for, and the crowd retreated even faster when the gun was passed to Mary Churchill, who blazed away enthusiastically at the battered lorry.

After a while the Prime Minister looked at his watch. "Time for lunch," he remarked, and began to walk back up the slope, the onlookers forming a line along which he passed. Taking up a strategic position at the far end of the line, Goodeve looked round for Davies to support him, but he was nowhere to be seen, so when Lord Cherwell introduced the R.N.V.R. officer to the Prime Minister Goodeve hurriedly brought up the subject of the Hedgehog on his own.

Mr Churchill listened intently, and then, looking again at his watch, he said, "I'm sorry, but I haven't time to come and see this weapon now. We are late already."

He turned away, and was about to get into his car when his daughter, who had just walked up to the group, firmly grasped his arm.

"We must see Captain Davies's bomb-thrower, Daddy," she pleaded; "of course there's time." Jock Davies, with his winning manner, had not been idle!

Smiling ruefully, Mr Churchill gave in, and the procession of cars shot away to Whitchurch. Watching the Hedgehog give a highly impressive account of itself, the Prime Minister soon forgot all about his lunch.

The mortar was set to fire twenty-four rounds, two at a time in quick succession, until all the projectiles were in the air at once. Climbing the blue sky, they formed a strangely graceful pattern, and as they reached their zenith they turned lazily over, like well-drilled marionettes, before starting their swift dive to earth. Then came the bangs of the discharges as they landed round the target—the shape of a submarine outlined on the ground with white tapes.

The Prime Minister was enthralled. He asked for a second salvo to be fired . . . then a third. Here at last, it seemed, was the instrument which could turn the tide of the U-boat war, and Goodeve did not have long to wait for repercussions of this successful demonstration.

The following morning the First Sea Lord sent for him.

"This anti-submarine gun of yours . . . how soon can you arrange a trial for me?" asked Admiral Pound. And straightway he promised all possible assistance in getting the Hedgehog into operational use.

This new and influential support came at a timely moment. Although there had been no serious setbacks in producing the prototype, Goodeve knew that in certain quarters there was keen resentment at the intervention of his little department in a sphere outside its normal field of operations.

This opposition was expressed in constant sniping at the Hedgehog for shortcomings which had no foundation in fact. Again and again D.M.W.D.'s development officers were obliged to stage extra trials or waste time on elaborate calculations on paper in order to refute criticism for which there was no real justification. The reason for this became clearer when a man in a responsible position in another department arrived one morning at the office in Lower Regent Street and asked to see Goodeve. Point-blank a request was made that D.M.W.D. should abandon work on the new weapon altogether. Goodeve's visitor said bluntly that he wanted a clear field for the development of one of the competing anti-submarine weapons. The future of his own establishment depended on getting their own A/S weapon into service, whereas Goodeve had no need to enhance his own reputation. Clearly, added his caller, the only honourable course for D.M.W.D. was to cease all work on the Hedgehog forthwith.

Goodeve was flabbergasted. This astonishing request completely ignored the needs of the Navy, and he resented the imputation that he was striving to produce the new spigot mortar solely for his own glorification. He knew that his visitor had struggled for a long time to get into the field of anti-submarine weapons and had had little opportunity. The man had been working under great stress for some time, but nevertheless this emotional appeal for work on the Hedgehog to be abandoned showed no sense of proportion or responsibility.

Happily the Hedgehog had now progressed far enough for its merits to be known to a wide circle of naval experts. No amount of pressure from any vested interest could stop production, and after the Whitchurch demonstration Goodeve was in a much stronger position to deal with departmental rivalry. By May 1941 the Hedgehog was ready for its sea trials.

It had a formidable performance. The spigots could hurl their load of explosive fully 200 yards ahead of the ship, and when the bombs hit the water they formed a circular pattern 130 feet in diameter. With their streamlined casing, and their long-vaned tails to keep them falling on a true path, the bombs sank three times as fast as ordinary depth-charges, and a simple manual control enabled the whole mounting of the Hedgehog to be tilted by hand to offset any roll of the ship at the moment of firing.

While the finishing touches were being put to the first of these multiple-spigot mortars, fitted in H.M.S. *Westcott*, the initial batch of live bombs were filled and sent off by rail to Liverpool. To the dismay of Francis and other members of the Wheezers and Dodgers awaiting their arrival, the bombs then vanished into thin air.

It was found that they had got as far as Crewe, but not until a few hours before *Westcott* was due to sail came a message that they had been tracked down to a remote siding in North Wales.

Francis was dispatched in a naval lorry to pick them up at Chester. When he set off on the return journey there was no time for détours. Turning a blind eye to the ban on explosives, Francis rushed his precious load through the Mersey Tunnel, reflecting a little apprehensively that a sub-lieutenant's pay would hardly meet the fine if he was caught.

Westcott slipped from her moorings on a brilliant early summer morn, with the calmest of seas. The firing trials were to be carried out against a submerged wreck in Liverpool Bay, and, after a few single rounds had been fired to check the functioning of the electrical gear, the destroyer—her Asdics trained on the sunken vessel—headed in for a full-scale attack.

On the bridge hardly a word was spoken. To the waiting scientists this was the culmination of months of anxious preparation—of constant consultations at the drawing-board; of interminable arguments with detractors of every feature of the Hedgehog, from the spigots, which were its nerve centre, to the bombs, with their ingenious fuse; and of countless trials which had gradually buoyed up the spirits of the Wheezers and Dodgers to optimistic certainty of success. Now their claims were about to be put to the test.

The command to fire was given, and they saw the bombs climb the sky in front of them. They could follow each individual projectile quite plainly, and they watched them do their slow, deliberate somersaults before they began to fall—faster, and faster. . . .

As they struck the surface in a perfectly circular formation Goodeve found himself counting the seconds out loud. It seemed an eternity before anything happened, and then came the heavy rumble of the exploding charges. Above the wreck the sea shuddered violently, and broke into a mist of droplets which rose and hung in the air.

A cheer broke from the watching sailors. On the bridge there was general rejoicing. In the midst of this Francis came up to Goodeve, saluted smartly, and said, "May I now be transferred to sea duty, sir?" "If that's what you want," said Goodeve, "you've more than earned it."

In relative silence the destroyer, her engines stopped, coasted into the centre of the huge ring of broken water, and then they noticed that the whole surface around the *Westcott* was covered with the white bellies of stunned or dead fish, which the crew began scooping aboard with every utensil they could lay hands on. It was the first time in the history of the Royal Navy that a submarine attack had been carried out ahead of a ship. And the Hedgehog had functioned perfectly.

Following the success of the *Westcott* trials the Admiralty went straight ahead with the Hedgehog, and in less than nine months from the day when Jefferis first travelled to Bath with his original drawings the weapon was in production.

In the interim period secrecy was more than ever necessary. If the enemy learnt that a new weapon firing contact charges was even contemplated it was thought they might well contrive some counter-measures in the construction of their U-boats. Several months after the trials in Liverpool Bay, however, came reassuring news.

An aircraft of Coastal Command, patrolling south of Iceland, surprised U 570 in the act of surfacing. The U-boat's captain was on his first patrol in command. Losing his nerve, he scrambled on to the conning tower and waved his white shirt in surrender. U 570 was captured intact, and when she was brought into port examination showed that no structural changes had been made.[1]

As it turned out, secrecy was a double-edged weapon. Many sea-going officers in escort vessels had never heard of the Hedgehog when it was installed, and had no real understanding of what it could accomplish. No trained crews were provided to maintain it, and when, perhaps after a long interval, the bomb-thrower was tried out something often went wrong, and the unfortunate Hedgehog was there and then condemned as useless.

Paradoxically enough, even when the weapon itself operated satisfactorily it often failed to win the confidence of its users. The average seaman is innately conservative. Used to weapons which fired with a resounding bang, he was not readily impressed with the performance of a contact bomb, which exploded only on *striking* an unseen target. The Hedgehog thus started with an initial handicap, and, to make matters worse, it was designed on principles unfamiliar to the sailor long accustomed to orthodox guns. Rumours began to circulate that the spigot mortar was unsafe. In point of fact it had been made as safe as it was humanly possible to make any weapon,

---

[1] This extraordinary incident is described in Wolfgang Frank's story of the U-boat war published in Great Britain under the title of *The Sea Wolves* (Weidenfeld and Nicolson, 1955). U 570 was later recommissioned for service in the Royal Navy as H.M. Submarine *Graph*.

and a remarkable illustration of the shock-proof qualities of both its fuse and explosive was given in New York Harbour. A whole salvo of Hedgehog projectiles was fired accidentally from the deck of an escort vessel moored at a jetty. They all landed on the concrete surface of the quay, and not a single bomb exploded.[1]

Despite its merits, however the results achieved with the new weapon in its first year at sea were distinctly disappointing. At the end of this period only one kill and three 'probables' had come in. The trials, using dummy projectiles against some of our own submarines, had indicated that 50 per cent. of the attacks should have been successful; in fact, only about 5 per cent. were proving effective, and this was little better than they had experienced with the depth-charge.

Proper training alone could dispel suspicion and mistrust, and this underlying reason for the Hedgehog's failure had just been realized in the Admiralty when Francis returned dejectedly to Lower Regent Street, having been put ashore on account of night blindness. For nine months after his transfer to patrol duties in the North Sea he had managed to hide this unusual physical defect, but by an ironic turn of fate he had been caught out in the end. Volunteering for the midget submarine operations against the *Tirpitz*, he spent several months of intensive training, and then his commanding officer decided to put all the crews through a night-vision test devised for air crews some years before by Air-Commodore Livingstone. Goodeve had been responsible for the introduction of this test to the Navy, but he did not disclose this to the disconsolate Francis!

No sooner was he back in D.M.W.D. than Francis was dispatched on a fact-finding tour of the escort bases, and soon afterwards he was posted to Londonderry as "Hedgehog Training Officer." Using the wreck of the *Empress of Britain* as a convenient target, he put the escort vessels through a thorough course in the use of the spigot mortar. Almost immediately the kills began to come in, and before the end of the war the Hedgehogs accounted for some fifty enemy submarines.

Once they understood its potentialities the men of the escort vessels became fervent supporters of the new weapon, and one day a macabre tribute to its efficiency arrived at the Admiralty addressed to D.M.W.D.—a parcel containing unchallengeable and rather gruesome evidence of a successful attack on a hunted U-boat.

To-day the Royal Navy has an even more ambitious ahead-

[1] Cited by J. M. Kirkby, M.A., Principal Scientific Officer, Admiralty Mining Establishment, in an address to the Institution of Mechanical Engineers, February 6, 1948.

throwing weapon in general use—the Squid, a huge monster, hurling 500-pound projectiles—but the Hedgehog, which still plays its part in the Service, paved the way for its formidable offspring. It also spurred the Wheezers and Dodgers to further successful incursions into anti-submarine warfare.

13

HIS MAJESTY'S PIER

THE acquisition of the pier at Weston-super-Mare, referred to in an earlier chapter, enabled D.M.W.D. to expand their operations considerably. Not only was Birnbeck, with its high rise and fall of tide, ideal for testing underwater projectiles, but on either side of the bay stretched miles of lonely headland, and beaches secure from inquisitive eyes.

Soon many unusual experiments were being conducted on and around Brean Down, a great grassy promontory to the south of the town. Others were staged in Middle Hope Cove, about four miles north of the pier, where two high-speed catapult tracks were laid down for testing missiles unlike any seen in the history of modern warfare.

Research at Birnbeck ranged out, in fact, to embrace every aspect of war. Secret weapons were fired along the beaches or into the sea, and a host of problems connected with amphibious assault—from the crossing of mined beaches to the scaling of cliffs—were examined there. D.M.W.D. were gaining a wide reputation for versatility, and before long they were asked to explore such un-naval projects as the clearing of jungles in Burma, the distilling of water for men and machines in the Desert, and means of adapting the P.A.C. to stop enemy tanks.

The pier which now became their second home was one of the few to survive the invasion scare intact. In the summer of 1940 an admiral had stumped into the little office next to the turnstiles, and said to John Wide, who was in charge, "I'm afraid we shall have to cut a large section out of your pier."

"You can't do that, sir," said Wide; "it's a continuous-girder pier; if you take one piece out the whole thing will fall down."

The Admiral looked at him suspiciously, and sent for technical experts, who confirmed the fact. So the dismantlers moved on, and the pier remained open for business. Few people visited it, however. War heightened the air of desolation which descends on all British seaside resorts in winter-time, and when Wide, who had spent much of his life in the Merchant Navy, left to join the Royal Naval Reserve the pier stood forlorn and deserted until the sudden arrival of Sub-Lieutenant Francis with his spigot mortar.

Birnbeck was more secluded than most seaside piers, for a neck of land hid it from the main part of the town, and one look convinced Francis that it was just what the Wheezers and Dodgers wanted. He cajoled the owners into leasing a small space just big enough for two men to stand on and operate the mortar, and when the first firing trials took place some R.A.F. ratings billeted in the Refreshment Hall helped to keep unwelcome visitors away.

Then more officers arrived from D.M.W.D. with Hedgehog fuses, and 'mudlarking'—an exhausting and chilly pastime into which every visitor to Birnbeck was initiated sooner or later—began in earnest. At high tide dummy projectiles fitted with live fuses were fired into some forty feet of water, and, six hours later, when the tide receded a team combed the odorous mud. The bombs were retrieved, and the fuses were then examined to discover whether they had functioned prematurely, either on leaving the mortar or on hitting the sea.

Officially the pier still preserved its civilian status, but in time word reached the Admiralty that a young sub-lieutenant with no proper authority to carry out deals in real estate was requisitioning more and more of it. An outraged member of the Admiralty department which looked after lands and buildings then called on Captain Davies, and said that if the Wheezers and Dodgers wanted a pier—or even a small part of one—they must apply through the Right Channels. So the position was regularized, and D.M.W.D. got the whole pier, inheriting at the same time an unusual asset for a scientific research station—a fully licensed bar!

Within a year Birnbeck became one of His Majesty's naval shore establishments. Having heard that he had gained an R.N.R. commission and realizing that his local knowledge would be invaluable, Goodeve successfully applied for John Wide to be posted there as First Lieutenant.

This West Country landmark soon became a recognizable offshoot of D.M.W.D.'s London headquarters. People arrived with mysterious packages containing jelly bombs or other strange contrivances which they wanted to try out, and far into the night loud explosions or blinding flashes of light came from the island on which the pier's far end was anchored.

At Paddington the stream of bombs, mines, and other lethal-looking objects bound for Weston-super-Mare aroused no more than passing interest among the railway staff after a while, but the Wheezers and Dodgers' fellow-passengers never seemed quite at ease when they found themselves sharing a compartment with a large bomb. To Goodeve, who always had work to do in the train on his journeys to and from Birnbeck, this could be a major blessing. Struggling into a crowded compartment, he would say politely, "Would you mind if we put this under the seat? It must ride crossways on the train." The projectile was then dropped with an ominous thud and levered under the seat.

On his way out to stand in the corridor he would remark to his companion with well-assumed anxiety, "You did remember to remove the fuse, didn't you?" It was never long before the passengers one by one found some pressing reason for deserting their hard-won seats, and for the rest of the journey Goodeve and his companions could settle down with their secret papers in splendid isolation.

In the early days there was an attractive air of informality about life on the pier. For the visitors from London camp-beds were set up in a vast, draughty room filled with discarded slot machines, beer engines, and dismantled side-shows. It could be bitterly cold, for the strong winds from the Atlantic blew in fierce gusts through the uneven boarding, but before long Naval Stores, who normally viewed heaters as an unnecessary luxury, supplied a Tortoise stove. Unversed in the wiles of R.N.V.R. scientists, they were no doubt impressed by the explanation that it was urgently needed "for boiling pitch to fill projectiles."

In the autumn of 1941 several officers were posted to Birnbeck for full-time duty. Among them was James Close, who had been working at Exeter on wire devices, and who was to direct affairs at Birnbeck for some eighteen months. He was later succeeded by Lieutenant-Commander C. N. Boswell, R.N.V.R., a member of the department from its very early days. Boswell had first helped to develop the Parachute and Cable, and later he had joined forces with Richardson on the task of producing a revolutionary new type of anti-submarine flare.

To help with the Hedgehog trials two ratings arrived and slung their hammocks in the Tea Room. One of them, Leading Seaman Johnson, became a mainstay of the establishment. Although he was apt to complain that the rigours of mudlarking brought on his "rheumatics," he accepted his strange new environment and duties philosophically, and he soon showed himself to be a man of resource. The messing arrangements for the ship's company were somewhat erratic at first, but Johnson would supplement his own meals from time to time by the simple expedient of emptying a basket of stones on to the heads of surprised seabirds as they fought over offal tipped from the end of the pier. Before they recovered from the shock the bemused victims were lassoed and roasted!

For all development work the pier party were answerable to D.M.W.D., but locally H.M.S. *Birnbeck* came under the general control of the Naval Officer-in-Charge, Appledore—a retired Rear-Admiral serving temporarily in the rank of Captain. To make matters more complicated still, their immediate superior was the Resident Naval Officer, Watchet—a retired Vice-Admiral serving in the rank of Commander. This was John Casement, an Irishman of great charm, who took a close interest in the pier's activities from the start. A tall, wiry man with greying hair, he was a strict disciplinarian, and the unconventional way in which some of his new charges went about their duties—mudlarking prompted the strangest of attires—disconcerted him a little at first. He realized, however, that for all its unorthodoxy the organization on the pier worked well.

It became a tradition of Birnbeck that all hands 'mucked in' together when there was a pressing job to be tackled, and because the ratings were put into the picture as much as possible, and understood the nature and objects of the trials, there was never any shortage of volunteers to work right round the clock if necessary.

After a while Admiral Casement moved his headquarters to Weston-super-Mare, and immediately life became full of surprises for him. Among the ingenious devices undergoing trials was the "Expendable Noise-maker," designed to foil the enemy's acoustic torpedoes. This was fired from a mortar, like the Hedgehog bombs, and on sinking below the surface it caused a series of rhythmic detonations.

For some unremembered reason the first trials of this cleverly conceived gadget were entrusted to the Army, who planned to fire the early rounds into shallow water just off the beach. With great care they measured the range, but they entirely overlooked the fact that the mortar itself, mounted on a wing of the pier, was forty feet above sea-level. To their intense surprise the first round sailed clean over the water and exploded in mid-air outside a cliff-side café, which emptied rapidly.

Much puzzled, the soldiers made a slight adjustment of elevation, and dropped the second round a yard from Admiral Casement's office. The outburst of wrath which followed led Boswell to search for fresh fields when a more advanced type of Noise-maker came up for trial. The improved model was a formidable affair—a large, rocket-propelled container which burst open, ejecting various exploding objects—and, noting with some misgivings that no fins had been fitted to stabilize its flight, Boswell and Jesse Wyllie, an R.N.V.R. lieutenant who enjoyed experimenting with infernal machines, decided to try it out on Brean Down. As a precautionary measure the first round was fired directly out to sea, but, as this flew reasonably

THE LONELY SETTING OF ONE OF D.M.W.D.'S TRIAL GROUNDS ON
THE SOMERSET COAST

One of the catapult tracks can be seen in the right-hand corner.

CLOSE-UP VIEW OF THE CATAPULT TRACK AT MIDDLE HOPE COVE

H.M.S. "BIRNBECK," THE WAR-TIME EXPERIMENTAL STATION OF
D.M.W.D. AT WESTON-SUPER-MARE, AS IT IS TO-DAY

Photograph by the author

DICK CROWE (RIGHT) AND LIEUTENANT-COMMANDER C. N. BOSWELL, R.N.V.
IN ONE OF THE LAUNCHES USED FOR TRIALS WORK AT BIRNBECK

straight, they aimed the next along the edge of the water to give the
recovery party on the beach below a chance to salve the wreckage for
examination.

To their astonishment the second rocket behaved quite differently.
After flying perfectly straight for several hundred yards it shot off at
right angles to its original course, disappearing inland at high speed.
They heard it explode in the distance, uncomfortably near to a farm,
and with some misgivings they set off to investigate.

It was not long before they met an irate man carrying a tangled
mass of blackened metal.

"Where did it land?" they asked.

The farmer glowered. "In my chicken run ... that's where it
landed."

"What a lucky thing," said Wyllie, trying to get the conversation
on to a more genial plane. "Where were you at the time?"

"Where was I?" bellowed the aggrieved farmer. "In the bloody
chicken run!"

After that all experiments with the Noise-maker were removed
even farther from the environs of Weston.

In point of fact, however, it was not easy to find trial grounds
remote enough for some of the more unpredictable weapons and
devices. A convenient area lay above Middle Hope Cove, where a
belt of rough moorland sloped down to the sea, but beyond this, over
the brow of the hill, lay Woodspring Priory, farmed by two brothers
named Burrough, who stoically endured the most startling incon-
veniences.

Having stampeded their horses and cattle unwittingly on several
occasions with the more lethal version of the P.A.C., Close felt that
some friendly gesture was due to the Burrough brothers for carrying
out their daily tasks under fire, and one day an opportunity presented
itself. The farmers reported that damage was being done on their
land by badgers, and Close promptly assured them that H.M.S.
Birnbeck would be only to glad to remove the marauders by the
most up-to-date methods.

From the store on the pier he collected an impressive assortment
of 6-inch cordite tubes, old flares, and rockets, and half a hundredweight of these was stuffed into the badgers' lair. The operation was
a humiliating failure. Although the pillar of fire, earth, and stones
which erupted should have discouraged every living creature for
miles around, the badgers seemed impervious to explosives, and only
a few days later they were sighted busily tidying up their shattered
premises!

By the time the big explosive P.A.C. called "Type J" was ready
for service the enemy were carrying out low-level raids on the Bristol

K

Channel area. The bombers passed close to Weston-super-Mare, and the pier was heavily armed with Type J's in the hope of testing them in action. News of the device on the pier reached the War Office, and a novel query came to D.M.W.D. Could their new weapon—designed to operate against aircraft—be used to ensnare German tanks?

The Brigade of Guards supplied a Valentine tank, which was driven to the foreshore below Brean Down. It had some difficulty in completing the last stage of its long journey, for as it turned off the main Bridgwater road into the narrow, winding lane to the sea a fault developed in the clutch plate and the tank embedded itself in the side of a small hostelry.

The trial of Type J in its new rôle was, however, a great success. Smothered in 600 feet of immensely strong wire, the Valentine was brought to a grinding halt, and its tracks became so hopelessly enmeshed that it took two days' hard work before the tank was able to struggle off the beach.

Projects under examination at Birnbeck became more and more varied. The team on the pier worked on a "Water Hammer"—a device for absorbing a weapon's recoil in the sea. There were dropping trials of 600-pound bombs with hydrostatic fuses which had to be laboriously recovered from the depths of the bay. Development work was also carried out on "Weasels"—tracked vehicles for negotiating snow and mud—and one of these overturned on the way to Brean, killing the driver and trapping Lieutenant Ritchie in a water-filled ditch, where he was all but drowned.

Ritchie's main activities were concerned with research into a new method of distilling water for ship's lifeboats, and another important task was the evolution of the new anti-submarine starshell invented by Richardson. Elaborate silhouette tests were staged with dummy submarines, and at night teams fired shells from Flat Holm, a small uninhabited island six miles out to sea, the illumination being measured with special instruments on the pier. On one occasion Close and a D.M.W.D. party, marooned on Flat Holm for a considerable period, discovered to their cost that the island was not, after all, entirely unpopulated. They were attacked and mercilessly bitten by myriads of giant fleas!

Mudlarking continued incessantly off the north side of the pier, and a stalwart performer was Donald Lamb, a tall, hawk-nosed R.N.V.R. lieutenant with inexhaustible energy and the strength of an ox. He could carry two Hedgehog projectiles, which weighed over 60 pounds each, across the mud and wet sand without any apparent effort—a feat which much impressed the ratings—but perhaps he was happiest when conducting researches with high explosive. He once startled Boswell by firing some shaped charges into the very foundations of the pier, which, one way and another, took a good deal of punishment from its temporary occupants. Perhaps its severest test came, however, when Wyllie elected to drive a three-ton lorry laden with gravel down the pier's entire length of frail planking!

The Wheezers and Dodgers had their own workshops on the pier, but many of the small engineering jobs which cropped up were carried out ashore by a local firm, the presiding genius of which was Dick Crowe, a vigorous, grey-haired man in his fifties who also owned one of Weston-super-Mare's leading hotels. An amazingly resourceful engineer, he readily undertook the welding of Hedgehog rounds, the making of rocket trolleys and catapults, the machining of spigot mountings, and anything else which came to hand. When he was first enrolled as an unofficial recruit to D.M.W.D. a slipway was badly needed for hauling some of the small trials craft up the steep gradient to the boat-house on the pier. Crowe solved this problem by adapting an old catapult track, and, salvaging the masts from a derelict ship, he used these as sheerlegs to lower the track into position. A wheeled carriage was built, and the slipway had just been successfully tested when an official arrived from the works department of the Admiralty.

Inspecting the slipway, he pronounced it quite impracticable. It could not possibly work, he said, and when Crowe proved to him that it functioned perfectly he demanded to see the drawings. Fumbling in his pocket, Crowe unearthed a very dirty envelope covered with hieroglyphics which were completely incomprehensible to the astonished official. After much argument the slipway was allowed to remain, and it served its purpose admirably for the rest of the war.

It was the resourceful Crowe, too, who extricated the D.M.W.D. party from an embarrassing misadventure with a 200-ton mine-recovery vessel which they put well and truly ashore one day when trying to get up to moorings in the river Axe on the highest tide of the year.

A rescue team arrived to find the vessel high and dry in a meadow, with several cows unconcernedly grazing around her, and although they waited hopefully for the next spring tide this failed to reach her by a good five feet. Among his many activities Dick Crowe was a member of the Auxiliary Fire Service, and, borrowing Weston-super-Mare's biggest fire-engine, he first cut away the ground from under the ship with a hose, and then carved a channel right back to the river-bed. The mine-recovery vessel thus regained the open sea before news of her stranding reached the Admiral at Appledore, but thereafter she leaked like a sieve, and could only be kept afloat with the aid of a trailer fire-pump, installed on the upper deck and manned continuously!

Minor contretemps of this kind did much to dispel the monotony of the heavy trials programme carried on day in and day out. For the most part the testing of weapons and devices was a laborious process of trial and error, calculation and analysis, which called for unlimited patience and meticulous attention to detail. There was, in truth, little glamour in the routine work carried on at Weston-super-Mare, but the very nature and object of the trials provided a stimulus which kept every one at concert pitch. Gradually the emphasis in D.M.W.D.'s programme shifted from defensive measures to preparation for attack, and, although the part played by the Wheezers and Dodgers in the war's final phase will be dealt with later, some of Birnbeck's activities in this phase can be described more appropriately here.

Looking ahead to the invasion of Europe, it was plain that the Navy would have to find means of clearing the mines from enemy beaches. When ports were captured they would also have to demolish blockships and other obstacles sunk in the approaches to enemy harbours.

At Whitchurch Brinsmead had long been concentrating on this wreck-dispersal problem. A way of focusing the explosive effect of underwater charges so that the destruction was greatly magnified, had been discovered, and Brinsmead, using this method, carried out exhaustive tests against the submerged hull of the *Fernwood*, a steamer filled with reinforced concrete and sunk off Weston-super-Mare.

The Wheezers and Dodgers were the only organization in the Navy pursuing experiments with shaped charges, and the trials attracted much attention in scientific circles. One day Dr Guggenheim arrived from London with an American professor who was anxious to study the results, and Boswell told them that at low water springs they would be able to walk right out to the wreck. The sands, however, were extremely treacherous, and only by following the path of a small rill running across the beach could they reach the ship in safety.

The two scientists plainly thought that too much fuss was being made about a simple seaside ramble, and struck out boldly on what they considered to be the most direct route. In next to no time they were in serious difficulties, and the American professor sank up to his knees in the shifting sand. The tide turned, and in the end they only just managed to drag him clear before the sea reached him.

To explode minefields laid on enemy beaches Dr Guggenheim invented an apparatus which was given the code name of "Hedgerow." Very similar to the Hedgehog, it was designed to be fired from a special type of landing-craft, the beaches being drenched by salvos of bombs which exploded just above ground-level.

To test its lethal radius the Birnbeck team laid specimen German minefields beneath the sand on Berrow Flats, and when some sixty mines had been buried in mathematically precise patterns a Hedgerow bomb would be detonated in the centre of the field. Hundreds of actual German Teller mines—lifted from the Western Desert, cleaned and reset—were used, and day after day fresh minefields were laid, first on the beach and later in shallow water.

The work grew increasingly hazardous, for it was known that the Teller mines deteriorated dangerously after six months, and the Birnbeck trials parties were using some at least two years old. When the early reports of the countermining experiments reached London a redoubtable woman scientist, Dr David, queried some of D.M.W.D.'s figures, and volunteered to take part in the trials herself. She had several narrow escapes, once counter-mining a field from which the detonators had not been withdrawn, and eventually instructions came from the War Office that all Teller mines of a certain vintage should be destroyed. As the development of Hedgerow had such a vital bearing on the fate of any invasion attempt, and the Wheezers and Dodgers were then on the brink of success, the order was boldly 'misinterpreted.' Hedgerow made its first appearance at the Salerno landings, and we shall return to its career in action later on.

Considering the large part which explosives played in the daily life at Birnbeck, there were singularly few mishaps. The one accident which became a legend in the naval history of the pier was not, in fact, directly related to any experiment at all.

A prominent member of the Birnbeck team was Dr H. S. Hatfield, a physicist and a clever inventor who did many of the higher mathematical calculations for D.M.W.D. In appearance he personified the scientist of fiction, with his spectacles, his luxuriant moustache, and his vague manner, and, being a somewhat Bohemian character, the happy informality of life on the pier strongly appealed to him.

He set up a laboratory in the confectionery shop, which thenceforward became known as Hatter's Castle, and long into the night he would work there on problems which Goodeve sent down to him. One particularly dark night he emerged, deep in meditation, and after pacing up and down for a while he turned to lean on the railings of the pier. Absent-mindedly he chose the one spot where the railings had been removed to enable the Hedgehog mortar to be fired, and he fell forty feet on to the rocks below. Later in the night some one woke, and, noticing that Hatfield's bed had not been slept in, went to investigate. By a miracle, Hatfield, unconscious and badly injured, was discovered just before the sea covered the rocks on which he was lying. Happily he made a rapid recovery, but to this day visitors to the pier are shown the site of "Hatter's Leap" with understandable awe.

It was a visit by Lane to Dr Barnes Wallis, chief designer to Vickers, which led indirectly to the most spectacular series of trials carried out at Birnbeck.

At the end of 1942 D.M.W.D. became interested in the possibilities of a pilotless aircraft for laying smoke over invasion beaches, and Lane remembered that much earlier in the war Wallis had put forward a suggested design on these lines—for a small 'plane which could be catapulted from the deck of a cruiser, and then controlled by radio.

He went to see Wallis, and soon they were talking about a very different project. Wallis had evolved an earthquake bomb, which operated on entirely new principles, and the targets he had in mind for this giant missile were Germany's great dams—the Mohne, the Eder, and the Sorpe—which fed power to the whole of the industrial Ruhr. But he could get no support for this revolutionary development in bombing technique.

As he told Lane of his vain fight to interest people in high places Lane became more and more fascinated by the scheme. He reported the conversation to Jock Davies and Goodeve, but they pointed out that D.M.W.D. were powerless to secure the aircraft which Wallis needed for trials of the earthquake bomb. Goodeve, however, suggested that Lane should approach Rear-Admiral E. de F. Renouf, who at that time was working with a small staff on secret projects concerning human torpedoes and midget submarines. Renouf was always receptive to scientific proposals, and he had the ear of the Board of Admiralty. When he saw a demonstration of the small-scale version of Wallis's bomb in a tank at the National Physical Laboratory at Teddington he acted immediately.

On the following day he brought members of the Board of Admiralty to watch a further trial in the tank, and Wallis was told to go ahead with the production of eight half-size prototypes of his bomb. A special naval Wellington was secured, straight off the production line, and Lane arranged with the Flag Officer, Portland, for dropping trials off Chesil Beach. D.M.W.D. also laid on torpedo nets, buoys, and all the other gear needed for the trials.

Weeks of intensive experiment followed. There were more trials in the big tank at Teddington, and so much activity with the Wellington and Wallis's secret projectiles at Chesil Beach that some one in authority complained that the breeding of the King's Swans, at near-by Abbotsbury, was being seriously disturbed!

Films taken at Chesil Beach finally convinced the Air Council that the bomb could achieve all Wallis claimed for it, and the whole project was then taken over by the Ministry of Aircraft Production. By this time Lane had become an indispensable member of the Dambusting trials party, and to enable him to continue his work on the project Jock Davies agreed to his temporary transfer to M.A.P.

The story of the later stages in the development of Wallis's bomb and the successful attack on the German dams has already been vividly described.[1] D.M.W.D.'s part was now at an end, but research work on the Wallis bomb led to some remarkable experiments in a different direction at Birnbeck. It was proposed to apply certain principles in the operation of the dam-busting bomb to a naval version fired horizontally from motor-torpedo boats, and trials began at Woolwich.

The early results, using a cordite propellent, were not encouraging, for the projectile—an explosive sphere like a monster football—could only be induced to amble a mere fifty yards. When operations were transferred to Birnbeck a different method of propulsion was suggested.

A catapult track was laid on the northern wing of the pier, and down this it was planned to fire a rocket-propelled trolley on which the projectile was mounted. Protruding from the front of the trolley were two tapered steel rams, designed to enter hydraulic cylinders acting as a buffer at the far end of the runway, so that the trolley came to a dead stop while the missile hurtled on its course.

When this scheme was explained, Dick Crowe, for one, had serious misgivings, for the trolley alone weighed six hundredweight, and even in the short space of the track's length it was expected to reach a speed of 200 m.p.h. It seemed probable that the shock of bringing it to a dead halt would carry the whole jetty forward. And even if the pier itself stood the strain some of the Wheezers and Dodgers feared that the hydraulic buffers would burst asunder.

In an attempt to take some of the stress off the pier the track was anchored back to the rocky island below by six huge hawsers, but before the secret missile could be fired from this somewhat precarious position Higher Authority decreed that the project was insecure on more grounds than the safety of the pier itself. Too much might be seen by onlookers from the shore.

So they moved to Brean Down. High above the sea, it was not an

[1] Vide *The Dam Busters*, by Paul Brickhill (Evans, 1951).

ideal site, either for testing or recovering the missile, but there they could at least learn something of its behaviour, and the working of the rocket trolley, before they settled on a more suitable base for the trials.

Drenched by clouds of freezing spray, they set to work on the exposed headland, laboriously levelling a stretch of the rock-strewn ground. When the runway itself was ready, a blast wall of sandbags, filled with cement, was built up round the back of the buffers at the seaward end to reinforce the hydraulic stopping gear.

The stage was now set for the launching of the missile. The small party gathered on the ridge behind the trolley, with its twelve 2-inch rockets, waited tensely for the signal to fire, no one quite knowing what to expect. When Wyllie pressed the firing key the trolley, enveloped in flame, hurtled down the track like a meteor. With a shattering roar it drove straight through the buffers, and the massive blast wall behind just disintegrated. The air was filled with a whirling mass of sandbags, wire hawsers, and pieces of sheet steel, and the trolley, its rockets still belching tongues of yellow flame, vanished from sight over the cliff edge.

This was a chastening setback, and much discussion took place before the next move was made. They could not afford to cut down the speed of the trolley, but it was equally obvious that no hydraulic mechanism would stand up to the colossal impact. Neither would the trolleys themselves survive more than one high-speed run.

Both these problems were soon solved. In place of all the paraphernalia used in the first, ill-starred trial Richardson suggested that the trolley should be allowed to run into a wall of sand, and when this was tried at Middle Hope Cove it worked perfectly.

Two new tracks were laid at the Cove—one at sea-level and one ten feet higher, to allow for variations in the tide—and the new launching site proved better in every way. The giant ball could be fired roughly in line with the shore, and along its course marker posts were set up in the sea at 20-yard intervals. In line with these, high-speed cameras were mounted on the beach, and Hatfield, who by now had prudently exchanged his living quarters on the pier for a tent at Middle Hope, installed an immensely complicated electrical timing mechanism to record the velocity of every round.

Now began a long series of trials, which proved both hazardous and exhausting. The hazards sprang from the unpredictability of the rockets; it was exhausting work because, accustomed though they were to retrieving Hedgehog rounds, the Wheezers and Dodgers had a far more difficult problem at Middle Hope. The huge steel balls weighed more than 70 pounds, and they had to be recovered from mud which was 13 feet deep in places. Every time the lower track was used tons of shingle and seaweed had to be shovelled from the runway, and on one memorable occasion D.M.W.D.'s working party unearthed the odorous remains of two dead sheep!

Throughout its scale trials the secret missile achieved encouraging results. Its terrific speed across the surface of the water made it more impressive than a torpedo, and it had certain formidable idiosyncrasies which promised to complicate any attempts at countermeasures. After it had been put through its paces in front of Vice-Admiral Wake-Walker and other Admiralty observers D.M.W.D. were told to embark on full-scale trials at sea.

For these D.M.W.D. used an old barge called *Mary*. They fitted her with a special firing tube and towed her to Middle Hope, where she was then moored securely fore and aft. The rocket-catapult system hitherto used for propelling the secret missile was now discarded in favour of an explosive charge.

From this point, however, the development of the weapon slowed down. A long-term project, it had to give way to more pressing requirements, for by the time the Wheezers and Dodgers began trials on board the barge preparations for the invasion of Europe were being hurried forward. To D.M.W.D. came a flood of urgent tasks. They tackled more advanced designs of rocket landing-craft, components for Mulberry Harbour, explosive motor-boats, and the problems of mooring Pluto, the giant pipeline; they experimented with several different devices for beach clearance, including a canvas hose filled with nitroglycerine, and perfected ingenious rocket gear for cliff-climbing; they evolved incendiary floats, radar buoys for guiding the invasion fleet, and a novel contraption called the "Helter Skelter" which speeded up the disembarkation of troops. The story of all these endeavours will be told in due course. They called for intense efforts from the team on the pier, and as a result the experiments with the weapon at Middle Hope never came to full fruition.

Some headway was made with the firing trials on the barge, but great difficulty was found in reaching the required range, and in their efforts to increase the velocity of the projectile they finally stepped up the explosive charge far beyond the safe limit of the tube.

The outcome was almost as startling as the maiden journey of the rocket trolley at Brean, for the missile screamed past the marking post at the end of the range, and then, for some unknown reason, it swerved sharply towards the shore. Jumping a sea wall, it plunged across the headland at the end of the cove, putting to flight a herd of terrified cattle, and it was last seen heading out over the Atlantic.

Further intensive research was plainly necessary, but this was forestalled by the march of other events, and the war's swift climax came before the problems of the giant ball were fully solved. The same fate overtook another Martian missile—a flying-saucer bomb invented by a Norwegian naval officer—which was also put through catapult trials before the Wheezers and Dodgers left Birnbeck.

If the experiments with these secret weapons yielded no immediate and tangible success, however, D.M.W.D. were far from dissatisfied. The pier party had collected scientific data of considerable value. And future conflict is only too likely to reveal its significance.

14

HARRYING THE U-BOATS

THE story of the pier has taken us ahead of events. Invasion of Europe was a far-distant prospect when trials began at Birnbeck, for Britain and the remnant forces of her allies still stood alone, and very survival hung on the outcome of the war at sea. In the eight weeks of May and June 1941 enemy submarines sank 119 ships totalling 635,635 tons. From all causes the Allies lost nearly a million tons of shipping during this brief period.

In the Admiralty a special committee, under Professor P. M. S. Blackett, was formed to investigate all possible means of attacking submarines, and Norway, who attended several of its meetings, repeatedly pressed for the use of rockets. He had discussed with Goodeve, several months earlier, an idea for mounting 2-inch rockets under the wings of Swordfish aircraft, and using them to attack oil-storage tanks and similar targets, but at the time there was no scope for the Fleet Air Arm in such a rôle and nothing came of the proposal.

He now returned to the charge. The weapon he had in mind was a very simple affair—a rocket-propelled spear with a cast-iron, fluted head which would rip a large hole in the pressure hull of a U-boat—but perhaps its very simplicity told against it. The minds of the committee seemed fixed on more refined and scientific devices, and even Goodeve, who was attracted to the idea, was not altogether satisfied that Norway's theory could be translated into practice.

"Why on earth shouldn't it work?" said Norway testily, after one particularly abortive meeting in the Admiralty. "You can spear a fish quite successfully, and the principle is exactly the same. There was nothing wrong with the trials we did in the tank at Teddington."

"I know there wasn't," Goodeve admitted, "but I still don't think it will keep straight after impact. It will turn over."

They gave the Rocket Spear some more ambitious tests at Birnbeck. It emerged triumphantly, and after that Goodeve was no longer sceptical. But outside D.M.W.D. no one showed any interest in the weapon, and it was not until the Army asked for rockets to be tried as anti-tank missiles that Norway got a chance to justify his claims.

For the anti-tank trials the R.A.F. allocated a Hurricane, and somewhat reluctantly they agreed to test the Spear against submarine plating at the same time.

Among those who heard of the trials about to take place was Admiral Sir Max Horton, who as Commander-in-Chief, Western Approaches, was now directing the Battle of the Atlantic from his headquarters at Liverpool. Horton was "that *rara avis* among admirals, a technician who had completely mastered the scientific discoveries and devices brought in to aid ships and aircraft engaged in the battle against the U-boats."[1] And he immediately dispatched one of his staff, Commander Phillimore, to Boscombe Down to see if the Rocket Spear had possibilities. Phillimore was greatly impressed by the trials, and when he reported enthusiastically on the new weapon Horton at once urged the Admiralty to adopt it.

At first they were loath to hasten development, pointing out that no proper sight had yet been designed, but Max Horton was a determined and forceful man who generally got his own way. "It seems incredible," wrote Phillimore later, "but it is true that only eight weeks elapsed to introduce the new weapon, get aircraft fitted with it, crews trained in its use, and get a kill with it in mid-Atlantic."

It seemed incredible to Norway too. For months he had tried unsuccessfully to make people understand its potentialities. But even when his arguments were reinforced with evidence from the trials at Birnbeck few had listened. As soon as Admiral Horton's interest was known, however, the Rocket Spear was given immediate priority.

Norway paid one or two visits to the Royal Aircraft Establishment at Farnborough, to see that the weapon took shape on the right lines. After that there was nothing more for him to do but await developments. They were not long in coming.

A flight of Swordfish embarked in H.M.S. *Archer*, an escort carrier supporting Atlantic convoys, was armed with the Rocket Spear. At the same time the missile was fitted to an R.A.F. Beaufort squadron based at Gibraltar. It then became a race between the two Services for the first kill.

The *Archer* sailed for the United States, and had an entirely uneventful passage; patrolling in the Mediterranean approaches, the Beaufort squadron also drew a blank. Then, returning from the North American coast with a convoy eastward bound, one of *Archer's* Swordfish pilots sighted a U-boat. Before she could dive he

---

[1] Excerpt from a letter written by Commander R. A. B. Phillimore, R.N., to Horton's biographer, Rear-Admiral W. S. Chalmers, and published in *Max Horton and the Western Approaches* (Hodder and Stoughton, 1954).

got a hit with a rocket, which holed the pressure hull, and now there was no escape. "She tried to fight it out on the surface with her gun, but the Swordfish which had dealt the blow called up a Martlet fighter from the *Archer*. The submarine's crew, overcome by machine-gun fire, sank their boat and leapt into the sea."[1] When they were picked up survivors asked in amazement what had hit them. All they knew of the first attack was a sudden, tremendous bang on the pressure hull, and the spear passed right through the boat.

From other survivors—the crew of an Italian submarine sunk in the Mediterranean—came a graphic description of the devastation caused by the Rocket Spear.

In this case the weapon was fired at such close range that the rocket was still burning when the spear smashed its way into the engine-room. Once inside the hull of the submarine it ricocheted off the engines, and thrashed wildly about before tearing a way out on the opposite side of the boat. On its passage back into the sea it ripped a second hole three feet wide.

Norway was away from London when the news of the Rocket Spear's first kill reached the Admiralty. From Goodeve he received the following message:

> You will be pleased to hear, if you haven't done so already, that the Anti-Submarine Rocket Projectiles from aircraft scored a success the first time they were used. I am particularly pleased as it fully substantiates the foresight you showed in pushing this in its early stages. My congratulations.

It was, indeed, a happy sequel to the frustrating months when most of the Admiralty's advisers on U-boat warfare had refused to consider the Spear as anything more than an eccentric reversion to methods of the Stone Age.

As measures against them were intensified the U-boats began to rely increasingly on the cover of darkness. Homed on to our convoys either by signals from the big Focke-Wulf aircraft which ranged far out into the Atlantic or by directions transmitted from Doenitz's headquarters ashore at Kerneval, in Northern France, the German submarines would trail their victims at a discreet distance until night fell. Then they would close in on the surface.

During the final approach the U-boats were trimmed for diving, with decks awash, and only the conning tower was really visible. Even on a light night it was not easy to see them when they were much over half a mile away. On the other hand, the U-boat could sight its larger quarry at six times the distance.

[1] *Max Horton and the Western Approaches*, p. 194.

What was urgently needed was a method of turning night into day—both immediately over a convoy, to reveal any U-boat which might have penetrated the screen of escorting ships, and farther out on the flanks to a distance of some 4000 yards, so that fire could be opened on any submarine approaching on the surface. For the first task the Navy already possessed a large and brilliant flare called the "Snowflake," and to increase its effect D.M.W.D. were asked to find a way of projecting this to a greater height.

With the aid of the indefatigable Schermuly brothers Richardson solved this problem within a week, fitting the flare and its parachute into the head of a standard P.A.C. rocket, which carried the Snowflake to well over a thousand feet. But still the difficulty of illuminating the area *outside* the convoy screen remained. Searchlights could not be used, for they showed all too clearly the position of the searching ship, and the only alternative was the standard naval starshell fired from a 4-inch gun.

This latter method had two serious disadvantages. The 4-inch was the only gun which many of the escort vessels possessed for engaging a U-boat, and they were therefore in no position to strike at the enemy if their only effective weapon was occupied in another rôle. Secondly, the gun had a slow rate of fire—one round every ten seconds—and using it to search through an arc of 60 degrees with starshell was a dangerously protracted business. Fast-moving targets could escape far into the outer darkness before even a small arc had been covered.

Hitherto D.M.W.D. had never concerned themselves with illuminants, and Goodeve's team had only been brought into the Snowflake project because they were the Navy's acknowledged experts on rockets. Now, however, Richardson found himself worrying about this weak link in the protection of the convoys. For a fortnight he spent every spare moment studying technical reports of starshell trials, and the behaviour of different types of illuminant. Then, armed with some rough drawings, he went to see Goodeve.

"I believe I've got the answer to this starshell business. Do you think D.N.O. would agree to our trying it out?"

Goodeve looked at the drawings. "It's pretty revolutionary," he said. "Still, we can put it up to them and see what they say."

Then he stared at the notes in front of him again. Richardson's design—the result of brilliantly resourceful and patient research work—was unlike any other starshell ever invented. Planned for use in quick-firing 2-pounder guns, it had no parachute, and, falling fast through the air, it was to burn for less than five seconds. But the method of operation was ingenious, for Richardson was suggesting that five of these shells should be in the air at once, their paths of light joining up and reinforcing each other so that a continuous sweep could be made at the rate of three degrees every second.

"Currie has some useful reports on night-vision tests, and that's the fastest speed you can scan for small targets," he explained.

Goodeve nodded. "What about lighting the target once you've found it?" he asked.

"I think that will work perfectly well. If the gun is kept on the same bearing you will get a continuous light from a succession of shells."

"Well," said Goodeve, "I hope you're right about all this. I'll certainly put it up to D.N.O., but we shall probably be told it's quite impracticable."

As they had expected, the Director of Naval Ordnance's staff were decidedly sceptical. And the Ordnance Board, with their characteristic mistrust of novelty, produced several emphatic reasons why Richardson's starshell could not possibly function. But D.M.W.D. were allowed to go ahead, and Richardson roped in Swan, Boswell, Lane, and Dr Purcell to help with the development work.

As an initial target he aimed at producing a magnesium flare of some half a million candle-power which would burn for two seconds, but, to make certain that this would be powerful enough, teams armed with balloons and oxygen cylinders were sent to sea in the Bristol Channel. With the flares attached—they were actuated by a delay fuse—the balloons were then released, and cine-cameras on the pier at Birnbeck recorded the spreading path of light on the dark water. Prototypes of the flare were tested in wind tunnels, and, much to the alarm of Londoners, who feared that a new and dreadful form of air raid was imminent, Purcell even lit some on the roof of the Royal College of Science in Kensington.

In this preliminary stage no snags were apparent, but when the Ordnance Board made the first actual shells Richardson was puzzled to find that they gave nothing like the illumination he had estimated. Filming the trajectory, he discovered that the magnesium stars were jamming in the nose of the shell when it burst.

He explained this to the Ordnance Board, who claimed that if special tinplate cases were made for the flares this difficulty would not recur. The cases would instantly burn away when the shell exploded, and the stars would fall free.

The Wheezers and Dodgers had no facilities for making the shells themselves. They were entirely in the hands of the Ordnance Board. When the next batch came up for trial Richardson was dismayed to find that there was little improvement. Testing them exhaustively on his own, he saw that all this extra work had been wasted. As the shells burst large parts of the Ordnance Board's tinplate casing remained intact and masked the burning flare.

Once again D.M.W.D. had to go to the Ordnance Board and ask them to revise their design, but before doing so experiments were carried out in the laboratories of Imperial College. Purcell and Swan tried packing the 'stars' in a paper cover instead of the tinplate case, and immediately they found a remarkable improvement in the performance of the flare.

This suggestion was therefore put to the Ordnance Board—but it was flatly vetoed. Their pyrotechnic experts condemned it as unsafe and entirely unpractical, and the Board declined to have anything to do with the proposal. They were, they said, quite satisfied with the tinplate casing (which gave the low candle-power of 30,000), and refused to produce D.M.W.D.'s paper-covered 'star' for firing trials.

The arguments with the Ordnance Board had now taken the project well into 1942 without any real progress being made, and unless some way could be found to prove that the new type of cover for the flare was feasible there seemed no way out of the deadlock. Goodeve decided to bypass the Board, and he took the problem to Imperial Chemical Industries. Looking at Richardson's specification, I.C.I. said they anticipated no particular difficulty over the production design, and in a very short time they presented D.M.W.D. with a star which burned, not at 30,000 candle-power, but at 400,000!

Before the powerful new starshell could be issued for action, however, an important new development occurred in anti-submarine warfare. A new type of radar set which enabled rapid and continuous search for surfaced U-boats was fitted to convoy vessels in 1943. This deprived Richardson's starshell of the main rôle for which it had been designed. These advanced radar sets were, however, in short supply; there were none for frigates and light Coastal Forces engaged in the E-boat war, and since the M.T.B.'s and motor-gun boats had no form of illuminant at all the 2-pounder starshell was a godsend.

The earliest reports of its performance at sea surprised even Richardson. The captain of the M.G.B. which fired the first starshells in action ordered his gunlayer to aim directly at a German trawler. To his astonishment, the starshells caused instant and fierce fires. As they struck home a blazing white light illuminated the ship for several seconds, and immediately afterwards flames blazed out all over the superstructure.

Richardson had not suspected the starshells to have any special incendiary properties, and, much intrigued, he carried out some laboratory tests of his own. He found that the shells would, in fact, easily pierce wooden hulls and light plating; on emerging the star burst over a wide area with a bright glow which would undoubtedly cause fires in the presence of petrol or oil leaks.

It was therefore recommended that all Coastal Force craft should belt the starshell rounds alternately with their high-explosive ammunition, and on the night of October 24–25 they were thus used in a number of actions with E-boats. One commanding officer described the effect as devastating. Of three boats attacked in one particular sector that night one was rammed and sunk, and the remaining two were quickly transformed into blazing wrecks by the starshells.

Although the development of radar had limited the starshell's scope, over a million of Richardson's shells were used in the next two years, and with this experience behind them the Wheezers and Dodgers went on to tackle a number of similar tasks. The most important, perhaps, and certainly the most eventful of these projects was the "Water Snowflake."

Aircraft searching the night seas with their A.S.V. apparatus found they needed a special type of flare which could be dropped into the water when they detected a U-boat, and to meet this need D.M.W.D. designed a novel apparatus.

In a buoyant container was a rocket, a parachute, and a Snowflake flare. When this was dropped into the sea the aircraft had time to fly in a circle in the darkness until the U-boat lay between the dormant Snowflake and the 'plane. The rocket was then ignited by a cell operated by the action of the sea-water, and the floating object suddenly came to life, the parachute flare being hurled a thousand feet into the air, where it burned for a minute, silhouetting the submarine for the attack.

Translating this theory into practice, however, proved far from simple, for when the first containers were dropped during trials the parachutes which carried the apparatus down into the water from the aircraft generally wrapped itself round its load like a shroud and prevented the rocket from escaping. They got out of this difficulty by dropping the parachute head-first, with a weighted keel attached to it to drag it out of the way of the container, but problem number two was much more obstinate. When the rocket ignited sufficient power had first to be built up before it could climb out of its floating container into the sky. The delay was only a matter of seconds, but in a rough sea the whole contraption might well be swamped before the rocket emerged.

To test the Water Snowflake's behaviour afloat Boswell was lent an R.A.F. high-speed launch, and off Ramsgate they began preliminary trials, dropping the apparatus into the sea astern, attached to a line which was paid out while the boat moved slowly ahead. Boswell

L

explained to the coxswain that the rocket was expected to fire after thirty seconds in the water, but the first Snowflake went off too close to the launch for the coxswain's liking. When the next was lowered into the water he decided that discretion was the better part of valour, and, opening the throttle, he went full ahead, completely forgetting that the proximity of the Snowflake to his launch depended entirely on the speed at which the line could be paid out. In a few swift seconds he was towing the Snowflake container horizontally, with the rocket pointing straight at the helpless observers on board, and by the time Boswell had explained by frantic shouts and gesticulations what was about to happen the launch had so much way on that nothing could be done to retrieve the situation. So every one lay flat on the open deck and waited for the explosion. At point-blank range how it missed the launch was a miracle, but the effect on the coxswain was salutary. For the rest of the day he treated the Water Snowflake with the deepest respect!

To overcome the swamping danger the department designed special lids—known as "Bug-bafflers"—which fitted over the top of the containers and were only knocked off by the rocket itself as it shot out. Once these were ready the R.A.F. launch and its reluctant crew again went to sea. Their task this time was to retrieve any Water Snowflakes which failed to function when dropped from the air, so that Boswell and his team could examine the defects.

At first all went well. An elderly Fleet Air Arm 'plane flew up and down dropping the containers. Boswell timed them as they hit the water, and when any refused to go off the coxswain would bring the launch alongside and the gear would be hauled on board.

The pilot of the 'plane seemed unduly anxious to get rid of his load, and, flying in tight circles, he dropped the Water Snowflakes at such a pace that after a while Boswell could no longer keep track of them all. A dozen had been retrieved safely, however, when he saw, to his dismay, that an enthusiastic aircraftman had just pulled a perfectly good container out of the water. Lying on the deck, it was smoking furiously, and Boswell knew it was just about to detonate. He picked it up to hurl it over the side, but it was too late. The Snowflake climbed straight out of his arms into the sky, to the considerable alarm of the pilot, who had chosen that precise moment to fly low over the launch as he dropped the last of his containers.

One by one, however, the snags in the apparatus were cleared, and D.M.W.D.'s Water Snowflake was finally tested against a rival design sponsored by the Ministry of Aircraft Production. It came through with flying colours, although the preliminaries of the trial gave the Wheezers and Dodgers some uneasy moments. Instead of being staged at sea the demonstration was suddenly switched to a reservoir near London—and no one knew whether Purcell's sea-water cell, which was the nerve-centre of the whole apparatus, would function at all in a suburban reservoir. Humorists in the department suggested that he should insure against disaster by taking several packets of potato crisps with him, and doping the cells with the salt provided. Happily their fears proved groundless, for the Water Snowflake was a versatile device, and reassured them all by functioning even in Admiralty tap-water!

Many other flare devices, too numerous to mention in this story, were evolved by D.M.W.D. as the war went on. Among them was a "Rocket Sea Marker," which Coulson helped to develop for speeding attacks on submerged submarines; another was an apparatus formidably entitled the "Wave Amplitude Measurement Marker," which he produced with Francis to aid research into the problems of Mulberry Harbour. In D.M.W.D. this was the least popular of all the pyrotechnic experiments carried out by the department. Involving the use of bags of chemical compound, which produced a self-igniting gas, phosphine, on contact with sea-water, not only was it dangerous to handle—but it smelt quite overpoweringly of cats!

The U-boat phase brought rapid expansion of the department's activities in yet another field. Radar was in its infancy when the war began, and although Admiral Somerville's original responsibilities included the development of radiolocation for naval use, Goodeve and *his* research team did not become concerned with it until the need arose for tracking the F.B.B. units which drifted so recklessly to various parts of Southern England. Dove, Harris, and Purcell then set to work to explore different means of getting echoes from balloons.

As most readers will know, an object is tracked by radar through the transmission of radio waves which rebound from solid surfaces. The distance of the object is calculated by measuring the time which elapses between the sending out of the electro-magnetic signal and the return of the corresponding echo. A flat metal sheet reflects the radiation used in radar in much the same way as a mirror reflects light, but since D.M.W.D.'s experiments were mainly with balloons, which would not support any great weight, they had to search for different means of securing loud and clear echoes.

The first promising results in this direction came when they enclosed their balloons in a mesh of copper wire, but they were still casting around for a less cumbersome alternative, when an Austrian named Theodor Suchy arrived one day at the office in Lower Regent Street. He brought with him a strange collection of bric-à-brac, which at first sight had no bearing on the problems of warfare—some leaves from trees and bushes and some beautifully finished imitation jewellery which he had made for Miss Vivien Leigh to wear in the film of *Cæsar and Cleopatra*. As he examined them, however, Purcell saw with some excitement that all the objects were coated with a silvery substance he had never encountered before. Suchy explained that this was a metallizing process; it could be applied not only to firm, level surfaces, but to fabrics like calico. And calico was what the Wheezers and Dodgers were using for the covers of their balloons.

The new process revolutionized the technique of reflecting radar waves. Suchy, an inventive and resourceful man who had been driven from his post in a German chemical works and was now established in England as a successful maker of fancy goods, showed how the conducting film of liquid could be applied to the surface of several balloons they chose for immediate trials. When these were filled with hydrogen and sent aloft they gave off echoes as strong as any all-metal sphere.

The process was used for all manner of projects, and D.M.W.D. eventually became the chief authority in the Navy for developing radar counter-devices, the work absorbing the main energies of an entire section under Tom Swan and Lieutenant H. A. C. McKay, R.N.V.R. They produced aids to target practice, special buoys to help anti-submarine training, devices to give echoes from lifeboats, and submarine decoys.

It was known that German U-boats had their own type of Radar Decoy Balloon—an apparatus romantically christened "Aphrodite." This consisted of a small steel float which looked like two pie-dishes fastened together. To it was tethered a balloon bearing streamers of metal foil, which flew like pennants in the wind, and when released from a submarine it skimmed away across the wave-tops, laying a false trail for any radar operator scanning the sea.

Aphrodite was never very satisfactory, however, for it gave a fluctuating echo, the metal streamers tore in the wind, and the German scientists never overcame difficulties in adjusting the hydrogen for the balloons. Unknown to the enemy, the Royal Navy had a much better decoy called the "Peardrop," which the Wheezers and Dodgers evolved. This was fitted with a float of different design, which removed the problem of adjusting the pressure in the balloon, and it gave off a consistent echo. On several occasions it was known that British submarines, releasing the Peardrop as they dived, were believed to be still on the surface, and German operators happily continued to track the decoy without suspecting that their quarry had long since disappeared.

.   .   .   .   .

Before the concluding phase in the U-boat war was reached in the summer of 1943 Goodeve's team were to tackle many other tasks related to the Battle of the Atlantic.

They produced a short-range mortar weapon called the "Unicorn," designed to enable merchant ships to lob bombs at enemy submarines which managed to penetrate into the midst of convoys, but not all their efforts were directed to tracking and attacking the enemy. Science had a vital part, too, to play in saving life at sea. The Merchant Navy were suffering heavy casualties, and the indomitable spirit they showed in the face of continual hazard is well illustrated by a story which the master of one merchantman told to Commander Holbrook at an Admiralty interrogation.

His ship was torpedoed in a full gale in the North Sea, and as she began to settle fast he ordered the crew into the boats. Two men—the chief engineer and a greaser—remained with the master on the bridge.

When the ship sank a few minutes later the chief engineer was drowned, but after drifting helplessly for some time in mountainous seas the captain of the ship and the greaser came face to face. The convoy had gone on, and they were quite alone, with no hope of rescue to spur a last fight for life. But as the men passed each other the greaser called out cheerfully, "Kick your legs and enjoy yourself, skipper. . . . This is the last free bath we'll ever have!" Then he disappeared into the darkness.

By a miracle both were sighted and rescued not long afterwards, but Fate rarely spared men cast on the water in such circumstances. The crying need was for better boats, better quick-release gear to get them afloat, and better equipment to sustain life for castaways, who often faced a lone journey of a thousand miles or more to the nearest land.

In D.M.W.D. one angle of this problem was tackled by Cooke. He and two friends had spent the summer of 1939 at Fleur de Lys, on the shores of Newfoundland, building a 28-ton ketch which they hoped to sail back to England. Now he began to design another type of boat which could be towed behind vessels in convoy, and would be large enough to take off the whole ship's company.

H.M.S. *Hiker*, as she was known in the department, was a 75-foot steel boat, equipped with sails and a petrol engine giving a range of 1500 miles. She was fitted with bunks and fully stored with provisions, blankets, and medical supplies, and to reach her the crew of the parent ship had merely to climb down scrambling nets hung over the stern.

Cooke carried out exhaustive experiments with different keels and rigs on small copper models which he rashly endeavoured to test on the Round Pond in Kensington. The trials there, however, were continually interrupted by crowds of small boys, who kept challenging him to races with their own model yachts; so work was transferred to the greater seclusion of Staines Reservoir. The first full-scale prototype of H.M.S. *Hiker* did not get into production, unfortunately, until the perilous days for Allied ships at sea were almost at an end, but in another sphere of life-saving D.M.W.D. were able to make a very important contribution indeed.

One day towards the end of 1941 Goodeve sent for Norway. For some time he had been analysing the causes of casualties at sea, and when Norway entered the room he pointed to a paragraph at the end of one of Trade Division's interrogation reports.

"Is there any way we can help in this problem of fresh water for lifeboats?" he asked. "Time and again there's a reference in these reports to men dying of thirst before they can be picked up. Do you think your section could design a portable still for ships' boats which would really work?"

Norway frowned. "An awful lot of people have had a shot at that before, and they haven't got very far. It's difficult to make an apparatus which is small enough, and yet produce a reasonable amount of water. Do you happen to know what proportion of these boats are motor-lifeboats?"

"Not offhand—but we can easily get hold of the figures. Why do you ask that?"

"I was thinking of the airship days," said Norway. "When we were flying in fairly low temperature we used to be able to recover as much water from the exhaust as the weight of the petrol we consumed, just by condensing the exhaust gases from the main engines. With a boat I don't see why you shouldn't do the same thing. You could fit a long exhaust pipe, to run up and down the garboard strakes close to the keel. . . ."

"That's certainly worth trying," agreed Goodeve. "What about the still, though?"

"Goodfellow's the best man I've got to tackle that, and I'll put Ritchie on to the other job. It might be a good idea if he went to Southampton and had a talk to Cave-Browne-Cave, who's Professor of Engineering at the University there. He knows as much about the technique as anyone; he was in charge of the engine installations of R.101."

"By all means," said Goodeve. "We'll go ahead with both ideas. Let me know how you get on."

Goodfellow, an immensely competent engineer who had already impressed Norway with his work on rocket weapons, heard about the still project with some misgivings. His dejection increased when he visited the Patent Office, for, browsing through the files there, he discovered that in the First World War no fewer than 980 patents had been taken out for small-boat stills in America alone. In civil life, however, Goodfellow had specialized in problems of oil-refinery construction, and as he searched for a means of generating and recovering the heat needed for condensation he found certain welcome parallels to difficulties he had overcome in his pre-war job.

His terms of reference were to produce a still which would convert sea water to fresh water at the rate of one gallon an hour, and the apparatus had to be a small, compact affair fired by petrol or paraffin. Tackling every stage of the task himself, he spent several months in a small engineering shop attached to the chemical laboratory of King's College, just off the Strand. And there, with his own hands, he built a plant like a tiny distillation unit—a most ingenious and refined piece of engineering.

The still itself was only the size of a jerry-can, but it could produce twelve gallons of fresh water for every gallon of fuel. It was a revolutionary development; if the normal water-tanks of a lifeboat were filled with fuel the new still could produce twelve times the amount of fresh water hitherto available.

In a year Goodfellow produced three different 'marks' of still, steadily improving its efficiency, and both the Army and the R.A.F. became keenly interested. In arid country like the Western Desert the Army saw its possibilities for supplying distilled water for the batteries of their motor transport and fighting vehicles; the R.A.F. needed supplies of sterile water for medical purposes; and demands for the new still became so widespread that its development occupied Goodfellow for two and a half years in all. At the same time other research organizations under the supervision of D.S.R. produced another very simple method of making sea-water drinkable by passing it through a special filter-bed. This method was widely adopted.

Side by side with this task experiments proceeded with Norway's other project—the recovery of water from the exhaust of engines. At the start the team working under Cave-Browne-Cave at Southampton were by no means sure that water recovered from the exhaust of a petrol engine would not prove poisonous.

Although it had been common practice in airships to produce water in this way, no one had ever suggested drinking it, and Norway feared that the presence of tetra-ethyl-lead in petrol would affect any water drawn off from the exhaust system. It was discovered, however, that all the lead passed away with the carbon dioxide in the exhaust gases, and although the water they condensed was heavily contaminated with oil and carbon, it could be purified quite easily by using a special filter.

As soon as it became known that the Wheezers and Dodgers were on the verge of success with this alternative method of water recovery the Army again stressed the difficulties they were facing in the Desert, and asked for priority to be given to the experiments. Heavy fighting was then in progress in North Africa, and the supply of fresh water was a constant anxiety. Norway felt sure that the apparatus taking shape at Southampton would solve this particular problem, for Army trucks moved mainly at night, when temperatures in the Desert were low, and in these conditions it seemed likely that fresh water might well be recovered at the rate of at least a gallon for every gallon of fuel burned by the truck's engines.

A Bedford lorry was loaned to D.M.W.D., and on top of the cab was mounted a large, honeycombed radiator. Special tanks and filtering apparatus were installed, and under the chassis they fitted a set of long, air-cooled exhaust pipes.

Ritchie, who had been given a free hand by Norway, then set off on a "Round Britain Tour" of 5000 miles, running day and night to test the equipment under varied conditions. While these trials were going on the Admiralty installed another water-recovery unit in a Fairmile motor-launch and tested it at sea, for it was now realized that the apparatus might well remove one of the greatest difficulties encountered in landing operations in tropical countries. Transport of water for men and vehicles on the beaches was a major operation in itself, but Norway pointed out that, as any invasion was bound to be supported by large numbers of landing-craft, each of these could now generate fresh water continuously as they made their way to and from the beaches. They would therefore be in a position to land many gallons of water for the troops ashore without any extra transport at all.

Ritchie's marathon journey with the truck proved that the apparatus could do all that the Army required. They were, in fact, so impressed that a message came from the War Office: "Surely the Navy can go one stage further now, and give us an apparatus which produces unlimited quantities of gin!"

Like many of the projects carried to a successful technical conclusion by the Wheezers and Dodgers, the outcome of their researches into water-recovery had its disappointing side. Scientific developments cannot always keep precisely in step with the course of the war itself, and by the time this particular apparatus was ready for service the fighting in North Africa was at an end. Instead of the parched desert, the Allied armies were fighting their way slowly up the heel of Italy, where water abounded, and Ritchie and his helpers reflected a little sadly that their efforts for the Army might, indeed, have been more profitably employed in adapting their apparatus to produce gin! For the Navy, however, D.M.W.D.'s discoveries were of immediate value, and the importance of Goodfellow's work was later recognized by the Royal Commission on Awards to Inventors.

The story of the Wheezers and Dodgers' activities in this field would not be complete without reference to the Johannesburg experiment.

A young naval surgeon walked into Norway's office one morning and said he had heard about the stills for ships' lifeboats.

"I suppose you are aware that in certain abdominal operations where liquid cannot be taken by the patient in the normal way through the mouth, water is supplied by the injection of a saline solution up the rectum?"

Norway received the news with some surprise. It seemed hardly an engineering matter.

"I'm sure you're right," he remarked politely, "but I'll have to take your word for that."

"Very well, then," said the surgeon. "Why does anyone die of thirst in a lifeboat?"

This was a devastating question, and Norway could think of no appropriate answer. In any case, even if his visitor was correct, it seemed an unusual procedure to suggest to merchant seamen!

Discussion in the department led to a certain amount of ribaldry, but it did seem worth investigating, and eventually a programme of research was carried out—not in a naval establishment, but, strange to relate, at Johannesburg University.

Twelve medical students, who volunteered to act as guinea-pigs, were taken to a particularly arid part of the Transvaal. There six were supplied with sea water by this unusual method, while the other six were given no water at all. At the end of the given time the students who had had the sea water were, admittedly, in a worse condition than their companions—but not very much worse. From this it appeared that if the sea had about half its natural content of salt the human body might well adapt itself to the system of refreshment proposed by the naval surgeon. The Wheezers and Dodgers, however, had to deal with realities, and, reflecting that the ocean was not likely to discard its salt in the foreseeable future, Goodfellow and Ritchie went on with their own more prosaic researches.

15

THE MANTLE OF ELIJAH

ALTHOUGH, as befitted a naval research organization, D.M.W.D.'s chief preoccupation lay with the war at sea, several interesting projects unconnected with naval warfare were now being developed by Goodeve's team. Among these was an apparatus known in the department as "Hajile."

For security purposes every project launched by the Wheezers and Dodgers was given a code name. A complete cover plan was also drawn up, and where several different firms were providing parts for a weapon or device each would be given a plausible but entirely different idea as to the real function of the object they were manufacturing.

Ironically enough, the only occasion when this procedure was jeopardized followed a visit to Goodeve by a representative of the Naval Intelligence Department. Announcing his identity, he asked to see the MOST SECRET list of projects, and jotted down the names of all the contractors then carrying out work for D.M.W.D.

Three days later Goodeve was surprised to receive a 'phone call from him.

"I'm speaking from Ipswich," he boomed. "I say, you know the job this firm here are supposed to be doing? Well, they don't know anything about it. I've asked them for particulars, and it may surprise you to know that they're doing no work at all on the thing you mentioned to me."

Goodeve was so startled that he almost dropped the receiver. "Of course they don't," he shouted; "you, of all people, ought to have realized that."

The whole security of that particular project had been compromised by a member of the very Admiralty department responsible for preventing leakages of secret information, and the existing cover plan had to be scrapped there and then.

Happily, blunders like this were rare, and D.M.W.D.'s own security precautions worked well. Some of the code names they chose for their more unorthodox ventures must have puzzled the Intelligence experts (who had to vet them) as much as any enemy agent, and Hajile was a case in point.

The project originated with a request from the Army, who wanted to find a way of dropping heavy objects—vehicles, guns, and stores —from the air, and they stressed that a high speed of fall was essential; lessening the danger of drift, it allowed the load to be dropped more accurately, and it also cut down the risk of damage from ground fire.

Realizing that any contrivance depending on parachutes would be unsuitable for this purpose, D.M.W.D. tackled the problem from another angle, searching for a method of slowing up the falling load at the last minute, and eventually they hit on the idea of using the blast of a nest of rockets to cushion the impact of the loaded platform on the ground. The object to be dropped was fitted into a sort of harness, girdled by a huge 'candelabra' of rockets, and the plan envisaged this falling free through the air until it was a few feet off the ground. At this moment all the rockets would fire at once, decelerating the speed of the platform so powerfully that, in theory at least, it would touch down quite gently.

To the observers of its trials it was a highly spectacular affair. In the last crucial seconds of its flight to earth the whole apparatus was enshrouded in a pillar of smoke and flame, and Jock Davies, with the sailor's traditional store of Biblical quotations at his fingertips, instantly suggested its code name from the Second Book of Kings.

"Look at it!" he remarked as he watched one of the earliest trials. . . . "It's Elijah in reverse."

Guggenheim did the early mathematical calculations, and the task of developing Hajile was given to Duncan Bruce and "Paul" Roberson, a young research chemist who joined the department in September 1942. Others assisting in the trials of the apparatus included Rivers-Bowerman, an Irishman who helped to overcome many of the snags which cropped up with the switch-gear and the crash pans on which the loads were dropped, and Louis Klemantaski, renowned in the motor-racing world before the war as a high-speed photographer. Both were characters. Rivers-Bowerman had the typical Irishman's dislike of being hurried. He liked time to think things out, and whenever he felt anybody was trying to rush him over some problem he would pick up a newspaper, or any document lying to hand, and begin reading it slowly and ostentatiously, as if to say, "I'll do the job for you . . . but only in my own time."

Klemantaski had joined the department by the same route as Menhinick. He began the war in the Army, as an instructor in the R.A.O.C., but when the desert fighting had been in progress for some time he found himself detached to work at a factory in the Midlands producing filters for Army vehicles. The Army had found that engines were rapidly disintegrating in North Africa through sand wear, and photographic study of oil and air deposits was urgently needed. To carry this out they sought the services of a well-known photographer of fish and flies, but this specialist was occupied elsewhere, and the job fell to Klemantaski. He was much relieved when a summons from the Admiralty freed him for more eventful pursuits.

The first aim of Bruce and Roberson was to devise a means of setting off the rockets of Hajile at the right height above the ground. The obvious answer seemed to be some form of plummet which would dangle below the apparatus and fire the rockets as soon as it hit the earth. The problem was not as simple as this, however, for any type of plummet used would have to be heavy enough to run out ahead of the falling load, competing with a fierce upward wind, and yet be sensitive enough to react immediately it landed on any yielding surface like grass, shrubs, or heather.

To experiment with this unusual type of switch-gear they had to find a place where they could rig up wires and slide the plummet down them. Bruce thought of the lift shaft at Hampstead Tube Station, but this proved to be 30 feet short of the depth they needed to achieve the required velocity. Some one then suggested the great hangar at Cardington, and there Roberson spent most of November 1942 clambering precariously about on the catwalk high in the roof, and sliding plummets of different shapes, weights, and sizes down a long wire. A naval stoker had been detailed to assist him, but he proved unable to face heights, and after Roberson had had to rescue him from his first climbing attempt, when the stoker became paralysed with fright half-way up an 80-foot fire-escape, it seemed less trouble to carry on with the experiments unaided. In time Roberson got quite used to crawling about on the narrow girders, but he was glad when the trials ended. Perpetually shrouded in a dense, clammy fog, Cardington was a depressing place, and the only really contented mortal there that chill November was the resident observer, who used to ascend to 2000 feet every morning in a balloon, and spend the day sitting happily with a book in the autumn sunshine.

The initial tests completed, the Wheezers and Dodgers aimed for a higher velocity—which meant a greater vertical drop. Bruce took the plummet and its accessories to an airfield on Salisbury Plain where a fellow-scientist was busily engaged in dropping blood-plasma bottles from a captive balloon on to the concrete apron of the runway. The height there was all right for the plummet tests, as Bruce found with a sickening certainty when he went up in the swaying basket, but there was no variety in the surface of the ground below to give the fuse a proper test. It would have worked deceptively well on the hard concrete. So they loaded all the gear into a truck and drove to Birnbeck.

When Hajile had been adapted to fire over water they began full-scale trials, dropping the contraption, loaded with a large block of concrete, into the sea from a Lancaster bomber. On his early runs the pilot deposited it too far from the end of the pier for Klemantaski to film the descent, so he was asked to aim as close to Birnbeck as possible. This request proved ill-advised, for the pilot was now on his mettle. Taking off again, he made a couple of dummy runs, and then released the huge concrete block and its girdle of rockets from 2000 feet with alarming accuracy.

As it came screaming through the air the watchers on the pier gazed open-mouthed. Then, suddenly realizing that it was going to score a direct hit, every one started running for dear life down the long plank roadway. The concrete 'bomb' landed squarely on the roof of D.M.W.D.'s engineering shop. It sheared through a massive steel joist, and then demolished the covered way leading to the steamer jetty. Happily there were no casualties, though the Wren cooks preparing lunch a few feet from the wrecked shelter thought the end of the world had come.

After that the bomb-aimer was requested to temper accuracy with discretion, and the trials proceeded uneventfully. At first, with four rockets fitted round the concrete slab, the load hit the sea fairly heavily. They tried with eight rockets, and Hajile fulfilled all expectations. Hurtling towards the water, the slab was checked just above the waves, and then it slid gently below the surface.

These tests over the sea showed that there was nothing wrong with the general theory, but the gear now had to be adapted for land trials. By March 1943 the Hajile team had perfected the switch unit, and they offered to demonstrate this to Richardson from a tree in Hyde Park. For security purposes they took the gear to an enclosed Ack-Ack site, and the Prime Minister's youngest daughter, serving there as an A.T.S. officer, was greatly surprised to find Roberson, in his naval uniform, wrestling with a tangled mass of wire in the topmost branches of a tall elm.

When the plummet passed its test successfully D.M.W.D. had to find some practical task for Hajile to carry out. They knew from experience that the speed of getting any device into service depended not a little on rousing the interest of people in high places. A successful practical demonstration of what Hajile could do would hasten its progress, and Duncan Bruce recalled a remark made to him by Sir Denistoun Burney in the early stages of the Hajile experiments. Burney, inventor of the minesweeping paravane, had been concerned with the project from the start, and often attended D.M.W.D.

progress meetings on Hajile, for he was interested in developing a special type of rocket. He had the grand manner of the elder states-man, and after one meeting he awed Bruce by observing, "Young man ... you'll never get anywhere without Cabinet support"—some-what depressing advice for a junior R.N.V.R. officer who had never even set eyes on a Cabinet Minister!

As a start it seemed a good idea to drop a jeep from an aircraft, but jeeps were hard to procure—especially by people who wanted to throw them out of aeroplanes at 2000 feet—and Roberson had little success until he called on the American Navy in Grosvenor Square.

To a Commander on the supply staff he explained rather ner-vously why he wanted two jeeps, but he had hardly finished speaking when his new-found ally grabbed the telephone. "Say, Jake," he said urgently, "come on up. There's a guy here who wants two jeeps— and, boy, he's going to beat the living daylights out of them!"

So Roberson got his jeeps, and dropping trials began in earnest. The first of these was a singularly unsuccessful affair, held on a bit-terly cold winter's day. First the aircraft refused to start. Then snow fell heavily, damping the rocket fuses, and when, finally, they dropped the jeep the Hajile equipment failed to function at all. Falling at 40 feet per second on the small pilot parachute alone, Jeep Number One went straight into the ground with a shattering crash. A fortnight later they tried again, adding a lot more rockets. This time the jeep survived the drop relatively undamaged, but when the smoke cleared away they found the vehicle was upside down.

They designed a special crash-pan to take the initial shock of the impact, and altered the setting of the rockets, but still the load continued to somersault on landing. Hajile, in fact, was in a thoroughly obstinate mood, and the thrust of the rockets varied in such an unpredictable way that the Wheezers and Dodgers never knew what to expect. Only one rocket had to fail for the whole decelerating apparatus to be thrown out of gear, and sometimes when the plummet struck the ground the whole cargo on the crash-pan would be hurled violently skyward, falling back with a tremen-dous, earth-shaking crump which tore all the fittings apart. Close to the ground the gear was surrounded by so much smoke and flame that it was difficult to ascertain precisely what happened at the moment of firing.

After one sequence of fairly successful drops a demonstration was staged for representatives of all three Services on Newbury Downs, using large blocks of concrete again, for by this time jeeps were becoming a rather expensive item. It was a lovely still summer day, but the rockets were on their very worst behaviour. When Hajile was launched from the aircraft some of the rockets failed to fire at all, and others which did set alight to the pilot parachutes. The concrete block consequently hit the ground with terrific force, and buried itself—as Bruce succinctly remarked afterwards—"right up to the maker's name."

Much discouraged, the Hajile team realized that they would have to start almost from the beginning again, carrying out exhaustive tests with both the plummet and the rockets. For this purpose aircraft drops were not altogether satisfactory; when Hajile was released from a great height it was impossible to tell exactly where it would land, and the observers could not therefore get close enough to detect the precise sequence of events when things went wrong. Roberson still thought that the continued capsizing of the cargo might be due to the drift of Hajile in the wind, but another of the Wheezers and Dodgers, who had got near enough on one occasion to peer through the smoke, swore that he saw the crash-pan turn on end appreciably *after* it touched down.

Richardson decided to transfer the trials to Shoeburyness, and try suspending the whole apparatus from a giant crane. Roberson was therefore ordered to ring up "the Superintendent, Chatham Dockyard," and arrange for the necessary facilities.

Little versed in the organization of the Navy's shore establishments, he followed his instructions to the letter, and when he got through to Chatham he demanded to speak to the Superintendent of the Dockyard in person. After some delay a voice asked what he wanted, and Roberson began issuing a stream of orders about the crane, the storing of the gear, and the assistance he would need.

"I'm not in the habit of dealing with minor matters of this kind," came an irate response. "Do you know who you are talking to, young man?"

"No," said Roberson, "I haven't the faintest idea."

"This is Admiral —— here."

"Oh, is it?" said Roberson, much alarmed. "Do you know who this is at this end?"

"No, I don't," boomed the voice.

"Thank God for that!" remarked Roberson, quickly replacing the receiver.

The D.M.W.D. team had not been long at Shoeburyness when they solved the capsizing mystery. With Hajile suspended from the crane they could now get much closer to it with safety, and Rivers-Bowerman thought of an ingenious way of dispelling the rocket smoke so that every detail of the touchdown could be plainly seen. From some undisclosed source he obtained an old Skua aircraft, and this was placed end-on on to the crane. Whenever Hajile was to be dropped the Skua's engine was started up, and the slipstream blew the smoke sideways, enabling Klemantaski to film the landing in slow motion.

They then discovered that as the girdle of rockets fired the colossal jet of cordite which beat down on the ground was digging a cup-shaped pit in the soil. This, acting as a reflector, focused a fierce jet of air on to the underside of the crash-pan as it came to rest, and overturned it.

To counter this further research was needed, and by the time all Hajile's teething troubles had been cured there was no chance to test the apparatus in action. It was, in fact, D-Day when the last memorable incident in its long development story occurred—and Hajile itself could not be blamed for what happened on that occasion.

Roberson, Rivers-Bowerman, and Klemantaski were all at Shoeburyness that historic morning, and before trials began they stood beneath the crane, discussing the news which had filtered through about the invasion. Hajile lay on the ground alongside them, the framework of iron girders which normally held the concrete block resting on a raised platform of railway sleepers.

Not realizing that the switches were closed, an electrician making some routine test of his own connected up the firing circuit. To his astonishment, all the rockets fired at once, and the great mass of ironwork rose straight into the air.

Rivers-Bowerman was felled by a blow on the jaw, and Roberson, who was actually standing in the middle of the circle of rockets, had a miraculous escape, for he was completely engulfed in flames as the contraption took off.

Forty feet above the ground Hajile lurched sideways. It crashed back to earth almost on top of Klemantaski, who was staggering about, blinded by a blast of sand which had caught him full in the face. He did not recover his sight for several days.

To the Wheezers and Dodgers Hajile involved a seemingly endless programme of research which brought more than the normal share of frustrations and disappointments. But its importance amply justified the effort expended on it. Roberson—condemned to spend the whole of his naval career on this one laborious task—occasionally gave vent to uncomplimentary opinions about deceleration in all its forms. But when the war was over it was a thesis on Hajile and its problems which gained for him a prized degree.

16

THE TOYSHOP

So numerous and varied were the projects launched from the office in Lower Regent Street that changes in D.M.W.D.'s staff proved constantly necessary. But the department never became unwieldy. Goodeve had no intention of allowing it to get bogged down by weight of numbers. He wanted the Wheezers and Dodgers to preserve a constant sense of initiative.

He chose his officers with great care. And he instilled in them all the tradition of never accepting defeat ... never accepting without question the opinion of recognized authorities on any matter. Although junior in status the officers chosen for D.M.W.D. were often men of great experience and technical ability, and they found themselves bearing responsibilities out of all proportion to their actual rank. From Jock Davies and Goodeve they got all the backing they wanted, however, and the Wheezers and Dodgers were a happy team.

Goodeve himself had one curious trait. Even in the most critical times he rarely came into the office much before noon. Then he would slip gradually into gear, working with ever-increasing intensity until midnight or later. During the daytime at least 50 per cent. of his energy was spent in getting to know people, in making and refreshing contacts. His best brainwork was done at night.

People who did not know his methods, and saw him roaming round other Admiralty departments, chatting to friends and greeting new acquaintances with easy informality, got the impression that the task of Miscellaneous Weapon Development must be something of a sinecure. Here was one man at least with plenty of spare time on his hands. In point of fact this penchant of Goodeve's paid him and his department hands down. At any stage in D.M.W.D.'s negotiations or operations he always knew where to find an ally who could assist him.

Norway and Richardson were outstanding deputies. Richardson, the scientist, had much of Goodeve's restless energy, though with less physical reserves to sustain it. He was very patient, very efficient—

M

and he fought obstruction like a tiger. People liked working for him. and they liked working for Nevil Norway too.

Norway, the engineer, had a very practical approach to any problem, derived from an essentially practical training. He told his young officers what he wanted, and then left them to get on with it in their own way. "Go away and do it," he would remark at the end of a briefing; "come back when it's done, or when you want some help" —and they knew they had a free hand.

He had an active, independent mind, and a mordant wit which could quickly deflate pomposity. Putting on his bridge coat one day, he accidentally cuffed on the ear another lieutenant-commander standing next to him.

"Awfully sorry, old boy," said Norway.

"That's not the way to address me," came the petulant rejoinder. "I might remind you, Norway, that in civil life I'm the equivalent of a rear-admiral. . . ."

"With the accent on rear, obviously," said Norway dryly!

A good deal of Norway's time and energy in this second phase of D.M.W.D.'s activities was absorbed by glider targets and more intricate types of model aircraft. Admiral Dreyer, the Inspector of Merchant Navy Gunnery, had become concerned about training difficulties, for the Merchant Navy men sent ashore to undergo courses on the range had no proper aircraft targets to fire at. It was never easy to get hold of aircraft to tow a sleeve for them, and in any case a sleeve target was a poor substitute for an attacking aircraft.

On Dreyer's staff was a certain Lieutenant Stanley Bell, R.N.V.R., who in peace-time had run a small airline between Glasgow and Paris. He suggested to the Admiral that model gliders might be developed to fly over the range, and by an odd coincidence the requirement eventually came to Norway, who had known Bell before the war. It was Norway who had supplied the aircraft for his airline.

Norway roughed out a design for a target 'plane and took it to a firm at Wimbledon who made toys. With their help D.M.W.D. produced an aeroplane with a 6-foot wing-span which could be winched up into the air to a height of 200 feet, and could then circle the range in free flight for a minute and a half. A technique was evolved of firing at it with Sten guns, fitted with a Lewis gun ringsight. As the velocity of Sten ammunition was about a third of that of the Lewis, and the model flew at about a third of the full-scale speed, the same lay-off could be obtained as in the case of a real aircraft under fire from a Lewis gun.

The gliders themselves worked well, but the operators had to dash about on the range, laying out the towing lines and altering the launching points as the wind veered. This inevitably interrupted the firing practice, so Norway turned his attention to developing a rocket-propelled aircraft which would be capable of flying for longer periods without close attention.

Target aircraft became a major industry in D.M.W.D., and teams had to be found to operate them. Norway said bluntly that it was absurd to put men on to the job of flying model aeroplanes at a critical stage in the war, when manpower was already a serious problem. So he decided to select a Wren to help with the development trials.

She had to be intelligent enough to master a new technique quickly, and she had to be neat with her fingers, for there was a good deal of repair work to be done on the fabric of the 'planes.

When these points were explained to the W.R.N.S. organization they produced Frances Randall, a young South Londoner who had been working as a hat-trimmer in a big West End store. In appearance she was a very ordinary-looking working girl, but she seemed intelligent and anxious to learn, and Norway placed her in the charge of Alec Menhinick, who was still convalescing after his ordeal in the *Patia*. A little later more Wrens were drafted to the outside staff of D.M.W.D., for ten ranges had to be equipped and operated as soon as the first batch of gliders was ready. The obvious person to train the newcomers was Wren Randall, who, although she had not been long in the Navy, had quickly developed quite an air of assurance. In due course her promotion to Leading Wren was approved.

Difficulties began to crop up on the ranges. The officers in charge knew nothing about the working of the glider targets, and the Wren operators, being new to the Service, were unable to assert themselves or to present the case for the device. Clearly it was necessary that some one should travel round the ranges and get the system properly under way. Menhinick did this for a time, but then Norway read the Riot Act and said that D.M.W.D. could not spare a trained R.N.V.R. officer for a job of this kind.

Again the only logical candidate was Leading Wren Randall, and since she would have to travel all over Britain, visiting ranges and negotiating with officers, she had to be regraded in rank. So Frances Randall, who had developed into a very pretty girl with an impressive sense of authority, became a Petty Officer Wren.

By the time the rocket-propelled target aircraft emerged it was obvious that ranges in many parts of the world would soon adopt D.M.W.D.'s ingenious models as part of their standard equipment. The Admiralty planned to introduce them in Egypt and Canada, and some one had to supervise their initial operation.

Again Norway put his foot down. "I can't possibly spare an officer from the engineering section to go abroad and work this toy. There's nothing for it . . . Wren Randall will have to take it on."

So Wren Randall became Third Officer Randall, and set off for Egypt. She handled the job remarkably well; returned to D.M.W.D. for a short time; and went out to Canada. There she met a lieutenant-commander in the Canadian Navy, and married him. None of the Wheezers and Dodgers would have been really surprised if Wren Randall had finished the war as a member of the Cabinet!

D.M.W.D.'s most important venture in the toy-aeroplane field was the "Swallow," which Norway developed from the rocket-propelled target 'plane after the costly failure of the Dieppe Raid. In any beach assault the task of laying a smokescreen at a height of only 200 feet over a heavily defended area was sheer murder for the unfortunate pilots. So the Wheezers and Dodgers were asked if they could build a pilotless aircraft which could take off from the deck of a ship and lay a smoke curtain over invasion beaches by automatic means.

Armed with this proposal, Norway went off to see his friends the toy manufacturers, and many conferences were held at the Royal Aircraft Establishment at Farnborough. Finally the Swallow was born.

It was a brilliantly ingenious affair, propelled by fifteen slow-burning rockets and controlled by a 'mechanical mouse'—a clock-work machine, mounted in the tail plane, which did several different jobs in rotation. It fired the Swallow's own motor rockets once the 'plane had been catapulted into the air. It altered the ailerons, allowing the aircraft to bank or to fly level, and when the Swallow swooped over the invasion area the clockwork mouse switched on the smoke, laying a dense curtain for more than a quarter of a mile.

To launch the Swallow from the deck of a landing-craft a catapult had to be used, and an experimental track was laid down at H.M.S. *Kestrel*, the Fleet Air Arm station at Worthy Down.

Some of the problems of a high-speed catapult have already been described. To get the Swallow airborne at Worthy Down the trolley on which it was mounted had to reach a speed of 100 miles an hour in a distance of only 40 feet.

To bring it to a halt the Wheezers and Dodgers mounted on the front of the trolley a large metal cylinder filled with water. At the end of the track was a ram. When the trolley struck this, the ram pierced a copper disc on the face of the cylinder, and then drove against the cushion of water inside. It was, in fact, rather like the apparatus tested so spectacularly at Brean Down; the stress involved was not so great, but even so the trolley took a lot of stopping, for when loaded with the Swallow aircraft and the twenty rockets which drove it down the track it weighed more than 16 hundredweight.

The main danger seemed to be that the rough track, or any unevenness in the firing of the rockets, might swing the trolley sideways, and the tapered ram might fail to enter the cylinder. The only serious trouble, however, came from quite a different source. When the Swallow landed after its first trial flight its wings were found to be riddled with minute holes. The ram had plunged into the cylinder with such violence that a cloud of water droplets had been expelled like machine-gun bullets. To protect the Swallow the Wheezers and Dodgers built a steel shield, like the roof of a tunnel, over the top part of the ram, the idea being that the trolley itself would pass under this, and the aircraft, mounted above, would be safe from the water 'bullets' as it took off. Even so they underestimated the force of the spray. On the first run with the tunnel roof clamped in position it blew the big metal shield, weighing fully one hundredweight, sky-high, shearing off the eight bolts which held it as if they were made of putty. It was not, however, until the trials were transferred to the Beaulieu river that Norway's team ran into real difficulties.

There the catapult was mounted on an obsolete landing-craft, and it was planned to fire the Swallow down the long entrance reach of the river, so that it would crash on the marshes near Needs Oar Point.

First of all they had to discover the exact speed of the trolley at the point of the Swallow's take-off, and Hatfield was called in. He arrived with his immensely complicated timing apparatus, a galvanometer, and masses of wire, and when his magic box had been installed the Wheezers and Dodgers carried out a long series of 'dummy runs,' using 750-pound concrete blocks as a substitute for the aircraft. Any uninitiated spectator might well have wondered what strange purpose the timing trials fulfilled, for the trolley, its rockets blazing, would hurtle down the track ... there would be a terrific crash as it hit the buffer with a force of more than 80 tons behind it, and the big concrete blocks would pitch forward into the river.

Day after day this went on—and day after day the strangest calculations emerged from Hatfield's electrical timing gear. First it insisted that the trolley was travelling at not more than 40 m.p.h. Then it went to the other extreme, announcing a speed of several hundred miles an hour, which seemed equally improbable. Many tons of concrete had been hurled into the Beaulieu river before a suspicion dawned on Biddell that quite an elementary fault was to blame for the erratic readings. Telling the others to watch the pointer on the indicator dial, he walked to the end of the runway and stamped his foot on the deck. Sure enough, the timing mechanism recorded a positively startling performance by the trolley, which had not moved at all! So Hatfield reluctantly took his apparatus to pieces once again, and this time the wiring fault was soon remedied.

In war the scientist is for ever working against the clock, and when the early flights of the Swallow from the landing-craft brought failure after failure the team of naval officers working on the Hampshire river sensed they were losing their race with time.

Whenever they launched the robot 'plane it would fly satisfactorily for a certain distance. Then some gremlin would start tinkering with the automatic controls, and the Swallow would plunge to earth. It took dozens of trials, and the exposure of thousands of feet of cine film, before they found out what was happening. The immense acceleration of the catapult was upsetting one tiny fitting inside the clockwork mouse.

As soon as this was corrected the Swallow climbed, turned, and banked beautifully, but this final success came too near to D-Day for the aircraft to go into mass production. It never, therefore, met its baptism of fire. The research carried out by D.M.W.D. and the Royal Aircraft Establishment was destined, however, to yield important dividends, for data collected during the Swallow trials helped to produce some of Britain's earliest guided missiles.

That development, however, belonged to the future. For the Wheezers and Dodgers the last word on the Swallow was written one day in 1945. Miss Slade, a mathematician who was one of the three civilians on D.M.W.D.'s executive staff, was finishing off a report on a floating incendiary device for the Admiralty records when her telephone rang.

The call was from the firm which had built the Swallow. They were thinking, they said, that small copies of the aircraft might make popular toys. Would there be any Admiralty objection if a scale model was shown at a toy-trade exhibition?

Miss Slade said she could see no objection from D.M.W.D.'s point of view, but it was really a matter for the Naval Intelligence Department. She mentioned a certain officer who, she thought, might be able to help them, and thought no more about it until the following day, when the lieutenant-commander in question rang up.

"I understand that you have revealed my extension number to an outside person," he said. "This is a serious breach of security. Surely you know by now that here in N.I.D. we all work in the dark."

Miss Slade recalled the Ipswich incident. "I've always suspected so," she said crushingly, "but we've never actually had any official confirmation before!"

For the most part the staff of D.M.W.D. were split up into teams to tackle well-defined and relatively short-term projects. Donald Currie, however, immersed himself in a field of experiments entirely his own, and at this particular period his movements were more mysterious than usual.

To Jamieson, who from his desk in the corner of the big room in Lower Regent Street somehow contrived to keep track of every one's comings and goings, he would say, "If anyone wants me I shall be in the swimming-bath at Wembley." And off he would go, laden with model boats, paint-pots, and strips of coloured fabric. He spent much of his time these days in museums and the reading-rooms of public libraries, and after these visits obscure messages for him used to reach D.M.W.D.

"Lieutenant Currie? No, I'm afraid he's not in yet," Jamieson would say to some puzzled officer taking a 'phone call at the other end of the room.

"Know anything of his movements? There's a chap on the 'phone who wants to talk to him about coral formations in the Bay of Bengal."

"No, I don't. He said he was spending last night at Staines Reservoir. . . ."

Donald Currie was, in fact, engrossed in yet another camouflage problem. Ever since the memorable interview between Goodeve and Commander Pouter D.M.W.D. had assumed responsibility for most of the naval research into ways and means of concealing ships and small craft, either at sea or in harbour. And this had become Currie's special preserve. A bold experiment by Peter Scott, when First Lieutenant of H.M.S. *Broke*, had done much to upset preconceived notions about camouflage of ships at sea.[1] In the First World War efforts in this field had been concentrated mainly on schemes of dazzle painting in bold colours and designs; little attempt was made to merge a ship into its background.

Drawing on experience gained when stalking birds with a duck-punt, Scott advanced a new theory. He noticed that on starlit or cloudy moonlit nights a ship on the horizon appeared as a black lump jutting up from a darker sea against the lighter sky.

[1] Lieutenant-Commander Peter Scott, C.B.E., D.S.C. and bar, R.N.V.R., was awarded the M.B.E. for his camouflage research, and the Admiralty presented him with a model of H.M.S. *Broke*, painted in the off-white shade he had developed.

To counteract this effect he carried out certain tests. These showed conclusively that in such conditions a ship could not be painted too white. By day, however, a white ship was unpleasantly conspicuous to searching aircraft, but further experiment produced a satisfactory compromise. It was found that pale greys, blues, and greens were much less obvious by day, and only slightly less effective at night.

Scott therefore devised an off-white camouflage for the *Broke*, and this was such a spectacular success that she was rammed by a trawler while at anchor in the Foyle, the trawler's captain protesting afterwards that *Broke* was invisible! On another occasion *Broke* and *Verity* collided 300 miles out in the Atlantic, the latter ship failing to sight *Broke* at all until the last moment. Eventually all warships in the North Atlantic and Home waters were painted to this speci- fication, after the colour scheme had been somewhat modified. Always to the fore in adopting new ideas, Captain Mountbatten became a keen supporter of the change, and he had the Fifth Destroyer Flotilla disguised in a curious shade of pale mauve which became known as "Mountbatten pink." This particular colour earned understandable popularity with harassed First Lieutenants, for it showed up dirt and rust a good deal less conspicuously than Scott's off-white camouflage.

Currie's own observations from the air were directed to the camou- flage of merchant ships, and they enabled D.M.W.D. to recommend a uniform colour scheme. Producing exactly the right texture of paint, however, called for patient research. Flying over the Atlantic at dawn and in the late evening, Currie noticed that the hulls of vessels covered with high-gloss paints showed up alarmingly in the rays of the rising or setting sun. Using an ingenious gloss-measuring instrument, D.M.W.D. therefore set to work to evolve 'safe' paints which would tone down to a matt surface within a few days of being applied.

While these experiments were going on, intriguing reports came from the Canadian Navy, who had been experimenting on lines very similar to Scott's researches. They also had reached the conclu- sion that a ship painted sheer white would be extremely difficult to detect at night, and Goodeve was keenly interested. It seemed to follow from this that a vessel might be actually *illuminated* in such a way as to make her invisible. The Wheezers and Dodgers therefore staged an elaborate trial, mounting lamps on outriggers and con- trolling their power by a rheostat in an attempt to merge the ship with the horizon. This succeeded dramatically at short ranges, but they found that the expense of supplying and operating such equip- ment would be prohibitive.

From camouflage of ships at sea D.M.W.D. turned to the concealment of warships and merchant ships in port. Pilots of aircraft raiding Brest reported that the *Scharnhorst* and *Gneisenau* were so
cleverly hidden that even when they managed to pick out the vast
mass of the upperworks it was difficult to tell which way the
battleships were lying. The Germans had painted the bows and
sterns of the two ships the same colour as the ground, and they had
used vast quantities of netting. Our own chief need was to protect
valuable merchantmen unloading in the docks, so Currie went off
to Newport, in Monmouthshire, where a steamship called the *Marwarrin* was lying. Using nets and outriggers to break up the line of
the hull, he produced an effective enough camouflage, but it had one
fatal drawback. Ships like the *Marwarrin* had to get to sea again
quickly; they were seldom in dock long enough to justify all the effort
of swathing them in a vast cocoon of nets and booms. Once in place,
too, it would obviously slow down the work of unloading to a dangerous extent.

The Wheezers and Dodgers provided a camouflage scheme for
naval air stations—and at Worthy Down Currie operated on some
Scorpions[1] so successfully with paint and special netting that observers flying over the field were unable to find any of the dozen
vehicles parked round the perimeter. He went to Lerwick, in the
Shetlands, and rigged up a cunning contraption of dummy lighters
and oil-drums to hide the submarines lying alongside the jetty there;
he devised special coloured clothing for Commandos carrying out
limpet attacks on shipping in enemy harbours; and he produced
ingenious nets for the M.T.B.'s which crossed the North Sea to hide
up in the fjords of Norway. These nets were large enough to drape
right over the boats. On one side they suggested a typical background of rocks and vegetation; when reversed, they gave an impression of a similar surface after a heavy fall of snow.

For an artist like Donald Currie, who for years had studied the
sea and the sky, the effects of light and shade, and contrasts in
colouring, the creation of a camouflage scheme presented no impon-
derable problems once he had seen the setting for himself. But now
the Admiralty asked for something infinitely more difficult. They
showed him the plans of a secret craft designed for raiding purposes.
It could carry a small crew, two canoes, and a load of explosive, and
when its occupants paddled ashore for reconnaissance or sabotage
work the parent craft sank to the sea-bed. Several days later an automatic timing device came into operation, and the submerged boat
rose to the surface under cover of darkness, ready to receive the
raiding party when they paddled back.

[1] Vehicles armed with machine-guns and used for airfield defence.

These submersible craft, which could vanish without trace and return just as unobtrusively without human aid, were called "Mobile Floating Units."

"We can't tell you exactly where they're going to operate, but you can take it that it will be in waters controlled by the Jap. The main danger for the raiding party will come from air reconnaissance, for the sea in that area is very clear. We've somehow got to reduce the chances of these M.F.U.'s being spotted while they're lying on the bottom during the day-time."

That was all Currie was told.

He set to work systematically to learn all he could about a wide variety of tropical sea-beds in all weather and water conditions. In theory this seemed simple enough; many encyclopedias and other reference books purported to give this information. As so often happens, however, Currie found that the experts were not always in accord. Some had special knowledge of the highly coloured coral formations encountered in tropical waters, and stressed this aspect. Others emphasized the prominent characteristics of different kinds of tropical weed, and to reconcile all their conflicting impressions meant days of tramping from museum to museum, from one authority to another.

The Hydrographer's Department supplied facts about the turbidity of water. The staff of the Natural History Museum told him all they knew about various types of sea-bed. He talked to experts on seaweed, mineralogy, and sea-bottom deposits. And from the head geologist of a famous oil company he learnt about the geological formation of the coast in the operational area.

At the end of it all he knew a great deal about the appearance of coral sand and quartz sand, tropical weeds like Laminaria, and all kinds of rocks. He was also aware that the camouflage problem was even more difficult than he had imagined, for the M.F.U.'s might equally well come to rest against a background of dark, grey-green mud, light yellow sand, or glaring white coral.

Somehow he had to produce a scheme basically suitable for any of these conditions, and he began experimenting with small-scale models. As a start he mapped out the whole surface of the deck in irregular light and dark patches. He then took his small boats to the Vale Farm Swimming Baths at Wembley.

The water there was crystal-clear—as clear, in fact, as any sea water in the world. Off the Tonga Islands a 15-inch Sechi disc can be seen at 200 feet. Vale Farm might well have been in the Tonga Islands, and, musing on this incongruity as he towed his models up and down the baths, Currie only came out of his reverie when he saw the astonished look on the face of the Cockney swimming-bath attendant, who obviously thought his visitors were too old to be playing with toy boats.

With the help of a team of lighting experts from the research staff of the General Electric Company, whose laboratories were not far from the baths, a very successful colour plan was evolved for the topsides of the M.F.U. The decks were given a sandy background, and disruptions of light and dark shading broke up the slab-like appearance of the craft.

They then turned their attentions to the canoes, for it was equally vital that the approach of the raiding parties should not be seen by watchers ashore. Here full-scale tests were possible, and Currie and the G.E.C. team began spending their nights afloat on the cold waters of the reservoir at Staines, paddling slowly to and fro in their flimsy craft while chilled observers peered through the darkness. At dawn they would all gather in one of the pump-houses to compare notes, and Currie invariably produced a large bag of Spanish onions which, he claimed, would fortify and invigorate his exhausted companions.

Privately, G.E.C.'s research team considered that almost any hazard of war was preferable to a ration of raw onions at six o'clock in the morning, but since their resistance was lowered by lack of sleep and they liked Currie too much to hurt his feelings they suffered in silence!

Only one essay in camouflage developed into a combined operation involving a whole team of the Wheezers and Dodgers, and, oddly enough, Donald Currie—busy with other work at the time— took relatively little part in it.

Strictly speaking, the story of the attempt to obliterate the Thames belongs to the earlier phase of D.M.W.D.'s activities, but water camouflage had more far-reaching aims than the defence of the metropolis. The London Blitz was over by the spring of 1941, but there were other targets. It became vitally necessary to protect the great factories in the Midlands. Lakes, reservoirs, and canals all helped the air navigator to pinpoint industrial centres, and it was not until the advent of radar that such visual aids lost their significance.

At full moon, rivers and lakes can be seen from afar. R.A.F. crews bombing Kiel spoke of sighting the Elbe fifty miles away, and Currie, making an aerial reconnaissance himself on a night when haze had already cut down visibility, picked out the Mersey quite easily at a distance of thirty-five miles. It was the heavy raids on Merseyside which first focused attention on the need for water camouflage, for the German bombers attacking the docks at Liverpool were observed to check their final approach by a line of five reservoirs leading from the Trent Valley.

Admittedly, other objects such as wide roads, woodlands, and the dark ribbons of railway track showed up just as prominently in bright moonlight, but in certain quarters it was strongly urged that the task of the bomber crews would be made a great deal more difficult if some way could be found to mask the surface of water.

When the proposal first came to Goodeve, Professor Rideal[1] had already conducted some interesting experiments at Cambridge, where he had camouflaged a stream with coal-dust. Goodeve fore-saw greater difficulty in applying such a method to any tidal water-way, and for stretches of static water other types of camouflage were, of course, available. Nets, supported by cork floats, could be spread over the water, and if properly moored they would not be so vulner-able to the wind. Within certain limits, however, the coal-dust experi-ments had certainly proved promising, and D.M.W.D. could not reject the idea without giving it a fair trial.

A team, soon to be known as the Kentucky Minstrels, was there-fore formed under the leadership of Duncan Bruce to study the whole project, and work began on the Thames in a craft inappropri-ately named H.M.S. *Persil*.

From the start there was keen competition, for rivals were in the field. On Ruislip Reservoir a party from a research station which specialized in such experiments were already testing an apparatus rather like a Hoover (except that it worked in reverse). Towed behind a launch, this discharged large quantities of oiled coal-dust just be-neath the surface; but the system was not proving very satisfactory, for the dust was first injected into a stream of air inside the appara-tus, and when it finally met the water it tended to clog instead of spreading out freely. If, on the other hand, they sprayed the dust from a point just *above* the surface it blew away.

Bruce tackled the problem from a slightly different angle. After discussions with Dr Lessing, a well-known fuel consultant, he first fed the dust into a high-pressure water-jet, and then expelled the mixture through an ordinary fire-fighting appliance. In this way he could lay his inky screen ahead of the boat, and the method of discharge was faster and cleaner—though cleanliness was only a comparative term for any part of the Kentucky Minstrels' activities!

The trials began in quite a modest way, but soon the Ministry of Home Security began to take a close interest. So did the special committee set up by the Prime Minister to co-ordinate efforts in the

[1] Now Sir Eric Rideal, M.B.E., F.R.S., Professor of Physical Chemistry at King's College, University of London, since 1950, and Chairman of the Minis-try of Supply's Advisory Council on Scientific Research of Technical Develop-ment since 1953.

Battle of the Atlantic. Any measures which promised to protect merchant ships during their time in port received high priority, and so more helpers—a petty officer and a party of ratings—were drafted to speed the experiments on the Thames. The competing sprayers were installed in four large launches, which plied up and down the river at night, smothering its murky waters in a thick mantle of coal-dust or soot, and more than once Mr Churchill himself came out on to Westminster Bridge to inspect the results.

The experiments became extremely unpopular with Thames-side housewives, who wrote to their M.P.'s complaining that their laundry was being ruined. There were contretemps afloat, too, and when, as the result of a slight technical hitch, a passing tug was deluged in a hail of oily black particles Bruce was given some extremely lurid, if rather impracticable, advice by her crew!

Nobody, however, suffered more than the Wheezers and Dodgers themselves. The coal-dust settled on them in clouds, ruining their uniforms and covering them with a sooty grime which soap and water took long to dispel. After a while they scarcely noticed one another's appearance, and Coulson, returning to the office one morning after a whole night on the river, was quite surprised when he was stopped in Piccadilly by an immaculate young Commander R.N., who regarded him with extreme distaste.

"All you R.N.V.R.'s are the same," he said scathingly.... "Look at you ... absolutely filthy ... a disgrace to the Service! And you didn't even salute me. Why not?"

As it happened, Coulson was accompanied by Richardson, who had been promoted to Commander two days earlier, but had not had time to acquire his 'brass hat,' so he said somewhat smugly, "As this officer with me holds the same rank as yourself I did not think it was necessary." A trifle disconcerted, his interrogator abandoned all further examination of Coulson's shortcomings.

As the trials on the Thames progressed it became evident that the effort involved in blacking out large stretches of tidal water would far outweigh any possible tactical advantage.

To cover one acre demanded at least a hundredweight of specially prepared coal-dust, and as fast as they supplemented the initial discharge a strong tide would wash the dust away. If a wind was blowing the whole film piled up against the lee shore, and choppy water swamped and sank the drifting particles.

In the greater shelter of the Surrey Commercial Docks results were more encouraging, but the Wheezers and Dodgers had their greatest success at Coventry. H.M.S. *Persil*, which, after the early experiments on the Thames, had been used mainly for retrieving the dead cats and dogs which floated odorously round the dock area, was transported north for these trials, and, with no tide to hamper their experiments, Bruce and his team camouflaged Coventry Canal so effectively that both an old gentleman and a dog walked into it, under the impression that it was a newly made-up road!

By that time, however, it was realized that any success by the Kentucky Minstrels could have relatively little effect on the Luftwaffe. The enemy had switched to moonless nights for their mass raiding, and with the swift development of radar the most ardent advocates of water camouflage abandoned their faith in this expensive and somewhat unreliable form of protection.

Goodeve always spoke of his acquiescence in the strange experiments on the Thames as "one of my gross errors." But when the trials began no one could have foreseen with any certainty the speed and direction of the march of science.

PART III: KEYS TO THE FORTRESS

17

INVASION AHEAD

THE start of the war's fourth year brought a dramatic change in Allied fortunes. Alamein turned the tide in North Africa, and Operation Torch launched a new drive eastward along the Mediterranean. By January 1943 the German Army was in full retreat on the Don. Churchill and Roosevelt could now look far beyond the conquest of Europe's "soft underbelly"; when they met at Casablanca the possibility of invading Northern France as early as the coming August was discussed at length.

Invasion plans burdened the Royal Navy with heavy responsibilities, and from this time onward all D.M.W.D.'s own efforts were directed to problems of amphibious assault. Weird projects began to take shape: floating roadways and airfields, harbours created by streams of bubbles, and rocket-propelled monsters to blast a way through coast defences. There were explosive amphibians, invisible boats, and cliff-scaling devices.

In the preliminary stages many of these raised abstruse questions of higher mathematics, and new faces began to appear in the department. Goodeve had a free hand to enlist the aid of distinguished consultants in any field, and men like Professor G. I. Taylor and the youthful Dr William Penney were called in to advise on the creation of artificial harbours.[1] Guggenheim, the author of a standard work on thermo-dynamics, at last had opponents in argument worthy of his steel, and he would lure Penney into lively discussion on the subject, while his naval friends listened in awed and uncomprehending silence.

Another notable civilian recruit was George Kreisel, whose mathematical calculations were far above the heads of most members of D.M.W.D. Given a problem, he would retaliate with pages and pages of hieroglyphics which reduced even Richardson to stunned

[1] Professor Taylor was knighted in 1944; Sir William Penney was Assistant Professor of Mathematics at Imperial College throughout the war, and has been Director of the United Kingdom Atomic Weapons Research Establishment at Aldermaston since 1953. He was knighted in 1952.

perplexity. And once, when in desperation Richardson asked an eminent professor of mathematics to interpret an explanation of Kreisel's, the learned man confessed with some diffidence that it was altogether too advanced for *him*!

Kreisel was certainly a colourful addition to the department. He had his own decided views on the appropriate rig for Service occasions, and would turn up at official trials attired in an old pair of grey flannels and a sky-blue shirt, widely opened at the neck. This gave him the carefree appearance of a holiday hiker who had somehow strayed into the decorous gatherings of uniformed officers by sheer accident. But George Kreisel himself remained entirely oblivious to the critical stares of the admirals and generals, all of whom seemed to him uncomfortably overdressed.

On the naval side of D.M.W.D. there were several officers now firmly established on the staff who have not, nevertheless, been mentioned so far. Ron Eades, a tall, good-looking R.N.V.R. lieutenant with a brisk, energetic manner, was a close friend of Boswell. Both hailed from Portsmouth, and for years they had sailed and played rugger together. Eades was completely fearless, and his indifference to explosives roused no little apprehension at Birnbeck, where he experimented with a lethal device called "Bookrest." This was a canvas tube filled with plastic explosive and designed to blow up enemy minefields. Plastic explosive was a highly temperamental substance, and quite liable to react to the slightest rough handling, but Eades treated it with a cavalier disdain. Whenever he wanted to empty it out of its hosepipe container he resorted to the simple expedient of banging the pipe against the wall of the magazine which housed all Birnbeck's cordite, flares, rockets, and detonators!

The leader of D.M.W.D.'s research into artificial-harbour problems was Robert Lochner, a sturdy, bespectacled man with any amount of drive, who had joined the department after commanding an M.L. flotilla in Coastal Forces. He was an electrical engineer when war broke out, but, being also an ardent yachtsman, he naturally gravitated into the R.N.V.R. His first appointment was to one of the Q ships, with which the Admiralty hoped to emulate the success of Rear-Admiral Gordon Campbell, V.C., in the First World War, but in the end little came of this venture, and while he was kicking his heels at Plymouth he put up an idea for countering the magnetic mine.[1]

---

[1] This idea was successfully used in the protection of large numbers of warships and merchant ships against magnetic mines in the early days of the war, and subsequently a substantial award was granted to Lochner by the Royal Commission on Awards to Inventors.

THE GIANT PIPES LAID ON THE BEACH AT PORTSLADE IN READINESS FOR THE TRIALS OF BUBBLE HARBOUR

SOFT LILO, THE FORERUNNER OF THE BOMBARDON FLOATING BREAK-WATER, UNDER CONSTRUCTION IN THE DOCKS AT SOUTHAMPTON

"THE MOST FORMIDABLE WEAPON IN ALL THE LONG HISTORY OF
SHORE BOMBARDMENT"

A Rocket Landing Craft in action.

Imperial War Museum

"STRETCHING AWAY ALONG THE LOWER DECK FROM THE BASE OF THE BRIDG
WERE SERRIED RANKS OF HUGE ROCKETS, ALL INCLINED AT AN ANGLE, AN
LOOKING LIKE SOME STRANGE, STUNTED FOREST"

Imperial War Museum

This brought a posting to H.M.S. *Vernon*, and there he met Goodeve for the first time. When he moved on to Coastal Forces he must have surprised some of his brother-officers by his spare-time preoccupation. He had decided to read for the Bar, and returning from patrols off the Dutch coast he would often prop himself up in an angle of the upper deck and study Roman law!

Robert Lochner's sea time came to an abrupt end in 1941, when a picture appeared in a London magazine. This showed him on the bridge of his M.L., coming back from some operation—and all too clearly he was wearing spectacles. The Admiralty promptly inquired how it was that a commanding officer of an M.L. and senior officer of the First Flotilla came to be suffering, apparently, from defective eyesight, and even the considerate test which the local admiral applied—"Look out of that window, Lochner, and tell me the colour of that large advertisement for Gold Flake Cigarettes!"—failed to secure a reprieve for long. Goodeve brought him into D.M.W.D., and after a time Lochner took charge of several of the department's engineering projects.

Another member of the Engineering Section was Williamson, the doyen of the Wheezers and Dodgers. One of the most accomplished engineers on the staff, he entered into the rigours of trials work with such zest that it was difficult to think of him as a veteran. This, however, he undeniably was. He had joined D.M.W.D. on his fiftieth birthday; in the 1914 war he had served both as an Engineer Officer in the Navy and as a Flight-Commander in the Air Force. He had learnt to fly in the very early days—his mentor was a Flight-Lieutenant named Alcock, who later made the first crossing of the Atlantic —and Williamson also took part in a memorable airship attack on the *Goeben* and the *Breslau* with 112-pounder bombs.

In all, more than fifty officers were employed on research and development now, among them Laurie, who had spent the decade before the war in Antarctic research and held the coveted Polar Medal; Brookfield, a schoolmaster in civil life, who was Norway's chief assistant in the office; Abel, an interplanetary enthusiast who had set his heart on a journey to Mars; and young Urwin, who had come to D.M.W.D. in 1942 after a singularly eventful naval apprenticeship as a rating. He fractured his spine when H.M.S. *Jersey* was mined off Malta; he was also serving in the cruiser *Aurora* when *she* was mined; and finally he was a survivor from the *Breconshire* when that ship sank after a mass dive-bombing attack. He seemed, however, little the worse for this lively sojourn in the Mediterranean, and in the coming days he was to play a useful part both in developing rocket landing-craft and in helping Lochner with his artificial-harbour problems.

N

The wide net which Goodeve cast over the embryo sub-lieutenants undergoing training at H.M.S. *King Alfred* even enmeshed the author of this story, who, after a year of undistinguished service as a rating on board an armed yacht, was as surprised as Menhinick to find himself suddenly deposited in the midst of an erudite band of scientists. On first arrival in the Admiralty he felt somewhat self-conscious of his status as a Temporary Sub-Lieutenant among so much straight gold lace, but Goodeve quickly dispelled any anxiety on this score.

"From now onwards you can act on the assumption that one wavy ring is equal to two straight ones," he said reassuringly. "Before I came to this job I was once sent for by Admiral Wake-Walker, and asked to carry out an unusual mission. When I suggested that the task was rather irregular he said, 'Of course it is, otherwise I would have done it myself. You, as an R.N.V.R. officer, *needn't* know it's irregular. Go and do it!' So you see you've got quite an advantage over many R.N. officers a lot senior to you."

Much of the success of the Wheezers and Dodgers was made possible by the wholehearted co-operation of the Admiralty's Commission and Warrant Branch. Once they knew the type of recruit Goodeve needed to strengthen the department they went to work as enthusiastically as any old-time press-gang. Officers with special scientific or engineering training were sought out and spirited from ships and shore establishments with uncanny speed, and in some cases civilians found themselves screened for security and converted into naval officers in as little as forty-eight hours.

In addition to the C.W. Branch, assistance in the same encouraging way came from the Director of Scientific Research and the Director of Naval Accounts, who saw to it that the new department was given all the financial support it required. There was, in fact, a refreshing absence of red tape in all the Wheezers and Dodgers' dealings with recruiting and accountancy problems, and the fact that no exact complement was ever laid down for D.M.W.D. left Goodeve free to engage all the necessary experts he needed as new and widely different tasks presented themselves.

This freedom was never abused. Goodeve had no intention of allowing the department to become overstaffed and unwieldy. From every one who wished to remain a member of the Wheezers and Dodgers he demanded unflagging enterprise and energy. There was no question of resting on one's laurels.

Two women members of D.M.W.D. call for mention. Miss Ottley, a tall, auburn-haired girl, had been with the team from the start. Although officially she was appointed as Goodeve's secretary, she soon became the uncomplaining amanuensis of the entire department, typing out their reports, taking messages, and even doing urgent running repairs to damaged uniforms. Any trade union would have been surprised at the long hours she chose to work, but at least life in the office in Lower Regent Street was never boring. Even on the rare occasions when comparative peace descended on the department there was always a chance that Guggenheim, who had a strange passion for rearranging the furniture, would start moving all the chairs and tables about, or Lane or Richardson would blow up part of the building.

Another stalwart member of the staff was Miss Slade. The eccentricities of the Wheezers and Dodgers intrigued her more than most people, for in addition to being an able mathematician she was a qualified psychologist. As assistant to Alec Coulson she took part in many of the outside trials, and she caused something of a stir whenever she appeared on board His Majesty's ships. No one ever expected sea trials to be conducted by a woman, and, even ashore, naval establishments seemed uncertain of the procedure for victualling, accommodating, and entertaining a female civilian scientist of officer status but no known rank. At the same time an undefined status carried certain advantages in a Service environment, and Miss Slade, who waged a constant and energetic war on red tape, had no scruples over ringing up senior officers and taking them to task with a freedom which Alec Coulson, her own superior officer but a mere two-and-a-half-striper, never—in spite of Goodeve's dictum—dared to emulate.

As a department D.M.W.D. was very much the reflection of Goodeve's forceful personality. He inspired immediate confidence and initiative in the most junior recruit, and since Jock Davies had skilfully steered clear of all attempts to limit the Wheezers and Dodgers' field of activities their influence was felt in every sphere of the naval war.

In the Admiralty, however, it was realized by the autumn of 1942 that the many problems set by the naval planning staff would only be solved in the time available if all the Royal Navy's scientific resources were properly co-ordinated.

Working under the ægis of the Admiralty were a number of research organizations in addition to D.M.W.D.—the staff of the laboratories at Teddington, an anti-submarine warfare unit, and other specialized teams attached to the Director of Naval Construction, the Engineer-in-Chief of the Navy, and the Medical Director-General.

One new and outstandingly successful organization—often described since as the finest research unit the Admiralty has ever had—was the radar department of the Signals Division, with which

Wright had a great deal to do. The achievements of the Admiralty Signals Establishment are outside the scope of this story, but the speed and efficiency of their work was quite remarkable. Thanks to them, the Navy was given new eyes to see with.

The research section of the Mine Design Department had also done outstanding work, but in spite of the importance of all these varied units, strangely enough, scientific research had no representative on the Board of Admiralty. The Board included men answerable for planning and personnel, supplies and transport, the provision of weapons and the running of naval dockyards, the building and repair of merchant ships, and the swiftly expanding Fleet Air Arm—almost every aspect of naval life, in fact, with the exception of scientific development.

It was therefore decided to create a new civilian post, giving the holder effective control of the whole research and development programme for the Royal Navy. And to this key position Charles Goodeve was appointed on the first day of October 1942.

He heard the news with mixed feelings. It meant the end of his career as a naval officer, for to give him the authority he would need in his new appointment the Board ruled that he would have to surrender his naval rank. After so many years that was a sharp wrench.

It was obvious, too, that this sudden promotion in the Admiralty hierarchy—from Commander R.N.V.R. to the equivalent of a Rear-Admiral—might make his position difficult. Henceforward he would be senior to all the Directors of Departments with whom he had dealt as a subordinate, and a good deal of tact would be necessary if he was to secure ungrudging co-operation.

Last, but not least, the move would sever his close ties with the Wheezers and Dodgers. It was some consolation to know that in the new job he could at least hold a watching brief for them; he could ensure that they had freedom to carry on their work on the same lines under Richardson, who would take over the scientific control of the department.

No sooner had Goodeve become Assistant Controller, Research and Development, and handed over to his deputy, than Jock Davies also departed. He had completed his term at the Admiralty and was anxious to get to sea again. In March 1943 he was given command of one of the new escort carriers, and in his place came Captain F. W. H. Jeans, an officer of considerable technical experience and ability, who had been serving on the British Admiralty Mission in Washington.

Jock Davies had contributed more to the success of the department than most people realized at the time. Some officers in his position would have regarded D.M.W.D. as a backwater on the list of Captains' appointments. They would have considered it anomalous to be asked to take charge of a minor shore department staffed almost exclusively by junior R.N.V.R. officers, and they would not have understood the temperament and outlook of Goodeve, with his impatience which occasionally rode roughshod over convention and accepted Service practice.

With his keen natural interest in technical matters Davies saw his appointment to D.M.W.D. in a different light. He was attracted and stimulated by Goodeve's dynamic approach to problems which others, more set in their ways, rejected as insoluble. He liked the spirit of the young department, the zest and drive with which every new project was tackled.

His task was to forge the essential link between D.M.W.D. and other bodies in the Admiralty who were still a little suspicious of scientists in uniform.

As a senior R.N. officer Jock Davies not only understood the Admiralty organization better than any of his R.N.V.R. subordinates, but he could interpret the likely attitudes of heads of other departments to most proposals which the Wheezers and Dodgers wanted to put forward. At the same time he held a firm balance between the far-reaching enthusiasms of his band of scientists and the sternly practical requirements of the naval war machine, which had to weigh many factors not always evident to the specialist preoccupied in a limited field. His success was reflected in the growing prestige of D.M.W.D. after the initial teething troubles had been overcome, and the loss of both Davies and Goodeve on the brink of great events was keenly felt.

Towards the end of the year came one further change. The Wheezers and Dodgers had been growing more and more cramped in their quarters in Lower Regent Street, and, as the Fleet Air Arm, who shared the building, were in even greater need of living room, the department moved once again—to Fanum House, the home of the Automobile Association in Leicester Square. There they took over the whole of the first floor, near neighbours being the Admiralty's own Directorate of Scientific Research, the staff of Trade Division, and the Salvage Department.

Next door was the Green Room Club, where the leading actors of the West End stage forgathered. The premises of the Green Room had previously housed the Discharged Prisoners' Aid Society, and, as the door between the club and the offices of the Wheezers and Dodgers was for some obscure reason kept permanently unlocked, the naval officers never knew whether civilians they encountered in the corridor were eminent scientists, actors in search of refreshment, or burglars on ticket of leave!

Goodeve continued to take a close interest in D.M.W.D.'s progress, particularly as many of the projects now under way had been initiated long before he began his new duties. It was, in fact, a 'phone call from Sir Edward Appleton to Goodeve as far back as February 1942 which led him to a bombed-out wing of the Grosvenor Hotel and his first strange meeting with Ronald Marsden Hamilton.

18

THE MAN IN THE GROSVENOR HOTEL

ONE morning early in February 1942 Sir Edward Appleton rang up Goodeve. "I wonder if you could find time to see a man named Hamilton," he said. "He's an extraordinary fellow . . . an inventor . . . and he's got a laboratory fitted up in a bombed wing of the Grosvenor Hotel. He's working on some ideas which I think might interest you."

At that precise moment Goodeve was not keen to see anyone. He was leaving later in the week for three months in America, and there was the usual mass of paper-work to clear up, last-minute conferences to attend, and decisions to make before he set out on his journey. He knew Appleton well enough, however, to realize that any suggestion from that source was worth following up straight away. After lunch that day he collected Purcell on his way through the outer office, and they took a taxi to Victoria.

The main part of the Grosvenor Hotel is flanked by Buckingham Palace Road, but when they asked for Hamilton at the reception desk they were shown upstairs and into a wing which ran out at right angles to the main building, over part of the station roof. To all intents and purposes this wing was now derelict. Enemy bombing of the rail terminal had made it almost uninhabitable, and as they pushed through the door into the long passage way they noticed the plaster peeling from the walls. Over everything hung the musty odour of disuse, and their footsteps echoed loudly on the bare boards of the corridor. From one of the suites of rooms leading off the passage a man emerged and came forward to greet them. Shortish in height, with a good-looking, sensitive face, he appeared to be in his middle forties. He carried his right arm stiffly, and Goodeve noticed that he had a withered hand.

"I'm so glad you were able to come," he said, as he led the way down the corridor; "I'd like you to see some of my models. I've had to build my own experimental tank. Not a very neat job, I'm afraid, but it was a lot cheaper than getting people to build one for me. No money to spend on frills here."

He laughed a little harshly. Glancing at him again, Goodeve saw the tired lines round his eyes, and suddenly he sensed that Hamilton was under some considerable stress.

They came to the home-made water-tank—and Goodeve marvelled at the ingenuity of the man who had created it. It was fully 200 feet long, and it was fashioned out of nothing more complicated than a vast expanse of linoleum and a double row of old bricks. Overhead ran electric cables, and these supplied power to a number of strange model craft floating on the surface of the water. The whole thing could not have cost more than a few pounds, and Goodeve thought ruefully of the astronomical sums of money spent on more elaborate experimental tanks fulfilling a similar function.

Now Hamilton was speaking again, and the tiredness had gone out of his voice. He was talking quickly and earnestly, with almost boyish enthusiasm.

"I have discovered something which may revolutionize warfare. If certain laws are obeyed the surface of a fluid can be made to behave in many ways like that of a solid. You can lay a sheet of canvas on water and roll a wheeled object over it in just the same way as you could if the canvas was laid on the ground. Look at these pictures. . . ."

Goodeve stared, fascinated, at the photographs Hamilton handed to him. On a carpet of thin chestnut fencing stakes, supported only by a tarpaulin, a boy was riding a motor-cycle across a stream.

"My son Peter helped me with these experiments. Even carrying a passenger he could cross the water at high and low speeds quite comfortably. At the moment of starting from the bank the machine raised a wave in front, but after a few feet the motor-cycle accelerated out of the crest of this wave. After that it was riding virtually on the level. Now, you see what this means, don't you?"

He turned back to the tank.

"This theory of mine—I call it Rolling Dynamic Buoyancy—can solve one of your greatest problems in an amphibious assault. My floating bridge gives you the link between the ships and the shore. Perhaps you'd like to examine this model. . . ."

Goodeve leant over the tank. There, floating on the water, was a miniature roadway made of strips of wood and canvas and anchored by wires fore and aft. Hamilton began to run a model truck across it, and the hinged sides of the bridge turned up to form a narrow lane which extended threequarters of the lorry's length ahead and astern. As the lorry passed over each section the sides of the bridge dropped back again to their original recumbent position. Inspecting it more closely, Goodeve realized the brilliant quality in Hamilton's design. A given load was spread through tension fore and aft. All the stresses and strains had been so cleverly and accurately worked out that not an ounce of material anywhere failed to bear its appointed part of the burden.

Hamilton dived back into his workroom and produced a sheaf of drawings.

"You will see here that there is no problem over transporting the bridge. It rolls up like a length of wire-netting, and it will unroll just as easily in the water; the sea will take all the weight."

"What loads have you got in mind, and how far can this bridge of yours be extended?" asked Goodeve.

"It should easily carry a 10-ton truck a mile to the shore. As I see it, we can make the bridge in 1000-foot sections of Douglas fir planks. To support them we shall need flexible steel cables with a breaking strain of at least 19 tons."

"How are you going to apply the tension on your cables?"

"I think we may have to experiment a little further in that direction," said Hamilton. "To keep the tension constant during a rise or fall of the tide I don't see why we shouldn't use a simple hanging weight. If variation in the tide is not important an ordinary winch would probably do."

Goodeve glanced again at the model floating in the tank.

"What happens if a lorry breaks down on the bridge?" he asked.

"That shouldn't cause any real trouble," said Hamilton. "You saw the hinged sides rise up out of the water when the track was pressed down. They formed a sort of shallow boat round the truck which travelled along with it. If the truck stops in a choppy sea the depression will gradually fill with water, of course, but it will be several hours before that part of the bridge becomes waterlogged. There will be plenty of time to tow away any vehicle that has broken down. Normally, of course, the bridge is self-emptying. As soon as the load moves away all the sea-water flows out again over the flat sides."

There were more questions from Goodeve and Purcell, and then, as they were turning to go, Hamilton made a gesture towards the tank.

"I don't suppose you would be interested in the other things I'm working on here, but my Train Ship could bring the war in Europe to an end if they would give me the money to develop it. I call it Horatio. The idea came to me when I was doing the preliminary work on the Bridge."

He moved to the far end of the tank and pointed to a long object in water. It was the strangest ship Goodeve had ever seen. Enclosed in an endless belt was a train of twelve electric locomotives, and when Hamilton switched on the power they began to move rapidly along a track mounted on the inside of the belt, picking it up and carrying it forward over the roof of the train as the craft gathered speed.

"I have used an entirely new method of propulsion. This craft you see is driven by skin friction. The scale model corresponds to a full-sized Train Ship 370 feet long and weighing 3000 tons. . . ."

Hamilton paused, staring at Goodeve intently as if in search of encouragement.

"It will be able to travel at tremendous speeds over land or water. You will see from these drawings that the carriages are connected by large universal joints. Between each section are hydraulic jacks which can be locked when the train reaches a certain speed in the water. They will hold the whole train rigid, in the form of a girder. Then it will ride the waves like a sledge racing over rough ice."

"What will happen if you run into a gale? In certain conditions surely the length and height of the waves will impose undue strain on your girder. You will then get a dangerous sagging effect, won't you?" Goodeve asked.

"Not at all," said Hamilton abruptly. "Releasing the jacks will give complete articulation; the Train Ship will then ride the waves like a piece of seaweed. When the main swell is large and steady I can adjust the shape of the train, to allow for the combined harmonic motions of the train itself and the swell, simply by releasing or locking the jacks. They also steer the Train Ship; you will only have to extend them slightly to one side or the other for the train to turn in a circle."

A silence fell on the long corridor, broken incongruously by the dull rumble of a very different type of train as it entered the station below them, and Goodeve looked again at the strange, futuristic object in the tank. Reflecting on the engineering skill which had gone into the creation of the Floating Bridge, it occurred to him that Hamilton's weird amphibians might not be so impracticable after all. One day they too might be entering a London terminal.

"You talked about winning the war with this invention of yours," he said. "What is in your mind?"

Hamilton smiled a little wryly.

"You probably think this is all very far-fetched," he said, "but theoretically it is possible to produce a vehicle, working on this principle, which will travel over water at a speed limited only by the strength of the materials used in its construction—a vehicle which can move not only over firm land and sea, but over ice, snow, or marshes. From this country, and from as far away as America and the Commonwealth, a fleet of these high-speed amphibious trains could converge on the very heart of Germany. Some could act as mobile battering rams, flattening by kinetic energy a path across occupied Europe for other trains to follow. You could have destroyer trains, remote-controlled and carrying enough high explosive to lay waste to whole cities . . . and other trains for carrying troops and supplies far behind the enemy lines."

Then, as if the thought of engineering so great a devastation oppressed him, he began to talk of a world at peace.

"One of these craft could do the journey from the centre of London to New York in forty-eight hours. Aero engines driving dynamos will give me all the power I need, and fuel costs will be far lower than for the conventional liner. This discovery is even more important when applied to cargo-ships and tankers, where the bulk of the resistance comes from the water and not from the air. It marks the greatest advance in propulsion since steam succeeded sail."

Hamilton reached into the tank again and turned the Train Ship on its side. "Of course, this model demonstrates only the broad principle. Several features have not been incorporated here. For instance, I have designed an automatic pumping system to keep the ship buoyant when the waves are breaking over her. And I can increase the freeboard and control the vertical motion of the track by pumping fuel to and fro, from one tank to another."

Goodeve and Purcell saw other things in the corridor that afternoon. Among them was a torpedo unlike any so far devised for submarine warfare.

"Hercules here is another of my pet projects," said Hamilton. "He's a versatile chap. Works on the same principle as the Train Ship. . . . He'll do over a hundred miles an hour under water, and he can climb ashore and overcome any beach defences. . . ."

Hamilton paused. "I'd better not start telling you about Hercules, though," he said. "I've kept you far too long already."

Goodeve looked at his watch. Afternoon had merged into early evening. In the quiet of the corridor they had lost all sense of time, and he remembered that he still had much to do before midnight.

Hamilton led the way down the damaged staircase, and as they hailed a taxi in the dark street Goodeve said to him, "Send me all your data on the Bridge. I think we can do something with that. I shall be out of the country for a short time, but Dr Purcell will see that it is examined."

The cab circled to head round Grosvenor Place, and he leant forward to wave a farewell. But Hamilton had already disappeared, back to his strange experiments in the gloom of the deserted wing.

The idea of the Bridge had first come to Ronald Hamilton fully a year before Goodeve's visit. Like so many other ideas of his in the past, it had given him no peace, nagging at his mind and torturing him with visions of yet another failure.

All his life success had been a mirage, beckoning him on and on, and mocking him as he strained forward to grasp at reality. His pride rejected this constant failure, bitterly condemning the stupidity and lack of foresight of the influential men who came to look at his inventions from time to time, and who went away casting vague promises of future help as one might throw scraps to a starving dog.

His bitterness he strove to conceal under a cloak of arrogance, but the pose was alien to his real nature. Ronald Hamilton was a sensitive man and easily hurt. He was a brilliant and original engineer, but he had had none of the lucky breaks which even the genius needs to fortify his belief in himself, and often in these days and nights in the empty wing of the hotel Charlotte, his wife, who knew and understood him better than anyone else, wondered how much longer he would stand the strain—the strain of toiling to develop ideas far ahead of their time, and trying to interest people who seemed unable or unwilling to grasp their significance, while all the time the bills for bare necessities mounted frighteningly, and there seemed no hope of any change in the pattern of worry and insecurity which had been the background to their life together for nearly a quarter of a century.

He had been fifteen years old when the First World War began. A broken right arm, which had become crippled when he was still at Lancing, prevented him from playing games and sharing many of the activities of others of his own age; the small boy's dread of being different from his companions led him to draw further aloof.

As he grew older he conquered his physical disability to a remarkable extent by sheer determination, but the self-consciousness he felt about his useless arm was never to leave him.

He had a passion for the Navy. Unable to serve at sea, he left school early, and somehow he wangled his way into an Admiralty department dealing with ballistics. While still in his teens he discovered a formula for speeding range calculation; he also invented an ingenious device for correcting errors in gunnery elevation.

The war over, he went up to Oxford, and met and married Charlotte, a good-looking, clever girl who was reading Economics there. Ronald Hamilton was a brilliant mathematician, but even then his mind was beginning to focus more and more on invention. His first brain-child was a self-changing gearbox for cars. Like so many of his later inventions, it was years ahead of its time; it worked perfectly, but, owing to lubrication problems and the fact that metallurgical knowledge was not sufficiently advanced, the Hamilton gearbox would not stand up to heavy wear. This was to be the first of many setbacks.

Oxford gave him an honours degree in Mathematics, and for a time in the early twenties he taught at a succession of public schools ... Rugby, Durham, and Malvern. As a schoolmaster he was out of his element. He preferred to work on his own, and the pattern of school life, with its set hours, its somewhat mechanical demands on his brain, and its restrictions on his freedom, soon became intolerable to him.

His instinctive flair was for inventing, but here he was hampered by the lack of a thorough engineering training. A highly original thinker, his mind would reach out with a leap into the unknown, searching and probing for an answer to some problem he had set himself. Then he would work back reluctantly to the fundamentals, often losing patience before he had tied up the many loose ends in his chain of calculation. Characteristically he scorned the more effective but less original procedure of accepting an objective and then working forward, step by step, from the known into the unknown.

He abandoned schoolmastering, and plunged into a new venture, under Sir Felix Brunner's sponsorship—an automatic laundry at Greenwich. He invented a method of determining the price of 'bag wash' by volume instead of weight, and sold it for £300. Then he began to study the mathematics of racecourse betting, and designed a totalisator, working on logarithmic principles, which was installed at Hurst Park.

This gave him his first taste of commercial success, but, though the ideas continued to flow, income never kept pace with expenditure. Hamilton invented a pick-a-back aircraft ... an automatic telephone system for rural areas which saved 80 per cent. of the wiring then used ... an electric razor ... and a radio set which recorded the programmes as they were broadcast. In all his researches, however, he was handicapped by lack of capital. He lacked too the business sense which was needed if his ideas were to be exploited to his own advantage.

As often as not he found himself unable to carry them to a successful conclusion through insufficient financial backing. Then he would be forced to drop them altogether, or sell his rights for a song to others, who reaped the benefit.

It was a relief to Charlotte when he abandoned the precarious existence of a free-lance and joined the General Electric Company to work on design and development. At long last—it seemed to her —here was something stable; but the slump came in the early thirties, the department closed down, and Ronald Hamilton was back where he had started.

He was ill-equipped to face the heartbreak years which followed. To make ends meet he worked in a laundry again, despising the dreary monotony of the job, and despising himself too for his failure to find better employment for his talents. With all his capital gone he no longer had any outlet for the creative urge which was still strong within him, and he grew unhappy and disillusioned.

His injured arm was a constant handicap, and, although Moynihan had operated skilfully on the elbow joint, Hamilton knew he would be permanently crippled. He kept a boat at Burnham-on-Crouch, and there they used to spend every week-end they could in the summer months. Sailing her was often acutely difficult for him, but the physical challenge only made him all the more determined.

The week-ends afloat acted as a safety-valve. His passionate love of the sea alone seemed to assuage his bitterness and still the sense of failure which oppressed him. And it was the sea which gave Ronald Hamilton a new lease of life.

When war broke out it seemed useless to volunteer. No Service medical board would look twice at him, he reflected. But as a yachtsman he offered his services for Dunkirk, and then, miraculously, he found a way into the Patrol Service, a kindly naval surgeon turning a Nelsonian gaze on his crippled arm.

He could handle boats and men, so he was given the rank of Petty Officer, and, blissfully happy to be of some use at last, he remained at sea until early 1941. Charlotte was away, teaching at a country school; his two boys were also at school, and, in the vacuum of war, life seemed, for the first time, strangely free from complications. He might well have been content to remain indefinitely on the Lower Deck if a scientist, pursuing some experiment at sea aboard his patrol vessel, had not started questioning him one day. Hamilton was then given a lecture on the sin of wasting his abilities, and the scientist passed his name to the Ministry of Aircraft Production. Before long they applied for his temporary attachment to a department of their own dealing with the vetting of inventions.

Slowly at first, his own inventive brain became geared to the problems of war. It was then that he began to experiment on the stream which flowed close by his cottage at Churt, exploring with growing excitement the principle of Rolling Dynamic Buoyancy.

By May 1941 he felt sure he was on the brink of a major achievement. He asked for official facilities to continue his researches, but M.A.P., who considered that the investigation of the surface tension of water was well outside their field of operations, declined the request. His reaction was characteristically impulsive. Without pausing to consider whether he was a free agent he informed the Ministry that he was leaving. The development of the Bridge was too important to the war effort to be delayed by routine demands on his time, and henceforward he intended to devote all his energies to it, he informed them. Before they had recovered from their surprise Hamilton had gone.

He sent for Charlotte to join him in London, and for no particular reason they decided to stay at the Grosvenor.

"How long will you want the room for?" asked the reception clerk as they booked in.

"We haven't really thought about it," said Hamilton. "We might stay indefinitely. . . ."

A heavy air raid had just begun. The guns were thundering from the Park, and even the great, solid hotel building seemed to lift and rock as the bombs exploded near by. The clerk looked at them curiously. It seemed a strange moment to be contemplating an indefinite stay in the heart of the battered city.

He showed them to a big double room on the second floor. The beds were pushed to one side, and they got hold of a couple of large deal tables. Then they shut themselves up and began working on the models.

After two months an official from the Admiralty came to inspect Hamilton's plans for the Train Ship and the Bridge amid the disorder of the bedroom. He was reserved and non-committal, and when he left Charlotte said, a little despairingly, "We shan't get anywhere without larger models and better facilities for experiment and demonstration."

They then discovered that a whole wing over the railway booking office was out of action. They asked if they could take it over, and the management, who plainly thought they were mad, said they could live there rent-free.

When their elder son, Peter, came back from Eton at the end of July, and joined them at the hotel, they moved into their new quarters. Early one morning, before any of the staff were awake, they carried the models down from the bedroom, across the hall, and up into the deserted wing. "To save a double journey they were all placed on a stretcher and covered over with a blanket," Charlotte recalled later. "We felt like conspirators removing a body!"

Half-way down the wide corridor were two rooms which they decided to occupy themselves. Procuring a pile of old bricks and the linoleum, Hamilton built his experimental tank in the passage, and they settled down to attack the problems of Rolling Dynamic Buoyancy as a team—Peter helping his father with the models, Charlotte doing the typing, making her erratic genius of a husband keep appointments, and generally acting as a safety-valve. Ronald Hamilton worked as if under an inspiration, grudging any moment spent away from his researches, and Charlotte literally had to drag him from his laboratory at meal-times.

All through the summer holidays of 1941 Peter worked with him. After that he was given special leave from Eton to assist with the experiments. He was a brilliant mathematician, who had won a scholarship to Eton and was later to get a Double First at Cambridge. Through him the team expanded, for he sought the aid of his tutor, J. S. Herbert, a former Cambridge rowing blue, to solve some particularly intricate calculations connected with the Bridge, and thereafter Herbert became a frequent visitor to the Grosvenor Hotel. At the start the schoolmaster found Hamilton far from easy to get on with. The overbearing arrogance he could understand, and he could make allowances for it, but Hamilton's petulant impatience with the groundwork which had to be put in before his ideas took logical shape and form was a sore trial to those around him. Obstinate problems of higher mathematics would often infuriate him, and, like a spoilt child, he would vent his irritation on the very people who were trying hardest to solve his difficulties. At times a fleeting sense of humour banished the tension, but this could be deceptive; leg-pulling he invariably took with bad grace.

When Herbert first arrived at the hotel Hamilton explained the main projects he was working on, and then, leading him to the tank, he unwound a roll of toilet paper. As it floated on the surface of the water he rolled tennis balls along it to demonstrate the possibilities of the Bridge.

Herbert went back to Eton to work on the main theory. The problem of tensions in the side-skirting of the Bridge had to be closely studied, and an answer, too, had to be found to the lateral effect of the tide flowing against the floating roadway.

Meanwhile others had joined the *ménage*. Stanley Hunter, a pleasant, shortish, grey-haired man in his forties, was a brilliant designer and draughtsman who had worked with Hamilton on the Tote project years before. In character they were exact opposites, for Hunter was self-effacing to a degree—a humble, very modest man who shrank from the limelight. He worked long hours without ever losing his mental quickness and accuracy under fatigue, and no problem of practical engineering ever seemed to defeat him.

Ralph Jenkins, a friend of Hamilton's who was working at the Air Ministry, also helped with the making of the models, and Toby Belfield, a lecturer in engineering at Oxford, spent a great deal of his spare time devising and testing mathematical formulæ. It was odd, in a way, that Hamilton should have been able to gather round

THE BOMBARDON BREAKWATER IN POSITION AT ARROMANCHES

CROSS-SECTION VIEW OF A BOMBARDON FLOATING BREAKWATER UNIT

LIEUTENANT GUY BOISSARD, R.N.V.R., AND SURGEON-COMMANDER C. L. G. PRATT, R.N.V.R., DRESSING IN THEIR WOOLLEN AND STOCKINET SUITS BEFORE DESCENDING TO THE BED OF HORSEA LAKE, MAY 1944

209

ONE OF THE TEAM WEARING A PROTECTIVE CAP WHICH RESEMBLED A JUDGE'S WIG: JUST BEFORE DIVING

CASE DRESSED IN ONE OF THE SPECIAL SUITS WHICH WERE EVOL AFTER THE HAZARDOUS EXPERIME WITH EXPLOSIVE CHARGES ON T BED OF THE LAKE

him such a devoted team, for he himself was the complete individu-
alist, who found it difficult and irksome to work with others. Often
he resented their criticism, but undeniably it acted as a stimulant.
He badly needed, too, friends around him who could share the burden, for the months to come brought little tangible success, and
optimism gave way to a sense of acute frustration.

The first crisis developed when a branch of the Admiralty discovered that Petty Officer Hamilton was no longer serving at M.A.P.
Pointing out that he had only been loaned from the Navy for special
duties there, they directed him to return to the Patrol Service forthwith.

Absorbed in his experiments, Hamilton had completely forgotten
about the Patrol Service. The drafting order placed him in a quandary, for although he knew he could gain an immediate discharge
from the Navy by revealing his disability, this would, he knew, have
unpleasant repercussions for the kindly naval doctor who had passed
him as fit, at his urgent request, at the time of Dunkirk. After frantic
deliberation he set off for the Patrol Service base at Lowestoft. On
the way he thought up an ingenious formula which eliminated any
risk of trouble for anyone, and, to his vast relief, he found himself
demobilized in a matter of hours. He was now completely free to
work on his inventions, but almost immediately the financial situation produced a further crisis. The bombing of London had ceased,
and the Grosvenor Hotel began to fill up again. Soon a suggestion
came from the management that they might have to reopen part of
the damaged wing.

Hamilton compromised by offering to pay a weekly rental of £10,
but whenever their total bill dropped below £20 polite inquiries were
made as to how soon they would be able to vacate their rooms. "As
we have the two boys still at school, and no money coming in, there
are moments of extreme financial tension," Charlotte wrote to a
friend. The tension was not alleviated by Ronald Hamilton's own
complete vagueness about money matters in general.

He had a tiny income of his own—not more than £150. Charlotte
had about the same. When things looked blackest there came a sudden windfall. They inherited £1000 from a relation, but it went
straight into the pool and was soon swallowed up. Between May and
December they spent £976. Of this, hotel bills and the purchase of
materials for their experiments accounted for all but £200. With no
sponsors, and the bills for bare necessities mounting steadily, it was
an anxious time.

They were convinced that the inventions must succeed. So a small
syndicate was formed to raise a few extra hundred pounds in cash.
They sold nearly all their wedding presents, and then Charlotte,

o

confined to a sick bed with jaundice, wrestled so successfully with Income Tax Repayment forms that they got back a further £200.

This at last gave them breathing-space.

Early in November a relation of Ronald Hamilton brought a famous figure in the transport world to the hotel to look at the models. He was very influential indeed, but, to Hamilton's distress, he seemed to understand little of what they tried to explain to him. He prodded the home-made tank somewhat suspiciously with his walking-stick, appeared annoyed that he had got it wet, and left without vouchsafing anything. The Hamiltons were in the depths of despondency.

A well-known professor also called. He showed more sympathetic interest, but he was obviously engrossed in other matters, and, apart from sending them a formula which appeared to disprove the whole principle of Rolling Dynamic Buoyancy *in toto*, nothing more was heard of him.

In December hopes were raised again. Hamilton gave his largest demonstration so far to a group of very senior officers from the War Office. In the middle of it, however, one of the inspecting party remarked omnisciently that although Hamilton's theories were most interesting there was nothing new in them. A certain Captain Walker, of the Royal Engineers, had conducted experiments on similar lines in India many years before. They had not led to anything, he recalled. After this reminiscence the War Office delegation looked less impressed, and by the time Hamilton had tracked the suggestion to its source and disproved it the Army had lost interest.

He opened negotiations with a firm in the North of England who hinted that they might finance his projects; approaches were made to a boatbuilding company, the National Physical Laboratory, and Sir John Thorneycroft, who spoke to the Controller of the Navy about Hamilton's researches. When nothing came of this Thorneycroft did offer some practical help, suggesting that Hamilton might like to transfer his experiments to a small factory which he controlled.

Hamilton gratefully declined, preferring the peace and temporary security of the corridor. In spite of his anxieties he was intellectually at his best during this period. Working on the models, on which so much depended, he was, of course, greatly handicapped. He resented the constant need for some one to hold the electric locomotives, or the pieces of the Bridge, while he operated on them; but he had overcome his disablement so fully that once, when Charlotte was asked how her husband had injured his hand, she had to think quite hard before she realized what her questioner was talking about. Nevertheless Hamilton suffered a good deal throughout the model-making phase. He insisted on doing all the intricate conversion work

on the standard toy trains himself, and one evening, struggling vainly
with a minute coupling, he cried out in exasperation, "Oh, God,
how I wish I had two hands!" That was the only time Charlotte
ever heard him complain.

Somehow they struggled through the month of January 1942,
continually contacting fresh people at the various Ministries without
making any appreciable headway. Then, when they were almost at
the end of their resources, came the meeting with Goodeve and
Purcell.

19

SWISS ROLL AND THE LILY ISLANDS

BEFORE Goodeve set out for America he had a long talk with Purcell. Obviously there were possibilities in several of the inventor's unusual projects, but the Wheezers and Dodgers had to concentrate on immediate requirements. Any effective link between ship and shore could play a vital part in the coming invasion, and it seemed to him that the floating bridge was a practical proposition, well worth developing. Purcell was therefore instructed to persuade Hamilton to drop his Train Ship researches, and he was taken on to the strength of D.M.W.D. as a consulting engineer, with a directive to concentrate on the bridge alone.

Finding a code name for the project was not difficult. When the prototype of the Bridge was wound up on its spindle and ready for launching it looked just like a monster Swiss Roll.

Hamilton proposed to build his bridge in thousand-foot sections. At each junction of the separate lengths there were to be rafts which would float under the two ends, and on these rafts he planned to mount windlasses for handling the anchor cables. In all, six lengths of Swiss Roll and six rafts would make up one floating roadway.

To lay the roadway on the surface of the sea special barges equipped with cranes would be needed. The sections of Swiss Roll would be carried to their destination in landing-craft; 6000 feet from the shore the crane barge would be anchored, and from this seaward base the floating roadway would be unwound to the beach. While the bridge was in use Hamilton calculated that a tension of some 20 tons would have to be applied at the seaward end by winching on the anchors of the barge.

The first step was to build an experimental, full-scale version of Swiss Roll, and by June 1942 this was taking shape in the dockyard at Portsmouth. There were problems to be overcome with the securing of the Bridge, for if normal anchors were used these would prevent ships from coming alongside. Hamilton got over this difficulty by designing sheerlegs which were flexibly mounted at each end of the runway. He then tackled a more awkward snag.

The Bridge would have to be used at all hours of the day and night and in all weathers. Adequate headlights might well be forbidden, and drivers of trucks trying to make the journey across the narrow, swaying track in pitch darkness, and perhaps heavy rain as well, faced the danger of running their vehicles into the sea. To rely on visual steering was obviously out of the question.

Hamilton then had a brainwave. He went to the L.P.T.B. depot at Chiswick, where all sorts of ingenious stability tests were carried out with London buses. There were kerbs of various heights and widths, and when the buses were run up against these obstacles special instruments measured the force exerted on the wheels as the kerbs turned them.

After discussing his problem with the technicians of the Passenger Transport Board he designed a kerb for Swiss Roll which could be placed in position after the Bridge had been anchored. To his delight he found that this steered the truck perfectly. The driver could, in fact, negotiate the floating roadway blindfold, or with his hands off the steering-wheel, and no amount of skidding caused by the waves placed the vehicle in any peril.

Other experiments were carried out to test the stability of the Bridge in rough seas. An M.T.B. was brought into the tidal basin where Swiss Roll lay, and while a lorry started down the track in one direction the M.T.B., proceeding at high speed on an opposite course, deliberately raised seven-foot waves which hurled themselves against the frail structure. The lorry rode the waves like the most seaworthy of boats, and Goodeve was able to report jubilantly to Jock Davies, "I am satisfied that the Bridge will be unharmed by storms, and will be usable in all but the worst weather."

By midsummer they were no longer living permanently at the Grosvenor. Most of the work was done at Portsmouth, but they retained the wing in the hotel, and frequently stayed odd nights there. Peter Hamilton spent much of the summer with them at Portsmouth, and proved a tower of strength. He would work all day on the development of the Bridge, and then study until late into the night, preparing for the two scholarship examinations he faced at Cambridge. He won both of them.

Although work on Swiss Roll was proceeding satisfactorily enough at this stage, Hamilton himself now began to have doubts about its development. Never a calm man, he was living on his nerves. He drove himself at such a pace that the strain inevitably told on him —and on those around him. When he was tired and on edge he lost his self-control, making slighting, bitter criticisms of his closest friends and helpers. They, in their turn, would react violently at times, so that each side was unfair to the other.

His greatest handicap, however, was his inordinate passion for inventing, which, oddly enough, surpassed his interest in the successful completion of any of his projects. With Swiss Roll this tendency of his grew to a positive mania, and as the summer of 1942 wore on the trials at Portsmouth produced continual rows, culminating in a violent scene on the eve of the first full-scale demonstration of the Bridge to a host of senior officers from the Admiralty, the War Office, and the headquarters of Combined Operations.

For several weeks Hamilton had been in a particularly temperamental and exasperating mood, and Goodeve had found increasing difficulty in keeping a firm grip on his ideas. He was hysterical and emotional—and he could not *stop* inventing. One design would prove perfectly satisfactory. Then Hamilton would go away and think up a series of complicated snags, a whole chain of new mishaps which might befall the Bridge unless he embodied counter-devices in its construction. To him the Bridge was never really ready for demonstration; there was always some 'improvement' to be made, and on the evening of Thursday, September 24, this led to a dramatic impasse.

During the day the M.T.B. had been brought back into the basin again, and it had charged backward and forward between the wall of the jetty and the long strip of floating roadway, while Belfield, suspended from a crane, took photographs of the effect of the waves.

Hamilton then decided that further modifications must be made before Swiss Roll was shown to the V.I.P.'s next day, and on his own initiative he gave orders for the Bridge to be dismantled. His intention was to incorporate an additional form of stabilizer which had just occurred to him, and he asked for a special night shift of dockyard workers to carry out the job.

When Goodeve arrived from London that evening, and found out what was happening, he was furious. He went to the dockyard, ordered the dismantled part of the Bridge to be reassembled, and left it under armed guard. He then warned Hamilton that he was not to re-enter the dockyard that night.

Hamilton was in a frenzy. Bitterly he accused Goodeve of sabotaging his plans, and he threatened to sue him. Reasoned argument was impossible with Hamilton in this hysterical mood, and Goodeve went to bed.

The demonstration next day was, in fact, a complete success, but for some time afterwards Hamilton refused to be consoled. There were several further trials to be staged, and Goodeve, disturbed at the prospect of what Hamilton might still try to do, telephoned Charlotte and asked her to calm her husband down.

"I've seen so many projects ruined because the inventor has refused to stop tampering with them," he said earnestly. Charlotte, to whom her husband's modifications seemed, at the time, so simple to carry out, disagreed with him. But Goodeve had seen the red light.

By the end of the month the trials of Mark I had been completed. Hamilton, however, had had yet another new idea, and he was so obsessed with the belief that Swiss Roll could not work without its incorporation that he refused—for the time being, at least—to have anything more to do with D.M.W.D.'s plans for the Bridge.

The Wheezers and Dodgers had to go ahead without him, and an additional trials programme was drawn up to cover such points as the drag produced by cross-tides, the rolling up and retrieving of the sections of Swiss Roll from the water, and the resistance of the floating roadway to cannon and machine-gun fire.

Tests made by experts at H.M.S. *Excellent* proved that the planks of the Bridge, being awash, were very difficult to damage by gunfire. The water cushioned and reduced the blast, and only six hits were scored in 180 cannon rounds. *Excellent* also reported that Swiss Roll would be immune from torpedo attack and an unprofitable target for dive-bombing.

In his attempts to justify the modifications which Goodeve had condemned as impracticable Hamilton continued to experiment on lines of his own. After toiling for several weeks he himself came to the same conclusion. And by this time he was having second thoughts about his attitude to the department employing him.

Swallowing his pride, he wrote to Jock Davies, apologizing for the "differences and difficulties" and attempting to explain the reason for his actions.

> During the Small Wave trials I saw that a cross sea caused the lorry to swing across the roadway, and the kerb arms, at a tension of 24 tons, rose to a height which allowed too great an eccentricity of the wheels from the centre of the wires.[1] I therefore added two more tension wires on each side, and this alleviated the trouble for small waves.

He went on to raise other problems which had come out of the Large Wave trials—mainly the anchoring down of the kerb arms to strengthen the automatic steering under difficult tide and wave conditions, and the reduction of a bending moment in the bridge.

---

[1] It was important that the wheels of any vehicle travelling on the bridge should remain as far as possible directly over the tension wires.—AUTHOR.

One day shortly before he wrote to Davies he had journeyed to London to report how these faults could be put right, but he was incensed to find that a conference on these very points had been held without him. Whereupon he had again lost his temper with Goodeve.

He accused D.M.W.D. of wasting time by working on the wrong lines, and when Goodeve passed the ball to him, listing several points which still demanded an answer, Hamilton had attempted to provide snap solutions without sufficient thought. His extemporary answers were quickly faulted by various people present, and Hamilton, trying to improvise still further, had got himself into a worse tangle than ever.

Jock Davies replied to his apologia pleasantly but firmly, pointing out in conclusion that *he* was directing the development of Swiss Roll by instructions from the Board of Admiralty:

> While giving yourself and other consultant engineers as free a hand as possible I have got to criticize as well as listen, in order that my decisions and recommendations to the Board and other high authorities may be the correct ones in the light of all available information.

After that Hamilton calmed down. It had been an agonizing period, particularly for his family, but on October 8 Charlotte was able to record in her diary the single, thankful phrase "Kiss and be friends!" The storm had spent itself at last.

Early in 1943 construction of Swiss Roll began in Bute West Dock at Cardiff, under Urwin's supervision. When the first full-scale sections were ready sea trials were carried out at Appledore.

There were destined to be further vicissitudes before Swiss Roll played its part in the invasion of Normandy, but reference to the Bridge at Arromanches belongs to a later chapter. It is fitting here, however, to follow the strange story of Ronald Marsden Hamilton to its end.

With the production of Swiss Roll now going ahead, Hamilton's inventive mind began to range out in new directions. He drew up preliminary designs of cross-Channel bridges, assault bridges, and aircraft runways. And he began to ponder the problem of the pier-heads which would be needed for unloading cargo from ships at sea during the invasion.

He maintained that the simplest and most effective type of pier-head would be a triangular, flexible, floating carpet, which could be made fast to the ship. From this was born perhaps his most important invention of all—Lily, the floating runway for aircraft.

Using the same principle as Swiss Roll, but making his floating carpet flexible laterally as well as longitudinally, he found that he could build whole artificial islands of any shape or size on the surface of the sea. They were made of hundreds of hexagonal buoyancy cans, 6 feet wide and 30 inches deep, which were linked and clamped together so ingeniously that they 'gave' in controlled undulations while retaining a surface rigid enough to take the weight of heavy aircraft. The flexibility of these man-made islands could be simply controlled by the action of underwater dampers.

Like Swiss Roll, the appearance of the structure inspired its code name. As Hamilton's Island lay on the sea the six-sided cans which composed its surface looked just like the pads of some giant water-lily.

His very first experiments were made with bundles of wooden spars, wired together and launched at Emsworth, near Portsmouth, but these disintegrated in the water. Then came the idea of using the steel buoyancy cans, and the swift progress of Lily revived dreams of Atlantic seadromes and cross-Channel bridges—schemes which had thwarted many an inventor over the years.

D.M.W.D. held the first full-scale trials of Lily off Lamlash, in the Isle of Arran. They found it was easily possible to assemble a strip 550 feet long and 60 feet wide in an hour, using a working party of 40 men, and from this runway a Swordfish aircraft made a series of rocket-assisted take-offs.

Lily's flexibility formed a saucer-like depression under the Swordfish's weight. This lengthened the take-off, as the 'plane had to climb out of its own depression, but it slowed the aircraft down very conveniently in the last fifty feet of its landing.

Pilots reported that touching down on the island was little different from landing on the deck of a carrier. They had, however, one or two tense moments, for an M.L. was used to make artificial waves, circling round and round the Lily field, and on one occasion the Swordfish's propeller tips, tilted down by the wave undulations, struck the metal surface of the runway.

The experimental strip at Lamlash was deliberately limited in size, and only Swordfish and Auster aircraft could use it, but Hamilton showed by calculation that a similar runway 1200 feet long and 90 feet wide would comfortably take a Hurricane fighter, and winds up to 60 m.p.h. would not put the airstrip out of action. When he had fitted his special dampers to the underside of the island Lily remained quite flat in waves up to 36 feet from crest to crest. The airfield could be easily dismantled, moved, and reassembled, and more than once in those wild waters off the Scottish coast an impressive demonstration of this was given. In a wind approaching gale force an entire island was laid down on the sea and made secure by only two men.

Maintenance was just as simple as installation, for Lily had only to be painted from time to time, and the hinge bolts on the buoyancy cans occasionally greased; after nine months in the water off Lamlash the floating runway showed little deterioration, and it withstood heavy seas.

The importance of Hamilton's discovery was plain. One ship could carry a whole airfield without difficulty, and with the idea of using these maritime runways during the approach to the Japanese mainland development was pressed forward. The islands could be built up in the sheltered waters of Pacific lagoons, and with their aid powerful reinforcements of fighter aircraft could provide cover for the ships and bombers closing in on Japan.

Hiroshima, however, forestalled many plans. Lily was never tested in war, but Hamilton realized the peace-time possibilities of his invention, and when he was handed back his patents for Swiss Roll and Lily he formed a small company to exploit them commercially. He took an office in Howick Place, Victoria Street—not far from the Grosvenor Hotel—and from there he launched an energetic campaign to secure orders.

He was certain that his luck had changed at last. Once again the mirage of wealth and success beckoned to him, and it did seem, indeed, that he could hardly fail. He saw many rôles for his floating islands—as pleasure promenades, artificial harbours, and safe bathing-pools at seaside resorts. His Lily strips could be used as loading bays for flying-boat stations, and he even put forward a suggestion for making additional car-parks with Lily units along certain stretches of the Thames.

These were the minor projects. His major plans were for the construction of vast floating airfields, and he went abroad—to Canada and Sweden—to sell the idea.

In a prospectus he issued soon after forming his company he reiterated the soundness of the principle of Rolling Dynamic Buoyancy:

> A rigid floating structure must be strong enough to withstand the large beam stresses set up by waves. Many people think that huge ships like the *Queen Mary* have almost reached the limit of length . . . the hogging and sagging forces as an Atlantic roller passes under them are enormous. . . . If, instead of resisting these forces, a degree of flexibility is introduced into the structure the forces diminish rapidly.

Hamilton stressed too the remarkable simplicity of his Lily islands.

They are completely stable. A man can stand on one unit while erection or dismantling is taking place. When erection takes place from a ship two men on a growing raft can assemble the units as fast as they can be lowered by derrick.

Ronald Hamilton had a strong sense of responsibility to all the people who had helped him in difficult times, either with money or advice, and he insisted on giving many of them large numbers of shares in the new undertaking. J. S. Herbert, who had never accepted any payment in all the time he worked with Hamilton during his holidays from Eton, was made a director of the company. To Goodeve Hamilton gave 200 shares.

He was buoyantly optimistic, and, indeed, success seemed within his grasp. Sweden sent an emissary to examine the possibilities of building a huge Lily island in the centre of Stockholm. They envisaged a terminal for transatlantic aircraft, and for long a £15,000,000 scheme was under serious consideration. But in the end nothing came of it.

Other inquiries seemed equally promising, but a malign influence dogged all Ronald Hamilton's endeavours. Negotiations rarely foundered on any technical snag; some extraneous factor would intervene, and plans would be shelved indefinitely.

At last, however, a concrete offer was made. He was invited to build a Lily bridge across the Severn for £25,000.

Hamilton was wildly excited. Here was a wonderful shop-window for his invention. It could sweep him to prosperity. But once again luck deserted him. Owing to the scouring effect of the tide in the river, he encountered unexpected problems with the anchoring of his bridge. While he was searching desperately for a remedy the backers of the scheme, alarmed at his slow progress, withdrew financial support. And on this setback the project folded up.

An award of £8000 was made to him for his war-time inventions, but it came too late to be of any personal benefit. He had already been forced to sell his patents, and soon afterwards his little company passed into other hands.

Undaunted, he turned his attention to a new sphere altogether, and began working on a scheme for eliminating wear and tear of railway rolling-stock. His plan called for the use of a new type of rail, and raised interesting problems of heat expansion.

In the latter days of 1952 he summoned Herbert to London to discuss the mathematical calculations involved, and when they met he announced with all his old optimism that this time he could not fail to succeed; on Goodeve's introduction British Railways had shown keen interest in his theories, and the first trials were to be held shortly.

It struck the Eton master that Hamilton was far from well, but he seemed temporarily buoyed up by enthusiasm for the new project. When they got down to intricate technical argument, however, Herbert noticed that he grew rapidly tired, and seemed to find difficulty in concentrating.

It was the last time he ever saw him. In January 1953 Ronald Hamilton died at the early age of fifty-four, and the dreams of a genius remained unfulfilled.

20

THE GREAT PANJANDRUM

As plans for the attack on the coast of Northern France took
shape D.M.W.D. were called upon to study a problem of
considerable complexity. The fate of the invasion might,
indeed, depend on its solution, for the task entrusted to the Wheezers
and Dodgers was the destruction of the Atlantic Wall.

It was reported that the enemy beaches were defended by an
enormous bastion of reinforced concrete ten feet high and seven
feet thick. Before any troops landing on the beaches could reach the
country beyond, this would have to be knocked down—or, at any
rate, a breach would have to be made in it large enough for a tank to
pass through.

To breach a wall of these dimensions meant that one ton of high
explosive must be placed at its foot and in close contact with it. The
beach itself would, it was assumed, be sown with landmines in front
of the wall, and the whole area would be swept by heavy fire from
small arms and mortars manned by the Germans. The problem
facing D.M.W.D. was how to get one ton of high explosive to the
base of the wall and set it off under these hazardous conditions.

Norway was puzzling over this one morning in the summer of
1943 when a Group Captain named Finch-Noyes, who was attached
to the headquarters of Combined Operations, came to see him. He
brought with him some rough sketches of a remarkable device.

It consisted of two enormous steel wheels, each 10 feet in diameter,
with a tread about a foot wide. They were connected by a drum-like
axle which, Finch-Noyes explained, would contain high explosive,
and the monster would be propelled by a large number of slow-
burning cordite rockets fitted round the circumference of each wheel.

The thing would be carried to the shore in a tank-landing-craft.
When the ramp went down the rockets would be ignited, and the
monster would propel itself through the shallow water and up the
beach to the wall like a giant Catherine wheel, reaching a speed of
perhaps sixty miles an hour by the time it struck the concrete bastion.
There the steel wheels would collapse, and the drum of T.N.T. would

be hurled against the foot of the wall, where a mechanical device would set off the explosive.

It was an ingenious and revolutionary conception. The more Norway studied it, the more it seemed to him that it offered the only solution to this highly difficult problem. Williamson, now a lieutenant-commander and one of his chief assistants, was called into conference with Finch-Noyes, and after a spell at the drawing-board the plans for the prototype were taken to a firm of engineering and building contractors at Leytonstone.

Norway christened the monster "Panjandrum"— "because the gunpowder ran out from its heels"[1]—and on August 3, 1943, its construction began in great secrecy in a special hut at the Leytonstone works. At the outset a major in the Royal Marine visited the factory. For security reasons he insisted on the hut being built round the Panjandrum. And he produced a typewritten list of seven names. "These are the only people you will allow into the hut while this thing is being built," he said to the works manager. Among those omitted from the Major's list—to the Wheezers and Dodgers' considerable amusement—was Williamson himself, the main Admiralty designer of the Panjandrum!

Within a month the prototype was completed—a considerable achievement, for it was a difficult thing to construct. It had to be strong enough to stand up to rough going on the beach, but weak enough to collapse against the target, for the rockets would be almost spent by the time it reached the wall.

Before they could remove it from the corrugated-iron shed in which it was housed the end of the building had to be taken out. In the early hours of September 2 the Panjandrum was rolled across the yard and loaded on to a transporter. The police had been alerted, and with an escort of motor-cyclist outriders the monster set off for its trials in the West of England, moving only under cover of darkness.

The precautions taken by the security authorities were somewhat peculiar. They insisted that the Panjandrum must stop only at approved Admiralty depots on its journey westward, and on arrival at these places it was hurriedly locked up before curious civilians could catch a close glimpse of it.

When it arrived at Appledore, however, Security abandoned all interest in it. The Panjandrum was rolled off the transporter on to the beach, where it was promptly surrounded by holidaymakers, who

---

[1] "and there were present the Picninnies, and the Joblillies and the Garyalies, and the grand Panjandrum himself . . . and they all fell to playing the game of catch as catch can, till the gunpowder ran out at the heels of their boots."—SAMUEL FOOTE (1720–77).

gazed with awe at the towering wheels and prodded the rocket-holders inquisitively.

In the region of Appledore the Combined Operations Experimental Establishment, known as COXE, had been set up to try out all manner of invasion projects. They tested different types of landing-craft, the discharge of vehicles from ships by pontoons and causeways, the swimming-off of amphibians, and the pentration and clearing of beach obstacles.

It was the ideal rehearsal area. The gradient of the open beaches off Westward Ho! and the tidal conditions were almost identical with those which would be encountered on the far side of the Channel. Near by the coast offered every kind of trial for a raiding party or a major landing force. Appledore had its long, open, sea beaches, with periods of high surf, and within the estuary were other more sheltered beaches, both flat and steep. Vehicles could be tested over mud, shingle, sand-dunes, or rocks, and demolition teams, too, had ample room for their hazardous experiments.

After some discussion the Great Panjandrum was taken to Westward Ho!, where at the head of the beach a great pebble ridge runs parallel to the sea, and on the morning of September 7 it was decided to launch the monster on its maiden run. First its central, explosive drum was filled with 4000 pounds of dried sand. Then the rockets were clamped in position. As no one was quite certain how the Panjandrum would behave only eighteen rockets were tried at the start, but even so it was an awe-inspiring sight.

Surrounded in clouds of smoke and flame, the Panjandrum thundered down the ramp of the landing-craft, ploughed its way through the water, and set off up the beach. It kept a relatively straight course until two of the rockets on one side failed to ignite, causing it to swing to starboard, but Norway saw it was much underpowered, and it came to a standstill after covering 220 yards.

The rolling resistance on the sand seemed a great deal higher than they had expected, and without more rockets it was obvious that the Panjandrum would never reach a speed of 60 m.p.h. at the head of the beach.

They decided to double the number of rockets, fitting them on to the inside of the wheels, and next day these extra rockets arrived by air. Anxious to get them fitted before darkness set in, Williamson went over to COXE to ask for assistance. The only British welding equipment was out of action through generator failure, but a 'phone call to an American Army unit near by produced instant results.

A large truck bearing a Chrysler generating set appeared in a matter of minutes, and with it a welding team headed by two non-commissioned officers smoking large cigars. They greeted Williamson with jovial informality, slapping him on the back and addressing him as "Bud," but as soon as they got down to work the job was finished in next to no time

The following day the Panjandrum was loaded into its landing-craft and taken round to Instow Beach, inside the Torridge estuary. With clouds of steam hissing around it, it negotiated 150 yards of water quite successfully, but just before it reached the target-marker on the beach a patch of uneven, loose sand slowed it up. Again some rockets failed, and it swerved aside, coming to rest after 406 yards. It was still far too slow, and more stability was obviously needed.

The Wheezers and Dodgers returned to London, and an inquest was held in the department. Captain Jeans presided; Finch-Noyes and Lieutenant-Commander the Earl of Antrim came over from Combined Operations; and Richardson, Norway, Guggenheim, and Abel were also present.

To reduce the Panjandrum's instability Williamson suggested the fitting of a third wheel, and this was agreed, but when they came to discuss the rocket problem there was some difference of opinion. Norway contended that the faster the Panjandrum travelled the straighter it ought to go; Guggenheim took the view that it should begin its run slowly, and work up gradually to its maximum speed. In the end it was decided to double the number of rockets once again.

The Panjandrum team returned to their temporary headquarters at Bideford, and on September 27 a three-wheeled Panjandrum was placed on a special wooden ramp erected near the waterline. Before they could try it out, however, a fault developed in the electrical wiring circuit, and although they worked desperately to clear this they were overtaken by the tide. Rolling in across the bay the sea engulfed the great machine, and, to Williamson's dismay, the centre wheel collapsed. Some of the rockets were salvaged, but it was three weeks before the juggernaut was again ready for action.

Powered by more than seventy rockets on its third outing, the Panjandrum gave a sensational display. No sooner had it reached the water's edge than it swerved violently back towards the sea, heeling over until the wheel flanges caught in the sand. The Panjandrum lurched and overturned, the crash dislodging several of the rockets, which flew low over the beach in all directions, while others, still secured to the perimeter of the outer wheel, continued to explode under water, sending up fierce jets of steam.

When they examined the wreckage they found that the centre wheel had become badly distorted. They therefore abandoned the third-wheel experiment and tried a different stabilizing scheme.

A steering system was rigged up, cables controlled by naval kite balloon winches acting as brakes on the large axle of the Panjandrum, and on October 26 the monster was given its fourth trial, at Westward Ho!

Two one-ton cables, 2000 feet long, were used, and Norway and Williamson each took charge of a winch. The beach was ribbed, soft, and very wet, but this time the Panjandrum worked up to a tremendous speed, and when Norway applied the brake to steady it, the cable on the port side snapped off close to the machine. It came whistling back like a bullet, and both the steersmen had to hurl themselves face downward on the wet sand. The working of the starboard wire showed that the steering system had possibilities, but when they tried it out next day again one of the cables snapped. Trials were therefore suspended to await a heavier wire.

With this fitted, and new winches operating, they launched the Panjandrum once more on November 12. It was a fine autumn day, and this time the beach was hard and smooth. A marker post was erected 250 yards down the beach, and they tried to demolish this. In spite of a cross-wind there was no difficulty in steering the Panjandrum, but the target was hidden in smoke as the machine thundered towards it. At the half-way stage one rocket burst from its clamps and released another, but on the whole the Panjandrum gave quite a satisfactory account of itself.

Norway was still worried, however, by the stability problem. At length it dawned on him what was happening. The power needed to make it reach the desired speed against the rolling resistance on the sand exerted so much torque that wheel-slip was developing. The steering-gear showed some promise, but he felt that this would never hold the huge machine with any certainty. The real basis of directional control was the grip of the wheels on the sand, and on an uneven surface the Panjandrum might well run amok.

The Wheezers and Dodgers realized that the experiments were becoming extremely dangerous, and the hazards were increased by the erratic behaviour of the rockets, which were not designed to withstand a lateral centrifugal force while burning. When the speed of the Panjandrum rose to over 50 m.p.h. it was common for one or two rockets to burst. This usually destroyed the attachment of adjacent rockets, which began darting all over the beach. These rockets were formidable pieces of ironmongery, each weighing some 20 pounds and burning for 40 seconds with a thrust of 40 pounds. When one broke away from the side of the Panjandrum it would scream across the sand in a series of hops at a height of only two or three feet, its progress lasting half a minute or more. A trial run was therefore a thing which had to be seen to be believed, the Panjandrum—a hurtling mass of smoke and flame—often careering straight for the spectators, or at the cine-operator, who usually thought he

P

had chosen a safe position, while rockets which had burst free from the wheels flew in all directions.

The hazards, however, had to be accepted. On the afternoon of the same day—November 12—they decided to test the monster over a chain of small craters, three rows of mines being detonated to make them.

The Panjandrum travelled at a higher speed than ever before, and right from the start the steering became erratic. The machine took a sinuous path, with violent swings at each touch of the brake, and after covering 140 yards it lurched wildly to port.

Norway threw up his hands to release all the burden from the steering apparatus, and this caused an instant overrun which locked both winch wires. The Panjandrum pivoted towards the sea and came to a halt. They found that this last fierce turn had badly distorted the starboard wheel.

The D.M.W.D. team returned to their hotel thoroughly dejected. The Panjandrum was quite unpredictable, and there seemed to be no end to its fits of temperament. Talking things over, they decided that the new band brakes were too powerful, even if controlled with a light touch. A different type of brake must be designed. If, too, an angle was introduced on the steel tyres this might give the machine a firmer grip on the sand.

No more trials took place before the end of the year. Various modifications were made, and two new Panjandrums were built in London. While they were being made ready word came to D.M.W.D. that close accuracy of steering was no longer considered imperative by the invasion planners.

When they next assembled at Westward Ho!, early in January 1944, the Panjandrum which they loaded into the L.C.T. was almost a reversion to the original prototype in appearance, with just the two 10-foot wheels, the axle chamber (ballasted with two tons of sand), and no steering-gear fitted. In the morning the Panjandrum was given a preliminary run with forty-eight rockets in position. Norway hoped for a speed of 65 miles an hour, but this time it mysteriously failed to reach even 50 m.p.h. over a measured 800 yards.

After lunch a resplendent gathering of admirals and generals made their way to the pebble ridge. There were a number of distinguished scientific observers present too. Whitehall had come to pass judgment on the Great Panjandrum, and the Wheezers and Dodgers sensed that this trial would decide its fate.

First, two minefields were detonated to provide the craters which would be encountered on an enemy beach. Klemantaski, who was to photograph the run, chose a position about half-way up the course.

As he got his cine equipment ready he was joined by several Brass Hats, and an Airedale dog, owned by an Army officer and rejoicing in the name of Ammonal, which had somehow discovered what was afoot.

Far down the beach lay the L.C.T. Through his binoculars Klemantaski could see the Panjandrum being brought to the head of the ramp. Then the signal was given, and Abel, crouched behind a wall of sandbags on the deck of the landing-craft, pressed the firing key.

The Panjandrum made a slow, impressive start. As it began to move towards him it reminded Klemantaski of a photograph he had just seen of one of the new German rocket missiles leaving its launching platform.

In the first few yards the inevitable rocket burst from its clamps. Two more broke free, but now the Panjandrum was moving at a terrific speed. To Klemantaski, with his long experience of motor-racing, it seemed to be nearing a hundred miles an hour—a rushing inferno of smoke and fierce jets of fire.

At 80 yards the monster crossed one line of craters, and the shore-side wheel dipped ominously. At 120 yards the awed watchers realized it was out of control. The Panjandrum began to swing in a great curve to starboard. Hypnotized by the vast Frankenstein object roaring across the sand, Klemantaski continued to photograph it until it was heading straight for him. Then he sprang to his feet and ran for his life, following the V.I.P.'s as they flung themselves headlong down the far side of the pebble ridge into a mass of barbed wire.

"At any moment we expected the monster to come hurtling over the brow and crush us all to death."

But the seconds passed and nothing happened. So they crawled back up the stony slope. From the crest of the ridge they saw an amazing sight.

The Great Panjandrum was in its death throes. It had swung back to seaward and crashed over on its side on the sand. This smothered the rockets which were underneath, but the others continued to explode, wrenching and distorting the whole frame, until the remainder burst from their fittings and screamed off along the the beach in every direction, some vainly pursued by the Airedale dog!

When the pyrotechnics were over, and the awestruck admirals, generals, and scientists descended cautiously to the beach, all that remained of the Great Panjandrum was a twisted and blackened mass of wreckage. Round it lapped the incoming tide.

Various eminent authorities were consulted, but it proved impossible to overcome the two major defects. To cure the instability of the Panjandrum some suggested putting special treads on the steel tyres; others wanted to remove the tyres altogether and let the machine run on spikes. But it was the peril from the rockets which really sealed the fate of the monster. The risk of them breaking loose while the machine was still on board its landing-craft was too great to accept, and the project was reluctantly abandoned.

The official reason for the genesis of the Great Panjandrum may never be told. Even to-day there is still some mystery about it, for the Atlantic Wall, which it was called into being to demolish, never in fact existed in the form outlined to D.M.W.D. The beaches ultimately assaulted by the Allies in Normandy had no defence of this kind, and the proposal may well have been put up by the Staff in the hope that it would leak out to the enemy, thus convincing them that we intended to attack that part of the coast where such walls had already been built.

The Wheezers and Dodgers' work on the North Devon coast was, however, turned to good account. It stimulated and advanced research in the department on a much more tractable engine of war, the Alligator, and before long this amphibious counterpart of the Great Panjandrum was swimming happily in the Solent.

21

THE GRASSHOPPER AND THE ALLIGATOR
TAKE TO THE WATER

THE task of launching 100,000 men against a hostile shore produced problems in such array that even in a relatively small research organization like D.M.W.D. it was far from easy to chart the progress of every project examined and tackled as the invasion drew nearer.

In addition to work on the major undertakings like assault craft, cliff-scaling gear, the clearing of obstructions from beaches and ports, radar deception measures, and Pluto, the gigantic cross-Channel pipeline, a host of minor problems were brought to the Wheezers and Dodgers. All were vital links strengthening the chain of preparations which had to be forged before D-Day.

Some of the earliest links in that chain were provided by small parties of men who paddled ashore in the darkness, landing on the beaches of Holland, Belgium, and France, and made surveys. Their job was to find out which parts of the enemy coast were most vulnerable to a landing in strength. Since they carried out their work right under the noses of the Germans it was impossible to use any of the normal surveying methods. And the task had to be done in complete silence.

Combined Ops therefore asked D.M.W.D. to devise a "Beach Gradient Meter." They wanted a small truck which they could push up and down the beach, and which would record on a paper drum inside it a graph of the slope.

To their request they added a pathetic little footnote. It was most important, they said, that the wheels should not squeak!

The Wheezers and Dodgers produced this device for them, and by walking about in the darkness, and pushing the wheeled cart before them, the surveying parties were able to secure a complete contoured map of the beach areas they visited.

It was also necessary to gauge with great accuracy the depth of water off the enemy coast. Existing charts might not be entirely reliable, and, since certain mathematical experts claimed that this

information could be secured by dropping large objects into the sea
and measuring the plume which rose, an aircraft was lent to the
department, and a series of photographic experiments were carried
out on a lonely part of the English coast.

Another minor project was the Invisible Boat. When Laurie returned from the United States, where he had been in charge of the
manufacture and fitting of Plastic Armour, he mentioned to Norway
that enterprising boat-builders in Florida were turning out small craft
made entirely of Perspex. It had long been the habit of tourists there
to go afloat in glass-bottomed boats and gaze down on the elaborate and beautiful coral formations off the coast. Then some one
had hit on the idea of building entire dinghies of Perspex, which
allowed holidaymakers to view the wonders of the deep from any
angle.

One particularly interesting fact emerged. When such a boat was
a hundred yards from the shore it became invisible; the occupants
appeared to be sliding over the water on their posteriors, with no
obvious means of support!

It seemed to D.M.W.D. that such a craft might be ideal for landing agents on an alien shore. They therefore made a Perspex boat of
their own, 9 feet long and 2 feet in the beam, and Norway was told
to find a suitably secret place for trials.

At that time he had a house on Hayling Island, with a garden
running down to a sea creek off Chichester Harbour. At the foot of
the garden was a secluded boat-house, and the Perspex dinghy was
taken there for observation tests. These showed that the Florida story
was well founded. In bright sunlight, with a clear blue sky and blue
sea, the boat was, indeed, practically invisible. It was equally difficult to detect at night with a black sky and black sea, but in overcast
conditions it was a different story. Against a background of white
clouds and a dull, leaden-coloured sea the dinghy showed up discon-
certingly plainly, reflecting the sky and looking almost glaringly
white. In spite of this snag, however, the very hush-hush organization which dealt with the landing of agents seemed most impressed
by the trials, and they spirited the boat away to use for their own
mysterious ventures.

Meanwhile John Dove had been at work on his own with quite a
different kind of craft at Dover. To attack the German shipping
which crept round Cape Griz Nez at night he had devised an explosive motor-boat. Powered by a Chris Craft engine, it needed no
crew, for it was the complete robot. Under radio control it could
start itself, slip from its moorings unaided, and set off on a gyro
course plotted by the radar sets which directed the big guns at
Dover.

He brought it up the Thames to demonstrate it to Captain Jeans. Although on that memorable occasion something went wrong with the remote-control system, and the boat charged the wall below the Houses of Parliament, he eventually induced the robot mechanism to work with such uncanny accuracy that the craft could be homed on to a target twenty miles away with an error of only twenty yards. As things turned out, however, it was destined never to be used in its explosive rôle, for a much more important task cropped up. The development of the boat went forward as an invasion project, and, stripped of its explosive apparatus, it became a cog in the elaborate deception plans evolved for D-Day.

The Dieppe Raid had shown the need for close and powerful support for assaulting troops, and one of the major difficulties facing General Sir Frederick Morgan and his COSSAC staff was to find a way of swamping the enemy defences during the time-gap between the end of the naval bombardment and the touchdown of the first wave of men to reach the beaches.

It seemed to the COSSAC planners that the assaulting infantry must be accompanied by their own floating artillery—"guns, mortars, and batteries of rockets mounted in small craft."[1] From this vital need sprang the most formidable weapon in all the long history of shore bombardment—the "Rocket Landing Craft."

The original idea for a landing-craft crammed with rockets, which could loose a veritable cloudburst of high explosive over a limited area, came from Colonel Langley, who was attached to Combined Operations H.Q., and in due course the Wheezers and Dodgers were asked to draw up plans for a bombardment weapon of this kind which could be both elevated and trained.

A few days later Goodeve walked into the department. He had come to talk over the possibilities of a new gunnery recoil system with Richardson, but he noticed some one working at a drawing-board on the plans of "Grasshopper"—as the rocket craft was known in its embryo stage—and after studying the drawings for a while he said to Richardson, "Surely that must be the wrong approach. If you have to train and elevate the banks of rockets you'll run into all sorts of unnecessary complications. Why don't you point the ship at the target, and discharge the rockets straight from their stowage lockers by the ripple-firing system?"

D.M.W.D. had already used ripple-firing with great success. It was simple and almost foolproof. In front of the operator was a circle

[1] See Chester Wilmot, *The Struggle for Europe* (Collins, 1952). COSSAC was the chief planning organization for the invasion, its short title standing for Chief of Staff to Supreme Allied Commander.

of studs, each one connected to a group of rockets, and when an arm—geared to guard against over-rapid movement—passed across these an electrical contact was made, and each batch of rockets fired in quick succession.

Goodeve knew that this method was ideal for the job in hand, and quite safe to use for if the ship was rolling more than a certain number of degrees firing could be instantly checked by a special isolating switch. His intervention, however, led to much controversy. Both the Gunnery Division and the Naval Ordnance experts were strongly in favour of training and elevating the banks of rockets; indeed, a 'gun' which could not be trained or elevated must have seemed at first sight a startlingly revolutionary proposition for the Navy. But Norway and Brookfield prepared plans for a fixed projector, and Goodeve's powers of logical persuasion finally won the day.

This aspect apart, the Grasshopper raised a number of novel problems. The intention was to fire between 800 and 1000 rockets from the deck of one ship, but the vital question was, "How many can be discharged at the same time?"

In the first trial, which took place off Spithead in bad weather on April 11, 1943, the size of the salvos was gradually increased to 198 rockets, fired in groups of 33 at intervals of half a second. At each discharge blasts of hot air eddied back over the screen on the bridge, and by the fourth salvo the searing heat was building up so fast that Dr Bourdillon and Eades, peering over the side, had their hair, eyebrows, and clothing severely singed. So violent was the thrust of the rockets that the great tank-landing-craft began to go rapidly astern as the salvos left her deck.

From this experience it was obvious that members of the crew in exposed positions would become seriously burned if the complete mass of rockets was fired at once. At the same time hundreds of the rockets themselves would be subjected to flame and very hot gases; this might well detonate the cordite or buckle the projectors, thereby causing an explosion.

To ensure the safety of the Rocket Ship's commanding officer D.M.W.D. recommended the installation of an enclosed 'kiosk,' like a telephone booth, on the upper deck, and they suggested that the ship's Ack-Ack gunners should be issued with special asbestos clothing. The heat problem plainly required further examination, and on April 21 tests were carried out by remote control. The Wheezers and Dodgers planted a number of devices on board for gauging the temperature in the rocket tails—sensitive paints, alcohol thermometers, and certain crystals with a known melting-point which were sealed in small tubes.

This time 759 rockets were fired in the usual batches of 33. Great waves of flame swept over the bridge of the landing-craft, and the fierce build-up in temperature sent a flood of red paint pouring through cracks in the deck to smother the array of scientific detecting instruments which were thought to have been safely positioned below.

Temperatures of more than 800 degrees were recorded in the vicinity of the rockets, and when an electrical fault led to two salvos firing very close together the heat went up to 1000 degrees!

To close observers the Rocket Landing Craft in action was an unforgettable sight. Stretching away along the lower deck from the base of the bridge were serried ranks of huge rockets, all inclined at an angle and looking like some strange, stunted forest. In a few seconds the entire mass—hundred upon hundred of them—could be discharged into an area only 750 yards long by 240 yards deep, and when the salvos were fired the ship became shrouded in a swirling blanket of smoke and flame, out of which the rockets rose like flights of birds with fiery tails.

More protective measures were put in hand by the D.M.W.D. team, which included Brookfield, Byng, and Urwin, and trial number three was staged off Portsmouth on April 28.

This time a slight stern wind was blowing, and it was cooler on the bridge, but the deck and the projectors became hotter than ever before. It was apparent that on a warm day the risk of a general explosion in the landing-craft would be high, and if any technical fault caused a delay after the firing of a number of salvos there was a danger, too, that the remaining rockets would 'cook off.'

A few days later, therefore, they experimented in a new direction, flooding the deck with sea-water during the firing period. This proved a great success, and it was decided to go straight ahead with this formidable new assault weapon. Plans called for the conversion of 30 landing-craft to Rocket Ships by April 1944, and each would be capable of delivering a full salvo of 1080 rocket shells. The projectiles themselves were fitted with anti-personnel fuses—long sticks which protruded from the nose and detonated the explosive just above ground-level—and, although so many soared into the air at once, the ripple system, which followed a set pattern, prevented them from colliding with each other.

Apart from one further trial in the autumn, when for the first time they saw over a thousand rockets discharged from one of the more advanced types of Grasshopper craft, the Wheezers and Dodgers' exploratory work was now at an end, and the production of the Rocket Ships was handed over to the Naval Ordnance Department, one of whose staff, Lieutenant Hinton, had designed the original projectors from D.M.W.D.'s plans.

The Rocket Landing Craft, which carried more explosive for its size than any vessel ever used for bombardment, provided a terrifying and completely successful answer to the problem of destroying enemy morale at the most vital moment of a landing operation. It was regarded by many as the most valuable of all the projects on which the Wheezers and Dodgers worked, and both in the Mediterranean and the Normandy assaults to come it was to prove a devastatingly effective reinforcement to Allied gunfire.

Although it was now known that no Atlantic Wall, as such, girdled the coasts of Northern France, the planners considered it advisable to continue experiments with a machine for demolishing major obstructions on the enemy beaches. The Panjandrum had proved too intractable. Now D.M.W.D. turned to the "Alligator."

This was an amphibious vehicle, originally designed for rescue work in the Everglades swamps of Florida. It had tracks like a tank, and on these were little scoop-like spades which propelled it slowly through the water. The Americans had shipped many of these odd-looking beasts over to Britain, but so far they had not found a use for them. The Wheezers and Dodgers now proposed to mount on the bows of this amphibian a 'mattress' containing a ton of high explosive. This would be held by two compressed-air jacks, which would press it firmly against a wall or any other type of obstruction it encountered.

The explosive experts maintained that to get the best results the mattress would have to lie quite flat against the target. This involved the designing of a highly complicated mechanism, for the Alligator might strike the wall at an angle, and there was always the possibility, too, that the wall itself might be overhanging or sloping away from the vehicle.

From an American depot at Bedford D.M.W.D. procured an Alligator driven by a powerful Chrysler engine. They then sought the aid of the Hudson Motor Company, who had a factory on the Great West Road. With their co-operation Williamson designed the high-explosive mattress and the supporting jacks; Biddell tackled the intricate electrical problems; and Dove went to work on the radio-control gear which was to guide the Alligator from its landing-craft to the enemy shore. In quite a short time an automaton even more ingenious than the ill-starred Panjandrum began to take shape.

To assist the Wheezers and Dodgers Hudsons placed at their disposal two mechanics, Frank and Fred, and a Russian designer with a name so difficult to pronounce that he became known, for convenience, as George!

George was a refugee from Stalin—a pleasant, quiet man who

was much perplexed by the freedom of speech allowed to all and
sundry in the land of his adoption. During breaks in the trials he
would perch himself on the Alligator and steer the conversation
round to British politics and politicians. Then he would listen with
rapt attention. When all the British political parties had been rent
to shreds with complete impartiality by the naval officers present he
would grin delightedly and remark with evident satisfaction, "In
Russia you would all be shot for saying that!"

When the Alligator was ready for its first test they looked round
for a target on which to try out the hydraulic system. The explosive
mattress was slung on two pivots, attached to the outboard end of a
pair of huge hydraulic rams. These rams were linked in such a way
that if the Alligator hit an obstruction at an angle the ram taking the
first impact would be forced inward, breaking a copper seal. This
would bring into play the ram not in contact, and it would shoot
out, forcing the other corner of the mattress into position. The pivots
allowed the load of explosive to turn upward or downward according to the slope of the target, and the actual detonation of the charge
was effected by mine-detectors fixed on the front of the mattress.

Near the Hudson works they found a 10-foot wall. To reach this,
however, they had to drive the Alligator across the Great West Road
and down a bank on the far side. The amphibian was so vast that
they could not get it round the island outside the works, and after
several abortive attempts they sent for the police. The bypass was
then closed to traffic for half an hour, and the great beast was
manœuvred slowly to its destination.

This first trial went well. Williamson had been repeatedly reminded by the ballistic experts that the mattress must press tightly
against the target; to his delight, the hydraulic rams exerted such
pressure that the whole vehicle, which weighed 11 tons, was pushed
slowly backward.

Next the radio-control apparatus was installed, and, borrowing
two tons of 56-pound weights from a firm in the East End, they carried out loading trials to test the Alligator's stability in the water.
They then decided to take it for a cross-country run in Richmond
Park.

It was a lovely spring morning when they set off. The bank of the
Thames was safely reached, and they entered the water near Kew
Bridge. The Alligator's snout was then turned upstream, and it swam
steadily along until the weir at Teddington came in sight.

As they approached this obstacle the lock-keeper, who had been
observing them with evident alarm, shouted to Williamson, "You
can't come through here! We had a doodle-bug on us last
night."

On the other side of the river was a ramp for small boats, and Williamson gazed at it speculatively.

"You can't go up there either!" bellowed the lock-keeper. "I'm not having that thing stuck half-way."

So they headed downstream again, and, crawling out on the south bank, they rumbled across the bridge towards the Park. As they swung right for Richmond Hill, however, the port track of the Alligator suddenly came off. And there they were, well and truly marooned.

There was no hope of making any rapid running repairs, so a guard was placed over the machine, and it remained all night in the road, where its strange design and vast bulk—it was over 26 feet long and 11 feet wide—made it an object of much curiosity.

When they got the track back in place next morning they squeezed through the gateway into Richmond Park with three-eights of an inch clearance on either side. Waiting for them was a Ford station wagon fitted with the radio-control apparatus, and for the first time they sent the Alligator away on its own, guiding it on a complex route in and out of the trees. The remote-control system functioned perfectly, but the steering mechanism itself seemed erratic, and it was with some misgivings that Williamson, accompanied by the faithful Frank, Fred, and George, set out on the homeward journey.

The Alligator waddled back into the river near the Star and Garter, and it had been swimming downstream for some time before Williamson noticed that the generator had ceased charging. Almost immediately the engine stopped.

The rapid tide swung the ungainly craft beam on to the current. They tried to snatch at several barges as they passed, and then a tug came in sight. Realizing what was happening, the tugmaster swung his line of lighters across the path of the Alligator, and Williamson was able to get a line on board the last of the tow. The tug hauled them as far as Chiswick Bridge, where they were able to make fast to a buoy.

They were still trying to decide what to do when a police launch appeared.

"What's all this?" shouted a sergeant. "You can't make tie-up there."

"We've got to," said Williamson. "Our engine's failed."

"I shall have to report you," said the sergeant. "What *is* this craft, anyway, and where are you bound for?"

"It's Number H.49.... I can't tell you any more than that ... and we're bound for the Great West Road!"

When they had recovered from their astonishment the river police ferried one of the Alligator's crew ashore to collect spare parts, and they were able to complete the journey under their own power.

After modifications had been made the great beast was taken by road to Westward Ho! There Biddell did some brilliant work on the electrics of the amphibian, converting the remote-control system so that the Alligator could be directed from the air, and it was driven in and out of the sea and up and down the beach, guided entirely by one of the team flying high above the Devon coast in an Auster.

From Westward Ho! they moved back to the South Coast for extensive sea trials under the supervision of Alec Menhinick.

On the day of their arrival in the Solent the weather was foul, with blinding rain, and Menhinick, in charge of the rolling and pitching monster, was mightily relieved when a small landing-craft came out to Hamble Spit to meet them and help them to turn round in the river.

He was surprised to see that the crew of the landing-craft consisted of two Wren ratings, and when the Alligator was safely moored he invited them aboard the L.C.T. which was serving as parent ship to the amphibian. They looked as if they needed a hot drink, for they were soaked to the skin. One of them, known to her friends as "Spiffy," eventually arrived in the tiny wardroom of the tank-landing-craft. Her hair was plastered down with rain, her jersey and serge steamed gently in the reviving warmth of the small cabin, and the water dripped from a pair of tattered plimsolls on to the piece of matting proudly described as the wardroom carpet. She apologized for her bedraggled appearance, but Alec Menhinick thought she looked uncommonly attractive. A few weeks later they were married.

The Alligator was now attached to H.M.S. *Tormentor*, the small craft base in the Hamble, and in the ensuing trials Menhinick had D.M.W.D.'s own tank-landing-craft, L.C.T. 2119, at his disposal. The Alligator was carried in this, and the small landing-craft, commanded by Menhinick's future wife, acted as escort and tender. In it he made a number of journeys across the Solent to negotiate with the local authorities at Ryde, for he discovered that just outside the town was a sea wall which would serve admirably as a target for the amphibian's steering trials.

Each time he went to Ryde they made fast to the end of the pier, and it never occurred to him that he was not following a perfectly normal procedure until one afternoon the Commanding Officer of the Landing Craft Flotilla arrived on board bearing a staggering bill from the Southern Railway for 'berthing charges' at £2 a time!

"Look here, Menhinick," he said, "I can't possibly sign this."

"Oh, that's all right," said Menhinick, with reckless optimism. "I can. . . . Just leave it to me!"

He signed the bill with a flourish, and posted it to Waterloo Station. To his considerable relief, the Southern Railway accounts department were still puzzling over the identity of the organization which had so readily accepted liability for their berthing charges when the war ended!

The sea trials of the Alligator in the Solent brought the most alarming misadventures, and the amphibian was nearly lost on one occasion when returning from the target wall at Ryde. It had almost reached its parent ship when the engine stalled, and a large wave hurled it against the stern of the L.C.T. As soon as the mattress struck the side of the ship the copper seal broke, and the heavy explosive compartment—fortunately filled with harmless ballast— was carried forward to the full extent of the rams. For a second or two the Alligator seemed about to do a crash-dive. Although it then steadied itself, it remained at a terrifying angle. With the weather blowing up Menhinick thought it highly unlikely that he could keep his charge afloat, but after the V.I.P.'s watching the trials had been ferried ashore the L.C.T. began to tow him slowly towards the Hamble river. The voyage lasted all night, and ashore Wren Menhinick, just married to the Alligator's helmsman, spent an anxious vigil, certain that she was about to qualify for a widow's pension in record time!

The worst of the experiments with the Chrysler-engined model were over when the Wheezers and Dodgers got a new Alligator altogether—a most impressive monster powered by a Wright Whirlwind radial aircraft engine. It was delivered at Hamble in the dead of night, while Menhinick was in a sick bed nursing some ribs broken in a more recent misadventure with the amphibian. Since he was the only one who knew how to drive the newcomer off its transporter he was called out.

It was too dark to see the planks down which the huge vehicle had to crawl, and the Alligator and Menhinick soon became airborne. The resulting crash, and a blow from one of the steering levers as the monster hit the ground, sent him straight back to the sick bay with some more ribs out of action.

One by one the technical difficulties were overcome. The most formidable of these was the control of the Alligator from the air at night. To show which way it was heading in the darkness two lamps were mounted on short masts at either end of the vehicle, and facing aft. In theory all one had to do then was to keep the lights in line with each other, but in practice it was extraordinarily difficult to see the lights at all from an aircraft making wide circles at some distance out to sea. Menhinick was reduced to constant exasperation. "It's all very well for you to say it's easy," he said indignantly to Williamson in the wardroom one day. "I doubt if even Einstein would be able to make the right mathematical allowances if he had to work from a sighting base which never stopped moving either horizontally or vertically. And you know I can't even add or subtract!"

In the end, however, the Alligator passed all its trials with colours flying, but, exasperatingly enough for the Wheezers and Dodgers, who had created this strange and menacing craft, it suffered the same fate as the Panjandrum.

No promising targets could be spied for it on the vital stretch of the Normandy coast, and although development continued, in the hope that it might be given its baptism of fire in the Far East, it never found an enemy stronghold to destroy.

22

BUBBLES IN THE CHANNEL

IN January 1943 it was decided that the main invasion of Europe would be launched in the Baie de la Seine. And as the vast project took shape one problem dominated the thoughts of the men striving to piece together the elaborate jig-saw puzzle of plans for the coming assault. Without a harbour of some kind to protect the arrival of troops, weapons, vehicles, and stores the whole gigantic enterprise might well be doomed. In the chosen area of the Normandy coast little more than a summer breeze could produce surf conditions which, as Combined Operations H.Q. pointed out, would make "the landing of men an operation of great hazard, and the delivery of stores practically an impossibility."

The provision of a harbour was therefore vital to the success of "Overlord"; a report to the First Sea Lord called it "the crux of the whole operation." What form, however, should an artificial harbour take? As yet no one knew.

By strange chance a senior naval officer at Combined Operations Headquarters happened to glance at a back number of the *Scientific American*. One article was of absorbing interest to him, for it described a series of experiments carried out some thirty years earlier with an apparatus for reducing the waves of the ocean.

It appeared that an American citizen named Brasher—a swimming-bath superintendent—used to journey daily to New York across the Hudson river, and, being an observant individual, it was not long before he noticed an unusual phenomenon.

Although the surface of the great river was often choppy there were certain places along one bank where the water was always calm. This puzzled him considerably, and he decided to investigate. He then discovered that at each of the points concerned bubbles of air were escaping into the river from subterranean tunnels.

To Brasher this seemed highly significant. If bubbles of air, emerging so gently into the river, could calm the broken waters of the Hudson surely it might be possible to devise a high-pressure apparatus which could reduce the size of waves on the great lakes and oceans of the world. The discovery might entirely alter the existing conception of harbours and breakwaters; it might even set coastal erosion at bay.

In 1916 the first Bubble Breakwater equipment was tried out on the coast of California. Pipes were laid on the sea-bed, and compressed air was forced through them in an attempt to break up the rhythm of the waves. Sure enough, Brasher's apparatus succeeded in subduing short, steep waves, but it would only work in these limited conditions, and after much unavailing effort the project was abandoned.

On the face of it there was little to suggest that the ill-starred trials on the Pacific coast more than a quarter of a century before held the key to the Normandy landings, but the need to explore any clue which might solve the Invasion Harbour problem was urgent. Brasher's theory was therefore eagerly re-examined in London, and the Wheezers and Dodgers were directed to carry out some practical tests. A civilian scientist, Dr White, assumed technical control of the first experiments, and Coulson assisted him.

The first apparatus they built was one-fiftieth of full scale. It was laid on the bottom of the large tank in the hydraulics laboratory of the City and Guilds Institute, in South Kensington; then special machinery churned up vicious little 2-inch waves, which chased each other across the surface of the water towards a miniature beach, where they formed a tiny line of surf.

Gazing through the glass sides of the tank as the air-pressure was switched on, White and Lochner soon had visible proof that Brasher's initial optimism had been well founded. A thick stream of bubbles rose from the pipe. As soon as these reached the top of the tank the waves to leeward of this barrier of air magically died away, and the tiny, fretting line of surf disappeared. At first sight it seemed like some strange optical illusion, but closer examination showed a logical enough reason for this instant quelling of the waters.

At the moment of arrival at the surface the water rising with the line of ascending bubbles divided to form two distinct horizontal currents, which flowed away in opposite directions—one towards the little imitation beach, while the other met the advancing waves, sweeping their momentum from under them. It was like watching a man trying to mount a descending escalator. If the speed of the escalator is increased the perspiring victim will eventually make no further progress, even though his legs continue the motions of climbing.

So it was now with the waves in the tank. Individually the particles of water were still going through their wave motions, but as the bubbles generated their rival stream of power the waves themselves

Q

came to a standstill, dissipating their energy against this new opposing force.

It was an exciting revelation—but could it ever be reproduced in the open sea? And could the full-scale apparatus be made portable, durable, and seaworthy? Lochner was called in, and a thorough mathematical investigation of Brasher's theory was set in train, Professor Taylor undertaking to calculate the power which would be needed for a working plant. At this stage D.M.W.D. were only charged with the production of a breakwater one quarter of a mile long, but even so it soon became obvious that *power* might prove the decisive factor. A rough check showed that to keep quite a small bubble barrier in operation something in the region of 150,000 h.p. would be necessary.

To discover the effect of a tidal stream on the apparatus tests were carried out in the huge Admiralty experimental tank at Haslar. There Lochner had a larger version of the perforated pipe towed along beneath the surface at varying depths, while waves up to 15 feet in length were generated.

The trials then switched to Birnbeck. Three big Diesel road-breaking compressors were borrowed from the Army, and hundreds of feet of special pipe arrived. Holes were drilled, rubber joints were fitted, and at the outlet end of each submerged section of the pipe corrugated-iron screens were attached.

The first sea trials were spectacular—and somewhat inconclusive. They were carried out in lashing rain and rough seas, which repeatedly tore the iron screens from the ends of the pipes and twisted the unwieldy network of metal into such a tangle that frequent halts were necessary for running repairs.

Hour after hour Dr White crouched under the wall of the pier, entering data in a sodden notebook and occasionally signalling to James Close to give him more power from the compressors which thundered at the head of the beach.

Watching these efforts to tame the sea with the cynical amusement of a sailor born and bred, John Wide eventually remarked to one of the visiting scientists, "You'd get better results if you used oil!"

"Nonsense!" said the civilian. "Pouring oil on troubled waters? Complete illusion . . . no logic in it. Typical seaman's superstition!"

This nettled Wide. In his time he had been first mate in sail aboard one of the last of the old sailing tankers.

"I'll prove to you that it's nothing of the sort," he said, and, waiting for a suitably rough day, he took the reluctant civilian out in a small boat. To make the demonstration doubly spectacular he detonated an explosive charge on the sea-bed, and then emptied his supply of oil over the side. Seasick though he was, the scientist had to admit that he was much impressed!

The Birnbeck trials showed that a good deal of preliminary work had still to be done before the bubble-making equipment was ready for its first full-scale test. More powerful generating plant was needed, and some way had to be found of anchoring the pipes firmly to the sea-bed.

Dr White and his team returned to London, and Boswell was told to dismantle the makeshift apparatus. The three Diesel compressors were to be handed back to the Army. This, oddly enough, proved impossible, for the Army declared that they had loaned only two compressors to the Wheezers and Dodgers. It would, they said, be most confusing if three were returned! Boswell stuck to his guns, maintaining that even if the R.E.M.E. unit in question *had* made a mistake in their stocktaking there must be some recognized Army technique for disposing of surplus stock; in the Royal Navy such items were thrown overboard without any of this fuss! The owners of the compressor pointed out sarcastically that *they* worked on dry land, and after a final check of their stores they announced belligerently that H.M.S. *Birnbeck* would have to keep the third machine, whether they wanted it or not!

For the first major trial of the Bubble Breakwater D.M.W.D. began searching for a site on the coast where ample power was available. The type of air-compressing plant now envisaged would have to be driven by electricity, and Robert Lochner suddenly thought of Portslade, to the west of Brighton, where the great power station, with its tall, thin chimneys, was a prominent local landmark. He caught a train to Brighton and paid a call on the Borough Engineer.

War must have inured the Borough Engineer to surprising demands from the Services, for when Lochner, who could not explain why he wanted them, asked for the use of a stretch of beach, some workshops, and an unlimited supply of electricity this mysterious request was granted on the spot.

The first step was to clear several hundred mines from the beach where the Wheezers and Dodgers were to operate. It proved a dangerous job. One man was killed, and after disagreement with the Army over completion of the task the D.M.W.D. team devised their own mine-clearance system, setting off the buried mines by rolling loaded pipes across the sand.

A special pump-house was built on the shore, and a team which included Byng, Urwin, and Eades, assisted by thirteen divers, began laying a Bubble Breakwater 1200 feet long, roughly parallel to the beach and 600 yards out to sea.

Heavy though it was, the bubble pipe floated free as soon as it was filled with air, so it had to be sunk on to a bed of concrete blocks and weighted down to prevent it from sailing away on the ebbing tide. Then began weeks of arduous and heartbreaking experiment.

At the start it all seemed straightforward enough. They only had to contend with 400 feet of pipe, six compressors, and a high-voltage electricity supply, but the working parties were dogged by constant setbacks. Weather in the Channel was vile, and time after time heavy seas tore at the apparatus, wrenching the pipes from their moorings and hurling them back on to the shore. Whenever the equipment remained in position for any length of time a fresh snag developed. The holes in the master pipe became silted up and hidden by drifting sand. The divers then had to descend with underwater guns and punch more apertures to maintain the density of the bubbles.

The actual attempts to subdue the waves which came rolling in to the Sussex coast were far from encouraging. The available compressed-air apparatus never satisfied the increasing demands they made upon it, and reports reaching D.M.W.D. from American and British manufacturers warned that there was now considerable doubt whether the required quantity of more advanced plant would be forthcoming. Even if this did become available, however, no one could yet see, at this anxious stage, how the whole intricate layout of pipes and compressing machinery was to be embodied in a portable form.

It had to be portable, for in an invasion no reliance could be placed on shore-based power; the Bubble Breakwater must be fed from a vessel moored off the coast. And Lochner began to be haunted by nightmare visions of ships, half the size of the *Queen Mary*, with their holds crammed with bubble pipes and masses of special machinery. He wondered gloomily what would happen to such ships in a Channel gale.

In March the Combined Chiefs of Staff informed the Admiralty that unless some form of artificial harbour could be guaranteed the invasion would have to be called off. By now the planners had further complicated D.M.W.D.'s task by calling for a much larger stretch of protected water. They wanted at least a mile of calm sea behind the major breakwater, and additional Bubble strips to safeguard both the landing-craft lying off the open beaches and the ends of the special piers which the Army were designing.

The news of the decision by the Combined Chiefs of Staff coincided with the depressing discovery that to keep in being a whole bubble harbour of this size at least one and a half million horse-power would be needed, perhaps every minute of the day and night.

Lying in bed at his home near Haslemere, recovering from a bout of 'flu,' Lochner could not drive the harbour and its problems from his mind. Failing a miracle, it now seemed that the Bubble Breakwater was not going to produce the answer. But where lay an alternative?

He began to probe once again at the root of the matter. The planners were calling for a simple and portable barrier to stop waves. What was the nature of a wave?

The general idea was easy enough to grasp. Water was composed of small molecules which were capable of a certain amount of independent movement. Otherwise water would not fit into a glass. Tests in the experimental tank showed that the wave molecules moved on a circular path. But what precisely happened *beneath* the surface of the sea? Did an Atlantic roller roll all the way down to a thousand fathoms?

No! Of course it didn't! How dense they had all been! The ordinary wave which buffets the bather loses most of its power at 12 feet. At 120 feet Atlantic rollers no longer worry the crew of a submarine.

Jumping out of bed, he went to the attic. Rummaging about, he found an old buoyant rubber mattress—a relic of peace-time holidays at the seaside. He also found an iron bar, and, bending the mattress lengthways, he got his wife, Mary, to sew the two sides together, with the bar forming a rough-and-ready keel.

They carried this strange object downstairs. At the foot of their garden in the little village of Hammer, on the Surrey and Hampshire border, was a pond, and, launching the weighted mattress there, they spent all the remaining hours of daylight up to their knees in the cold, weed-ridden waters of the pool.

By nightfall Robert Lochner knew he had stumbled on a discovery which might revolutionize the whole approach to the problems of the Invasion Harbour.

In addition to their preoccupation with the artificial harbour, the planners were also carefully examining countless ways and means of ensuring the complete success of the initial assault. One of these, on which much depended, was the counter-mining of the defended beaches.

As early as 1941 tests had been made at Shoeburyness to discover the effect of exploding charges in the air or at ground-level against an anti-tank minefield. A year later Combined Operations H.Q. suggested that such charges might be fired from a weapon designed on the lines of the Hedgehog and mounted in a special type of landing-craft, and in the autumn of 1942 the Wheezers and Dodgers began work on the "Hedgerow."

In the next twelve months they carried out extensive trials against enemy mines laid on the beaches near Birnbeck. As with the Hedgehog, the vital factor in developing the Hedgerow projectile was the fuse. It had to be sufficiently robust not to actuate on contact with water at high velocity, but it had to be sensitive enough to go off on impact with the soft mud in which it eventually landed in the shallows close to the beach.

After much experiment the Wheezers and Dodgers solved this problem by fitting the fuse with brass domes of varying thickness. The tolerance between the two limits was found to be very small, and hundreds of rounds had to be fired before the right answer was forthcoming.

The fuse itself was carried on a long stick which protruded from the nose of the projectile. When they retrieved the early rounds from the mud they found that many of the sticks were bent, suggesting violent impact with the ground. This should have set off the fuse, but, strangely enough, none of them had actuated. Eventually they discovered that the bending was caused not by the shock of the projectile's striking the sea-bed, but by a peculiar wobble which the Hedgerow bomb developed as it entered the water. They strengthened the stick, and after that they had no more trouble.

To determine the counter-mining distances and the characteristics of the craters caused by the explosions Boswell and the team at Birnbeck staged trials against many different sizes and shapes of minefield, both dry and submerged, and eventually D.M.W.D. were ready to build a pilot model of the Hedgerow installation.

This had twenty-four spigots, mounted in two parallel lines just abaft the ramp of the tank-landing craft which housed them. The rounds were inclined at different angles on their spigot mountings, the steepest spigot commanding a range of 315 yards, while the one with the least elevation could hurl its projectile 475 yards. Guggenheim estimated that a salvo of Hedgerow rounds would blast a path through an enemy minefield 120 yards long by 8 yards wide.

The first firing trials, held off Hayling Island, were something of an anticlimax, for Combined Operations, who were responsible for the arrangements, looked up the tides for the wrong month, and the tank-landing-craft ran aground too far out! Consequently none of the rounds reached the beach. This contretemps had one practical result, however, for the idea of using tank-landing-craft was abandoned in favour of the smaller L.C.A. (assault landing-craft), which could approach closer to the shore.

In March 1943 the pilot model of the Hedgerow was transferred to an L.C.A. in Portsmouth Dockyard, and again they set off for the firing grounds off Hayling Island, accompanied by a technical expert from H.M.S. *Vernon*. On the way out they shipped a good deal of water. This short-circuited the electrical contacts, and the observer from the *Vernon* suggested calling off the trial. Trying out the new weapon with the installation saturated in sea-water was a hazard no one had bargained for, but time was precious, and Williamson decided to take the risk. Drying the electrical equipment as thoroughly as possible, they fired a full salvo.

The Hedgerow in action presented an impressive and unusual sight. Each projectile weighed 60 pounds, and as they climbed clumsily into the sky they all seemed to be proceeding at grotesquely different angles to each other. The terrific concussion as they exploded just above the beach not only set off the buried test mines; it threatened to paralyse any human being in the immediate vicinity.

On board the L.C.A., however, there was an unexpected development. The thrust as the big projectiles left the deck caused widespread damage to the mountings, and cracks appeared in the hull of the boat. At the technical inquest which followed the Director of Naval Construction's advisers recommended elaborate strengthening of all future Hedgerow craft.

The work was still in progress when an SOS came from the Commander-in-Chief, Mediterranean. He had seen plans of the Hedgerow, and asked that five of these special craft should be made available for an important operation. It was then the middle of May, and the pilot model had fired precisely one salvo; Admiral Cunningham's staff called for the delivery of five tried and tested craft, in fully operational condition, by June 15. It was a stiff proposition.

The Wheezers and Dodgers were given a free hand, and Williamson and his team toiled night and day. Helping him were Rivers-Bowerman, who had done yeoman work on the stick fuse; Duncan Bruce; Guggenheim, who supplied most of the advanced mathematical calculations; and Helsby, who had devised the ingenious crushable brass cap in the nose of the projectile.

An engineering firm at Egham, in Surrey, built the Hedgerows, and in exactly four weeks to the day a whole complex chain of developments had been completed. The pilot model had been redesigned, five Hedgerows had been made and tested in their specially strengthened assault craft, and H.M.S. *Vernon* had trained the crews who were to man them.

It was a remarkable achievement, but unhappily this technical efficiency was not matched by administrative foresight elsewhere. No adequate instructions for the reception of the Hedgerow craft reached the Mediterranean, and a series of disasters befell them.

In North Africa the L.C.A.'s were recognized as familiar craft, but no one, apparently, had heard of the new weapon they mounted. So the trained crews were removed and drafted to other duties; the equipment, installed with such urgency, was stripped from the boats, and when at last some one discovered the significance of the Hedge-row mountings only two of the five installations were retrieved. Nobody realized that the craft had to be specially strengthened to stand the stresses and strains involved, and the shipwrights at Algiers, who had no blueprints to work from, laboriously reassembled the spigots, mountings, and the maze of electrical wiring in unstiffened boats. To complete this unhappy catalogue of blunders the Sub-Lieutenant R.N. who was placed in command of the two ill-starred Hedgerow craft—L.C.A. 446 and L.C.A. 403—for the Salerno landing was provided with new crews who had no knowledge of the weapon at all! He discovered, too, that the Hedgerow rounds he embarked at Djidjelli had been submerged in five feet of water for a considerable time in the hold of an ammunition vessel.

On August 29 the Sub-Lieutenant held his first and only firing practice. It was a chastening experience. On board L.C.A. 446 the beams supporting the spigot mountings instantly split apart, and the sides of the craft opened up. She sank almost immediately in the rough waters of Bizerta Bay, and L.C.A. 403 only just managed to struggle back into harbour. This left only the one Hedgerow landing-craft to take part in the invasion of Italy's mainland.

At zero hour—0330 on the morning of September 9—L.C.A. 403 went into action forty yards from Red Beach in Salerno Bay.

No sooner had the first salvo been fired from the Hedgerow than they found that the mountings had split again. This severed the firing leads to the forward spigots, and half the projectiles were now out of action.

Under heavy fire the crew worked frantically for forty minutes with insulating tape and spare cable, and managed to join up all but two of the mountings. Then, in the half-light of approaching dawn, the L.C.A. headed in towards Salerno town. Here again they came under heavy shellfire, so the remaining salvo was aimed at the harbour. Such damage had been done to the firing circuit and the spigot girders, however, that six of the projectiles failed to leave their mountings, and the rest all fell within thirty yards of the boat.

They could do no more, but, anxious to discover the effect of the one salvo he had fired successfully, the Sub-Lieutenant landed and made his way to Red Beach. Over an area of ninety yards he counted the unmistakable craters of twenty-three Hedgerow bombs. The last six had exploded right in the centre of a dense minefield laid in bullrushes and scrub eighty yards from the water's edge, and had cleared a wide path for the advancing troops.

In the Admiralty the potentialities of the Hedgerow were quickly realized. Its failure in the Mediterranean, in craft entirely unsuitable for it, had been inevitable; properly handled, the new weapon could obviously play an important part in the greater invasion which lay ahead.

The Wheezers and Dodgers now set to work to improve its performance. Alterations were made to the elevation of the spigots, new projectiles were designed, and the mountings were further strengthened to take the thrust of more powerful ammunition.

In the invasion of Normandy the Hedgerow flotillas were destined to encounter difficulties and hazards of a different nature, but the story of their intervention in Operation Overlord must be told in a later chapter.

From the moment that the department became recognized as the authority on miscellaneous weapons D.M.W.D. were called upon to examine all manner of strange ideas for prosecuting the war. Some had a sound scientific basis, and if they seemed likely to meet a pressing Admiralty requirement they were eagerly explored. Often, however, the suggestions reached so far into the realms of fantasy that no serious appraisal was possible.

The cranks who found their way to Lower Regent Street or the Wheezers and Dodgers' subsequent home in Leicester Square could be roughly sorted into two categories.

The "Solidified Searchlight" school rarely brought any explanatory documents. They presented the department with "just the basic idea . . . you'll easily be able to work out the details." With them the Idea was the thing, and putting it into practice was always a "mere matter of research and development."

The rival school went to the other extreme. They arrived with a formidable array of drawings, intricate calculations, and other data, often supported by voluminous correspondence with various Ministries, which had, apparently, already rejected their weapons or devices. Such setbacks rarely seemed to discourage them.

At the time of the Blitz a plan was presented in all seriousness for the building of an enormous Anti-aircraft Mountain, thousands of feet high, in Kent. From this, its sponsor explained, gunners would be able to shoot down the highest-flying bombers raiding London! And at various times plans came to D.M.W.D. for a space-ship; a gun for merchant vessels which squirted columns of water at approaching aircraft, presumably with the object of drowning the pilot in mid-air; and a weird and wonderful machine for manufacturing artificial tidal waves in the Pacific. Its inventor claimed that this would disorganize the Japanese defence system by washing all their outlying garrisons off the smaller coral atolls!

While the invasion scare was still alive in the war's early days Goodfellow produced for the entertainment of the department some drawings of a splendid dual-purpose · contraption. This was a "Rocket Guide Rail," which would enable the Home Guard to fire 2-inch projectiles from the shoulder—but its great merit, as he gravely explained, lay in the fact that it could subsequently be used as a pike!

It was Goodfellow, incidentally, who alarmed the highest Defence circles during that same period by calculating that the Germans could, if they wished, build two Channel Tunnels in a matter of eighteen months if they used slave labour. As a result he was asked to prepare a memorandum on the various means available to the enemy for disposing of the soil. Before long rumour had it that advanced units of the German Army were busily burrowing their way towards Romney Marshes!

For the serious inventor war offered an opportunity and a challenge. In Britain, however, it was often impossible to experiment on a grand scale owing to dire shortage of materials. On his first wartime visit to America Goodeve was astounded at the contrasting conditions in which research and development was carried on.

Arriving in Detroit, he paid a courtesy call on the great American inventor Charles F. Kettering, who was directing the Research Division of the vast General Motors organization. Kettering, renowned in his own country as a second Edison, welcomed him warmly, and then delivered a trenchant lecture on the iniquities of scientists!

"What we need to win this war is more inventors," he declared bluntly. "All scientists ought to be torpedoed!" He then went on to discuss with Goodeve a remarkable project which he was developing on his own initiative. It involved the mass production of remote-controlled aircraft, each of which would carry 1000 pounds of explosive, and, to Goodeve's astonishment, he found that these had been already built in their hundreds. They were parked in serried rows in building after building, and even overflowed into the car-park outside.

Kettering explained that they could be turned out at the rate of one every minute. The engines were internal-combustion motors of simple design, and the wings were ingeniously made of hard, rolled sheet steel. Technically, this was a considerable achievement, for no aluminium was required—and aluminium was then a rare and precious commodity.

Kettering envisaged a non-stop bombardment with his robot 'planes which would bring Germany to her knees. Pointing to a map, he declared that a vast underground factory could easily be set up in Kent, the raw materials for manufacturing the aircraft and their bombs being fed down vertical shafts. As these expendable robots were completed—at the rate of one every minute—they would take off up a sloping runway, and fly out from the cliff-side towards Germany.

His small 'planes embodied a variety of control methods. Some, he explained, would fly straight. Some would zigzag. After a given time some would seek out their targets by using infra-red rays. Any large city emits infra-red radiations—particularly in winter, when buildings are heated—and Kettering planned to turn this to advantage in homing his pilotless bombers.

Already he had tested the flying performance of his aircraft at a secret experimental station in the desert, and he had taken elaborate steps to defeat any possible counter-measures adopted by the enemy.

At dinner that night the man who had invented self-starting, lighting, and ignition systems for motor-cars before the First World War talked with boyish enthusiasm of many other projects just as ambitious as his bomber fleet. On his own responsibility Kettering had already spent millions of dollars on developing various controlled devices. As it happened, the rapid expansion of orthodox bombing, which enabled a far heavier load of explosive to be directed at enemy targets, removed the need for his ingenious robots. But Goodeve was often to recall with envy the freedom which America's wealth in material and technical resources gave to her inventors. He remembered Kettering's 'doodle bugs' too when the first German flying bombs began to fall on London. It was the enemy V1's which led to one of Goodeve's strangest encounters with an inventor.

One morning, when he was presiding over a joint-Services meeting in the Admiralty, he received a message that a Very Important Person in the Whitehall hierarchy wished to see him immediately. He walked along the passage to the great man's room, and there he was introduced to a stranger—a civilian who, he gathered, was an engineer from the North.

"Mr Blank has an idea which I'd like you to look at, Goodeve," said the Great Man. "It's a counter-measure to these flying bombs. Would you take him along to your room and let him show you the details? Unfortunately I have to preside over a meeting in a few minutes' time, so I can't come along myself, but I'd like a report as soon as possible."

Goodeve thought regretfully of his own meeting. Plainly that would have to go by the board now.

He led the way to his office, and his visitor, opening a bulging briefcase, extracted a mass of papers which he spread all over the floor.

"It's really quite simple," he remarked. "You know the barrage balloons?"

Goodeve said he did.

"Well, then," went on the visitor, "you send up hundreds of those balloons across the normal route of the flying bombs, and to the cable of each you connect this apparatus of mine. It consists of a cylinder of oxygen joined to a small benzine tank by an electromagnetic release valve. On the other side of the benzine tank is a bath containing a soap solution. Do I make myself clear?"

"Perfectly," said Goodeve. "Please go on." He was thinking of his meeting; it must be nearly over now, and he wondered whether some one was taking a full note for him to read through as soon as he was free.

"Now we come to the crux of the whole scheme. The mixture finally emerges into the air in a series of huge bubbles. . . ."

Goodeve came out of his reverie with a start. "I'm afraid I don't quite see what these bubbles of yours can do to destroy the flying bombs," he said a little sharply.

"Come now, Dr Goodeve!" chided the inventor. "Surely it must be obvious. Over come the flying bombs, and as they pass they suck my bubbles into their intake system. Immediately the bombs will explode in mid-air."

For a moment Goodeve remained speechless. He had left a vital conference to waste time on a project which had no basis of scientific probability whatever. But then he relented. The inventor was so obviously in earnest that it would be unkind to dash his hopes there and then. Instead Goodeve thanked him politely.

"It's an interesting theory. I'd like to consult some of my colleagues about your apparatus," he said. "Perhaps you'd let me have your address?"

When Goodeve sought to dispose of the matter, however, he found himself in a quandary. The Soap Bubble Scheme was far too ludicrous to send to any Admiralty department for their comments; indeed, it hardly concerned the Admiralty in any case. But the Great Man was interested in it, and had asked him to vet the idea. Obviously it would have to be treated sympathetically.

After pondering for several days he had a brainwave, and dictated a letter to the inventor thanking him warmly for the public spirit he had shown in bringing his scheme to the notice of the Royal Navy.

> I would, however, like to point out [he continued] that flying bombs are themselves propelled by a series of explosions far more violent than would be created by the introduction of your bubbles. What your scheme would, in fact, achieve is a refuelling of the bombs in flight, and here you may well have hit upon a most important discovery. If you can increase the strength of your mixture it may be possible to *accelerate* the flight and range of the bombs so con-

siderably that they will pass right over London and land in the open country beyond. I am convinced that you should reconsider your idea in this light, and then put it up again—to the Air Ministry, not the Admiralty.

A day or two later the inventor rang up Goodeve. "That letter you wrote to me," he began cautiously. "I believe you are pulling my leg!"

"Why should you think that?" parried Goodeve.

"Well . . . I think you *are*."

"In that case," Goodeve remarked, with a chuckle, "I wouldn't feel disposed to contradict you."

The conversation ended quite amicably. And after that no more was ever heard of the Great Soap Bubble Scheme for countering Hitler's secret weapon.

23

THE FLOATING WALL

WE must now return to the problem on which the fate of the forthcoming invasion hinged. The creation of an artificial harbour was imperative for reasons which will shortly be explained, but the full magnitude of the task facing the COSSAC planners can only be appreciated if the unusual conditions prevailing in the Baie de la Seine are borne in mind.

The enemy had had four years in which to make their coastline secure against attack. They had had four years to plan the complete destruction of every port on the Channel shore which might conceivably be used by invaders. In other waters this might not have been an insuperable obstacle, but the Channel was a very different proposition. Admittedly the statistics showed that bad weather was rarely encountered in June—the month chosen for the landings—but the risk of trying to sustain the greatest amphibious assault in history over open beaches in the Baie de la Seine was too appalling to accept.

At least 5000 ships would be involved. The proposed assault front ran for nearly fifty miles, and with a wind anywhere between North-east or North-west the chosen beaches would form a dead lee shore. Not only would bad weather make it impossible to unload from the landing-craft, D.U.K.W.'s, and Rhino ferries now being built for this task, but such small craft—some 4000 of them—would be unable to retire to the safety of their bases in England, a hundred miles away. Indeed, with such a long front it was not certain that these small craft would even get sufficient warning of an approaching gale to enable them to reach any sanctuary available on the French side of the Channel.

When the planners came to consider the form of protection needed for the invasion fleet they ran up against an immediate technical difficulty. As a report to the Admiralty stated bluntly, "Nothing favoured the choice of this coast for the construction of artificial harbours." The rise and fall of the tide was exceptional—as much as 24 feet at spring tides. Any breakwater based in 30 feet of water at low tide would consequently have to be 54 feet tall to reach the surface at high water.

In peace-time, with all supplies at hand and no hostile action to hinder construction, it had taken seven years to build the harbour at Dover. Now, in vastly different and less favourable conditions, the Allies had to find a way of laying down two much larger prefabricated harbours—each the size of Gibraltar—in little over a fortnight.

The broad concept of Mulberry Harbour[1] eventually embraced an outer breakwater, an inner one composed of huge concrete caissons called Phœnix units, which could be towed across the Channel and sunk by opening release valves, and a series of floating piers—'Whales,' they were named—running out from the beach to pier-heads, at which ships could berth and unload their cargoes into lorries. These pier-heads were mounted on stilt-like legs, and were designed to rise and fall with the tide. Here Churchill's astonishing prescience was shown. As early as May 30, 1942, he had written a minute—often quoted since—to the Chief of Combined Operations in which he predicted the very shape of these ingenious mechanical monsters: "They must float up and down with the tide. The anchor problem must be mastered. . . . Let me have the best solution worked out. . . . Don't argue the matter. The difficulties will argue for themselves."[2]

More remarkable still, incidentally, was Churchill's anticipation of the need for concrete caissons. In July 1917 he had suggested in a memorandum to Lloyd George the construction of "a number of flat-bottomed barges or caissons, made not of steel but of concrete," which would float when empty of water and could be towed across and sunk off the Horns Reef: "By this means a torpedo- and weatherproof harbour, like an atoll, would be created in the open sea."[3]

For the inner breakwater and harbour there was, therefore, at least a line of thought to pursue, but at the time when Robert Lochner began puzzling once again over the behaviour of waves the planners of Operation Overlord, who had already visualized the need for an outer breakwater to protect the Mulberry Harbours, were still uncertain of the form this would take. By April 1943 it appeared

[1] The originator of the detailed Mulberry Harbour plan was Vice-Admiral John Hughes-Hallett, C.B., D.S.O., who in April 1943 was serving as an additional Chief of Staff to C.-in-C. Portsmouth in the rank of Commodore. Admiral Hughes-Hallett retired from the Royal Navy in 1954, and shortly afterwards became Conservative M.P. for East Croydon.

[2] Sir Winston Churchill, *The Second World War*, Vol. IV, *The Hinge of Fate* (Cassell, 1951), p. 66.

[3] The memorandum was prepared in connexion with a scheme for the capture of the Friesian Islands of Borkum and Sylt. (See Churchill's *Second World War*, Vol. II, pp. 215–216.)

very doubtful whether the Bubble Barrier would be a feasible proposition. The sudden realization, however, that waves only exerted their
force over a relatively short depth seemed to Lochner to alter the
whole situation.

What they needed was some sort of wall in the sea which need not
be carried right down to the sea-bed; it had only to extend to the
point where the waves lost their energy. Therefore they must build a
floating wall.

So far, so good. But walls do not normally float! So in the first
place this would have to be a very unusual kind of wall, and, to make
matters more complicated, it would have to remain permanently
stationary—or, if it moved at all, it must move only laterally, expanding and contracting with the waves, whose force it would cushion.
The top of the wall must, obviously, stay in the same place.

It was when he had reached this stage in reasoning out the problem that Lochner thought of the Lilo mattress. As soon as his wife
had sewn on the metal keel they launched it in the pond, and Mary
Lochner began making miniature waves with the lid of a biscuit-tin.
The experiments eventually came to an abrupt end when she lost her
balance and fell head-first into the water, but by then Robert Lochner had seen enough to know that he was on the right lines. As soon
as he got back to the Admiralty he drew up plans for more accurate
models. When these were tested in the City and Guilds' tank they
showed clearly enough that the principle was fundamentally sound.
A floating barrier *would* suppress waves.

It was an exciting discovery. In one bound the Wheezers and
Dodgers had, apparently, eliminated all the machinery, the pipes,
and the huge ships which would have been needed to operate the
Bubble Breakwater.

In D.M.W.D. a period of intense activity followed. By July the
mathematical theory had been evolved, over a hundred experiments
with models had been carried out, and the floating dock at Portsmouth had been cleared, ready for full-scale construction.

It was very much a team job. Penney and Price, from London
University, tackled the mathematical side; Urwin went off to the
Admiralty Experimental Establishment at Haslar to conduct further
model experiments, and Guggenheim analysed the results. One of
the big tanks at Haslar was 900 feet long, and it had mechanism for
producing 3-foot waves. Urwin was glad when the job was over, for
the water had not been changed for a long time, and recovering the
models from the noisome depths was not as simple as it looked.

When construction of the full-scale prototypes began Lochner
went to the Balloon Development Establishment of M.A.P. for
advice on the preparation of the vast air-bags which would be

LIEUTENANT R. F. ADES, R.N.V.R., WHO LOST HIS LIFE ON D-DAY, SUPERVISING THE INSTALLATION OF ONE OF THE DEPARTMENT'S ROCKET GRAPNELS IN A DORY

ROCKET GRAPNEL IN ACTION WEST OF OMAHA BEACH ON D-DAY

MERRYWEATHER FIRE-ESCAPE MOUNTED IN A D.U.K.W.

TROOPS USING THE LADDER TO SCALE A CLIFF IN TRIALS ON THE SOUTH COAST SHORTLY BEFORE D-DAY

CLIVE UPTTON

HEDGEROW CRAFT BREACHING THE ENEMY'S SHORE DEFENCES
ON D-DAY

An impression by Clive Uptton.

By permission of "John Bull"

needed to support the floating wall. It was his first experience of dealing with the Ministry of Aircraft Production, and he was greatly impressed. There was a spirit of urgency, a liveness about the organization, inspired by Beaverbrook's leadership in the war's early days, and D.M.W.D. were given all the co-operation they wanted.

It was Nixon, one of Beaverbrook's key men on the Balloon Barrage side of the Ministry, who found the men and the materials, and Bateman, a designer of balloons at Cardington, brought his considerable knowledge to bear on this strange marine object. Then Dunlops were chosen to build the vast, flexible rubber bags, and Dr Oscar Faber, a well-known consulting engineer, joined the D.M.W.D. team to design the reinforced-concrete keels which would weigh down these great sea balloons. A new code word began to appear in the progress reports reaching the Overlord planners, for the floating breakwater was given the title of "Lilo."

All was not plain sailing. There were plenty of critics ready to suggest that a skin of fabric less than one-eighth of an inch thick would never stand up to the task assigned for it. It was generally recognized, however, that Lilo offered greater possibilities than the Bubble barrier. Experiments still continued with the Bubble Harbour apparatus, but in D.M.W.D. and other quarters opinion was gradually veering away from the conception of waves tamed by nothing more substantial than bubbles, particularly in view of the immense power which would have to be generated.

Lochner was confident that they were now working on the right lines. At the same time he still had a nagging feeling that the basic design might be improved. He was worried about the obvious vulnerability of the fabric sides of the breakwater under construction. If only he could dispense with them it would be a great step forward. When he got home in the evenings he would fill the bath and experiment with different shapes of rigid-sided models. The results were not immediately encouraging, but he kept on trying.

The three full-sized Lilos over which workmen swarmed in the dock at Portsmouth during the month of August were unlike any floating object ever seen. They were 200 feet long and 12 feet wide. The gigantic air-bags were divided into three compartments, running the full length of the Lilo and separated from each other by canvas walls proofed with rubber.

The keel consisted of a hollow tube of reinforced concrete 8 feet in diameter, and when flooded with water it weighed 750 tons. The tube could, however, be pumped out quite easily, and then it floated without any assistance from its rubber envelope. A sunken Lilo could in fact be raised merely by attaching an air-pipe.

It was intended to inflate the massive sea balloons just enough to

R

balance the external water-pressure at various depths. Any increase in the pressure from the waves on one side of the bag would cause it to yield on that side, thereby preventing transmission of the wave motion through the Lilo.

The army of workers in the floating dock were baffled by the grotesque thing they were creating. They guessed that it had something to do with the Second Front so stridently demanded in crude lettering on walls and hoardings. Its purpose they were unable to decide, but they were unanimous on one point—it would never float!

While the prototypes were being built there was much activity in other directions. Possible sites for the Mulberry Harbours were being examined for wave analysis; talks were taking place with the mooring experts to determine the best method of securing long lines of floating objects close together off a lee shore; and patiently Robert Lochner was continuing his experiments with small rigid-sided model breakwaters. By now he was beginning to get results.

By the middle of that month the Prime Minister was in Canada, and the British and American planning staffs summoned to the "Quadrant" Conference were working together on the problems of Overlord. Suddenly word reached the Admiralty that a team fully conversant with the progress of Bubble Harbour and the floating breakwater was to fly to Quebec immediately. They would form part of a "British Extemporized Artificial Harbours Committee" which, under the leadership of Brigadier Sir Harold Wernher, was to take part in the Staff talks.

Before setting out for Prestwick Lochner told Byng to proceed with tests of a new rigid-sided breakwater conceived from the experiments in the bath. With Lochner on the journey north were Penney, Faber, Nixon, and Bateman. At the transatlantic air terminal they were joined by Sir Harold Wernher and two leading War Office champions of the Whale Piers, Brigadier Bruce White and Major Steer-Webster.

It was an uncomfortable journey. In the bomb bay of the Liberator the noise was deafening. No one was allowed to smoke, and reading was an impossibility. There was nothing to do but lie on one's back on a hard, narrow straw mattress and wonder what fresh problems lay ahead. After eighteen hours they landed in Montreal, and transhipped into a Dakota for the final stage of the journey.

When they reached Quebec and drove to the Château Frontenac they found, to their dismay, that a meeting on Artificial Harbours was due to start in precisely fifteen minutes. Sleepless and unshaven, they grabbed their papers and plunged into technical conflict with a large American contingent of Army and Naval officers on the building of Mulberry.

To the surprise of the British team the plan put forward by the Americans centred on the use of sunken Liberty ships to form the outer breakwater. It soon became evident, however, that they had based their calculations on a rise and fall of tide of only eighteen feet, and when this error was pointed out they immediately saw that this was impracticable. In addition to up-to-date facts about tidal conditions much of the information brought by the newly arrived party from London came as a complete surprise to the U.S. planners. Whale piers were a novel proposition; so were floating breakwaters. Lochner had brought with him cine-films of the Lilo model experiments, and he gave two lectures—first to the Mulberry planning staffs; then, under Admiral Mountbatten's sponsorship, to a distinguished and critical gathering which included the British and American Chiefs of Staff. Always receptive to new ideas, the Americans were keenly interested.

Various sub-committees were formed, each one charged with examining a particular aspect of the Mulberry project—logistics, the design and construction of piers and breakwaters, and physical factors. Gradually the Invasion Harbour took shape.

The Prime Minister himself was anxious to hear about D.M.W.D.'s researches, and he took the chair at a meeting in the Citadel at which Lochner again described the principle of Lilo.

The Staff talks then switched to Washington, and for the next fortnight the small D.M.W.D. team worked as hard as any of them had ever worked before. The routine was always the same: a call at 6.30 a.m.; the first meeting in the War Department at 8.30; lunch snatched in the canteen, followed by further conferences. At 6 p.m. they returned to their hotel for an early dinner, and then had a final working session at which the day's progress was reviewed and preparation was made for the morrow's programme.

On his last day in America Robert Lochner was summoned to the White House to give a twenty-minute talk on the floating breakwater to the Prime Minister and President Roosevelt. A signal had arrived stating that the tests on the rigid-sided models put in hand before the departure from England had proved successful. At this stage, however, Churchill was still intrigued with the possibility that the spectacular experiments with pipes and compressed air might yet yield results, and before Lochner began his talk he inquired a little aggrievedly, "What about my bubbles?" Lochner was loath to disillusion him with a description of the constant setbacks D.M.W.D. had encountered over Bubble Harbour, and, to his relief, General Ismay intervened, remarking tactfully that the trials were still inconclusive.

That night a signal went to England. It was from the Combined

Chiefs of Staff, and announced that Mulberry was to be a British responsibility. There were to be two main harbours, each formed from a combination of blockships, concrete caissons, and floating break-waters. Each was to have Whale piers, and the production of these and the concrete caissons was to be a War Office responsibility. The Admiralty, on the other hand, was to be responsible for the block-ships, the floating breakwaters, and the safe passage of the compo-nent parts of both harbours to the French coast.

A few hours after this message had been dispatched from the Quadrant Conference the Lilo team were heading out over the Atlantic for England. They arrived home to find that the first two full-sized floating breakwaters were nearing completion, but other more momentous news awaited them. The latest tests of the rigid models had exceeded all expectations.

They were thus confronted with an anxious decision. Should they go ahead with the sea balloons? Or should they stake everything on an equally untried floating monster made of steel? Whatever they decided, it would be too late to change their plans again if they were proved wrong. In less than six months the breakwaters would have to be ready for their final trials.

Although projects connected with Mulberry Harbour were claim-ing chief attention in the department, the Wheezers and Dodgers had many other tasks afoot.

Experiments were being carried out with two formidable explosive devices called "Bookrest" and Tureen"; there were trials of a mat for passing troops across soft mud; work was beginning on a "Store-carrying Rocket," which in its early stages behaved as eccentrically as the Panjandrum; and different types of cliff-scaling gear were undergoing rigorous tests.

Bookrest, originally developed to clear spaces in the dense jungle which came right down to the river banks in Burma, consisted of a long canvas hosepipe filled with plastic explosive. To the end of the hose was clamped a huge rocket, which rushed from its resting-place in the bows of an L.C.T. towing several hundred feet of hose behind it. When it fell ashore the explosive in the hosepipe—1700 pounds of it—was then detonated by remote control.

At every stage of its evolution hair-raising incidents occurred. Cooke used to fill the canvas hose by pouring in the explosive and ramming it tight with a kitchen mangle. Quite early on in the trials he discovered that it had to be treated with some caution, for a premature explosion on the beach at Saunton nearly wrecked the house of the local Naval Officer in Charge.

It was thought that the device might be useful for mine-clearance, so exhaustive trials were carried out against mines buried at various depths in wet sand or beneath shallow water. The first time Klemantaski filmed these experiments he emerged from the cover of a Sherman tank on the beach to find the surface of the sea covered with shoals of apparently dead fish. He and Cooke were returning to London that night, and the opportunity was too good to be missed. They borrowed a large basket, and, cramming it full of fish, they carried it to the station.

It was a warm summer evening, and an obliging restaurant-car attendant suggested that the fish would keep fresher if they were tipped into a basin in the bar attached to the coach. Unfortunately, however, the fish were only stunned, and in the cold water they quickly came to life. Soon all service in the restaurant car was brought to a stop, for the bar and the passageway became strewn with convalescent bream and pollack, leaping and squirming in all directions. Whenever Bookrest reaped a similar harvest after that the Wheezers and Dodgers distributed the victims locally!

The chief drawback of Bookrest as a device for mounting on board ship was, once again, the unpredictability of the rockets. There was always the danger of back-blast, which might imperil the landing-craft itself, and it was difficult to find a sure method of securing the rockets to the hose.

Tureen, a similar device, suffered from the same defects. In this case the hose was fired ashore empty, and then a liquid explosive was pumped through it by compressed air. No one was particularly happy about handling this highly temperamental mixture, and Eades had a nerve-racking experience when demonstrating it to a group of senior officers.

The explosive itself was stored in large rubber bottles, and as on this occasion he had to transfer it into a tall metal container he stood on a ladder and the bottles were passed up to him. The fumes soon made him dizzy, and he was only half-way through his task when a loud sizzling sound was heard.

His entire audience wisely took to their heels, but Eades, reflecting that he was too close to the explosive to have any chance of escape, if, indeed, it *was* on the point of detonation, remained in lonely isolation at the top of his ladder, and continued to pour in the remainder of the liquid.

To his vast relief the sizzling noise suddenly ceased, and one by one the spectators reappeared to congratulate him on his sangfroid. Not long afterwards a barge laden with the same substance blew up without any warning or apparent reason in the harbour of a South Coast town, tearing the end off the pier and causing heavy casualties. Tureen was eventually ruled too hazardous to be put into naval service, but a somewhat similar device was later destined to be used ashore by Canadian troops in order to clear a quick passage through a rubble-strewn street. In point of fact, the very reverse occurred, however, for when the hose went into action all the buildings still standing on either side of the street promptly collapsed inwards, rendering it impassable!

The Store-carrying Rocket apparatus consisted of a large container which was towed into the air from a special ramp by a number of 2-inch rockets. Having climbed to its zenith, the container was supposed to float gently to earth on a parachute. Strictly speaking, the development of this device is outside the province of this story, for most of the work took place after D-Day, but early on Richardson and Boswell watched a memorable trial on the south side of Brean Down. When the firing key was pressed the only immediate sign of activity was a feeble puff of smoke from one rocket. Then the container began to crawl laboriously up the ramp. It tottered on the brink, and fell to the beach with a thud. As it struck the ground, however, all the remaining rockets went off at once, and with the drag of the container on the sand most of them wrenched free from their clamps.

Boswell and Richardson, a long way off across the dunes, and well out of the expected line of flight, spent a very unpleasant couple of minutes face downward in the sand, three rockets screaming out of the sky to bury themselves only yards away.

After this the Store-carrying Rocket was treated with great respect by the Wheezers and Dodgers, and Duncan Bruce was all the more astonished when some American naval officers temporarily attached to H.M.S. *Birnbeck* suggested that it might be a good idea to see if a human being could be projected in the container.

"That's quite out of the question," said Bruce firmly. "He'd never stand the degree of G involved."

The Americans looked most disappointed. "I guess you know best, Commander," said their spokesman, "but we've got a man here who's all set to go!"

At Birnbeck experiments were also carried out with equipment for Pluto, the giant cross-Channel pipeline.[1] D.M.W.D. came into this project because the Petroleum Warfare staff needed sea trials in order to find out how the pipe would unwind. Captain J. F. Hutchings, R.N., was attached to the Wheezers and Dodgers to take charge of the pipeline's tests afloat, and the design side of D.M.W.D. made special marker buoys fitted with a mechanism which would bring them to the surface at a predetermined time.

---

[1] The code name was taken from the initial letters of "Pipe Line Under The Ocean."

With the invasion date coming ever nearer, and pressure of work increasing all the time, many of D.M.W.D.'s specialists found themselves roped in to help with jobs outside their normal sphere. An example of this was Donald Currie, the camouflage expert, who spent some time scouring London for a suitable canvas cover for Pluto. He eventually found what he wanted in a shop in the Old Kent Road which seemed to supply almost everything, including particularly fine ropes of Italian hemp, which, he learned regretfully, were not for sale. They had already been reserved for the Public Hangman!

Perhaps the most important of the department's ancillary tasks at this time was the development of cliff-scaling gear. Long before serious preparation for the invasion began Combined Operations had called for a device which would throw a grapnel on to the top of a cliff 200 feet high, trailing a rope which the Commandos could use to climb to the headland. This request was passed to Norway for investigation.

Immediately he thought of the P.A.C. rocket. Designed to carry a line in precisely the same way, it needed only a grapnel head to bite into the ground on the cliff-top, and a suitable launching tripod.

Plans were soon prepared, and when the rocket was fitted with a four-pronged grapnel and 500 feet of stout climbing rope it functioned perfectly. At the north-east corner of Portland Bill they found a suitable cliff to experiment on, and there D.M.W.D. gave a demonstration to a party of Commando officers. In quite a short time half a dozen ropes were dangling down the cliff-face, and ready to be climbed, but the Commando officers—powerfully built, broad-shouldered, and athletic young men—showed only mild interest.

One or two of them were persuaded to climb to the cliff-top, but when Norway asked afterwards if they wanted the device to be put into production they said cautiously that that was probably a matter for their commanding General. They would have to go back and write out a report. No doubt, they said, D.M.W.D. would hear more in due course.

Eventually the Wheezers and Dodgers were informed that, while the Rocket Grapnel was considered very interesting, it was now felt that in actual assault it would be preferable to capture such positions by landing airborne troops on the cliff-head. The Rocket Grapnel was therefore put on the shelf, and for a time D.M.W.D. forgot all about it. Several months later, however, Menhinick had occasion to visit Freshwater, in the Isle of Wight, and, to his surprise, he found a party of Commandos laboriously scaling a high cliff.

They had with them a Swiss guide, dressed in British Army uniform, and his job, apparently, was to climb the cliff first, with the assistance of an ice-axe, and carry up a rope which could be made fast at the top.

Menhinick asked innocently why they were not using the Rocket Grapnel, and when he explained how it worked the Commandos said they thought it was a marvellous idea. Why, they asked, had no one ever told them about it? The discarded apparatus was therefore reclaimed from the store, and a team which included Byng, Menhinick, and Eades held a series of trials near Beachy Head. First of all they fired up a wire bridle and a rope with loops for hand- and foot-holds. Then they experimented with a more ambitious version —a 50-foot rope ladder under which hung 300 feet of doubled line. Seated in a bowline, the climber could be hauled up as far as the ladder by men on the beach below.

Menhinick and Eades used to paddle out to sea in a dory which had a small rocket projector clamped to its side. They found it safest to lie flat on their faces when the rockets went off, but it was quite a feat to move at all in the boat, most of the space being taken up by two huge Schermuly line boxes, with the rope coiled on a series of pegs.

Inevitably there were minor mishaps. On one occasion the Wheezers and Dodgers put a rocket through the bedroom window of a cottage near the cliff-top. On another, Menhinick was trying out the bowline at Birling Gap when he got his battledress caught fast in the block at the foot of the rope ladder. And there he hung, a hundred feet up the cliff-face and unable to move in any direction. He was out of sight of the team below, but by a chance in a million he was spotted by a U.S. film cameraman suspended in a bosun's chair and taking pictures further along the cliff. The latter signalled to the beach party, and the exhausted Menhinick was cut free. The most spectacular incident occurred, however, when the Rocket Grapnel was almost at the end of its trials and ready for service.

In April 1944 a demonstration was staged for Brigadier Lord Lovat at Tennyson Down, in the Isle of Wight. This time Byng, Menhinick, and Eades all went out in the dory, which was then anchored by the stern some distance off shore. They fired the first rocket, and when the grapnel had safely engaged Byng volunteered to make the initial ascent.

Grasping the rope, he stepped off the bow, but there was a slight lop on the water, and as he had forgotten to allow for the slack in the line he disappeared instantly below the surface, only his cap remaining in sight. A second or two later he came up, coughing and spluttering; but, undismayed, he then began the long climb from the sea to the headland.

By the time he had got half-way the amount of sea-water he had swallowed on top of a lobster lunch began to tell on him, and he was almost at the end of his endurance when he saw an inviting grassy ledge on the face of the cliff.

Thankfully he hauled himself on to this and lay down to rest. The minutes went by, and the party on the cliff-top could be seen peering anxiously downward. There was no sign of the climber; only Menhinick and Eades, out at sea, could see what had happened. The ledge on which Byng had subsided had a sharp overhang, and he could get no further. Being a philosophical individual, he had decided that as progress upward was impossible he would take a short nap before making his descent! And there he remained quite happily on his insecure perch until the spring sunshine had dried his saturated uniform.

It was only a few weeks later that the U.S. Rangers used the Rocket Grapnel with spectacular success in their D-Day assault on a German coast battery commanding the assault beaches of "Omaha" and "Utah." Before then, however, Byng had helped to evolve another and far more elaborate kind of cliff-scaling apparatus.

One day in that spring of 1944 a Sapper captain named Holmes called on the firm of Merryweather, in Greenwich High Street. Since the start of the war Merryweathers had been making equipment for all manner of tasks, from the fuelling of ships at sea to radar and bomb-disposal, but for two centuries they had specialized in the building of fire-fighting appliances.

With this in mind their visitor asked if it would be possible to install and operate one of their 100-foot telescopic steel ladders in a D.U.K.W.[1] At first sight this seemed out of the question. They pointed out that the standard fire-fighting ladder and its mechanism weighed 5 tons, and a rough calculation showed that if it was to be installed in a small amphibious craft the weight would have to be cut by half.

When they went further into the problem, however, they found that by discarding the normal turntable and winch and using a different raising mechanism they could reduce the overall weight very substantially. Some tests were carried out with the Brighton Fire Brigade's 100-foot turntable ladder lashed to a landing-craft. Then the Admiralty took over, and to D.M.W.D. fell the task of progressing the job. Byng startled the firm by announcing that five of the special ladders must be ready in six weeks. Normally such an order would have taken nine months to carry out, but the job was given

[1] D.U.K.W.'s, or "Ducks" as they were generally known, were American amphibious trucks "designed to carry a load of 1½ tons in smooth water"— Commander A. B. Stanford, U.S.N.R., *Force Mulberry* (Morrow, New York).

top priority, and D.M.W.D. saw to it that there was no delay in getting the necessary supplies of steel and aluminium to the factory.

Currie had to find some means of camouflaging these large, unwieldy objects. He experimented with netting attached to the canvas covers of the escapes, but at first this gave a lot of trouble. It could only be anchored at the top, and tended to flap, so he went and explained his difficulty to an East End tailor who had helped the department with several previous camouflage problems. The tailor showed him how the material could be cut on a long curve, and as soon as this was done the netting, with its patches of protective colouring, fitted snugly in place.

Three days inside the stipulated time the last of the ladders was ready. They were highly ingenious affairs, each one having two machine-guns mounted at its head, special shields of armour-plating to give some protection to the gunners, and a beach-to-cliff-top telephone. The ladders themselves could be raised to their full height in the brief time it took the craft to clamber from the sea and race across the beach.

It had been impressed on the Greenwich firm that absolute secrecy was vital, and although 500 men and women worked in the factory while these unusual fire-escapes were being built not a hint of their purpose reached the outside world.

Early one morning they were taken from the works, their shape disguised by a dummy framework of baulks of timber, and were driven westward to the Amphibious Wing of the Royal Army Service Corps in North Devon. There they underwent successful trials.

The design and installation of these seagoing ladders in such a short space of time was a remarkable technical feat, for an entirely new method of operating them—using the D.U.K.W.'s winch drive —had had to be devised.

The team working on this rush job for the invasion received a special commendation from the Board of Admiralty. As it turned out, they had done more than fulfil an arduous contract; they had won a race against Fate.

Not long after their task was completed a flying bomb landed in Greenwich. It scored a direct hit on the factory, laying it in ruins.

24

PREPARING FOR NEPTUNE

WHEN the decision was taken at Washington to use floating breakwaters as the outer bastion of the Mulberry Harbours little more than eight months remained before D-Day. An unexpected postponement of the invasion was later to give brief respite to the hard-pressed teams involved in Operation Neptune, as the naval side of the invasion was now known; but even so D.M.W.D.—only one of countless naval organizations working desperately against the clock—faced a task of singular complexity.

In addition to all their other invasion projects they now had to build, assemble, and test more than two miles of an entirely new and untried type of sea barrier. And the highly promising results of the experiments with rigid-sided models, which floated on their own without the need for any huge and fragile balloon envelopes to support them, raised a fresh complication.

The Combined Chiefs of Staff had ruled that the floating breakwater must be sufficiently mobile to be towed across the Channel; it must be capable of being moored in water deep enough to provide shelter for fully laden Liberty ships; and it must be strong enough to withstand winds up to Force 6—the equivalent of 25–31 m.p.h. The Wheezers and Dodgers were told that the breakwater must be ready in all respects by the month of May.[1]

The results of the latest experiments indicated that a full-sized rigid breakwater would comply with all the requirements D.M.W.D. had already accepted for Lilo, and on September 13 the plunge was taken. Although they decided to go ahead still with the trials of the Lilo prototypes, which were expected to provide valuable information on mooring problems, the major effort would be concentrated from now onward on the design and construction of the radically different steel units.

---

[1] The plans called for the completion of two fully established artificial harbours by D plus 14. It was decided that the floating breakwaters should provide some measure of protection to shipping by D plus 4.

At first this improved version was called Hard Lilo, to distinguish it from the rubber-and-concrete structure now awaiting trial in the Channel, but eventually it was given the code name of Bombardon.

The design for the full-scale Bombardon breakwater envisaged a series of hollow steel objects which, viewed end-on, looked like monster Maltese crosses. They would be 200 feet long and just over 25 feet wide, with a draught of 19 feet. On launching, the bottom and side arms would be flooded with sea-water to give the necessary stability. To support this weight the top half of the vertical arm would contain a nest of watertight buoyancy chambers.

To appreciate the magnitude of the Mulberry Harbour project and the rôle which Bombardon was to fill, the complexity of some of the other components involved should be borne in mind.

The Phœnix concrete caissons which were to form the inner breakwater called for 15,000 workmen to build them, and no less than 630,000 tons of concrete. The responsibility for constructing these caissons devolved on the War Office, who were also making the pier roadways and floating pier-heads, but this was not the happiest of arrangements. It had come about because, in the initial stages, the staff requirements for the harbours had been put to the War Office and not to the Admiralty. Enterprisingly enough, the War Office had devoted some attention to the question of harbour design, and long before Mulberry took shape they had prepared plans for various component parts. The virtual monopoly which they eventually held in this field was destined to produce difficulties for the Navy as the date of the invasion drew nearer. It meant that the bulk of the vast construction programme for the artificial harbour was in the hands of a purely military organization with little experience of seamanship, and yet the final responsibility for moving the Mulberry components across the Channel and placing them safely in position devolved on the Royal Navy.

At first the War Office had planned to make the harbour entirely of Phœnix units, but the Admiralty pointed out that if this was done it would take at least a fortnight before any appreciable shelter was available. If during that period the wind blew from the North the whole expedition would find itself in great danger on a dead lee shore.

When Admiral Sir Bertram Ramsay took up his duties as Allied Naval Commander-in-Chief, Expeditionary Force (A.N.C.X.F.), in October he realized the need for a deputy who could co-ordinate all the naval requirements for Mulberry. His choice fell on Rear-Admiral William Tennant, the same immensely capable and imper-

turbable man whose leadership had greatly contributed to the success of the evacuation from Dunkirk in 1940.

Tennant studied the Mulberry plans with some anxiety. His mandate was to create in fifteen days a harbour which would last at least
three months—a harbour which could handle 12,000 tons of stores
and 2500 vehicles daily, while affording protection for Liberty ships,
coasters, and all manner of small craft.

Before building such a harbour in peace-time it would have been
considered essential to spend months surveying the sea-bottom. Here
this was impossible. Heavily mined and littered with obstructions,
the vital area of the Normandy coast was defended by E-boats, and
it lay under the very muzzles of the German shore batteries. The
Allied planners were therefore forced in the early stages to work from
scanty intelligence reports, aerial photographs, and old French charts
based on out-of-date surveys. Early in 1944 this knowledge was fortunately supplemented by a series of audacious raids on the beaches,
and six weeks before D-Day Lieutenant F. M. Berncastle, D.S.C.,
R.N., carried out a fuller survey of the Arromanches area in a small
boat and took a line of soundings. At the time when Admiral Tennant first took stock of the situation, however, there was little reliable
information available about the prospective sites for the Mulberries,
and he wondered, too, how all the ingenious machinery for the floating piers was to be safely delivered.

It seemed to him that insufficient attention had so far been paid to
the towing problem; no one yet knew whether Bombardon would
prove effective; and if they had to rely on the Phœnix caissons, what
would happen in the early stages of the invasion to the mass of
shipping lying off the beaches? Providing that the caissons could be
laid rapidly enough, there would be some shelter at least for the
bigger ships inside the breakwater. But there would not be room
there as well for the thousands of small craft supporting the assault
groups—craft particularly vulnerable to the weather.

Tennant therefore put forward a scheme for several independent
shallow-water shelters, inside which the landing-craft could take
refuge. They would be additional to the two main anchorages—Mulberry A, the American port at St Laurent, and Mulberry B, the
British port at Arromanches—and he proposed that they should be
formed by blockships, which could be sailed across the Channel
under their own power and then sunk in position. The scheme was
adopted, and these shallow-water shelters were given the code name
of Gooseberry.

The Gooseberry harbours added a major commitment to the naval
programme, but the Allied planners had a much greater headache
than this in store for them. When Field-Marshal Montgomery

arrived from the Mediterranean in January 1944 to take up his post as Military Commander he came to the conclusion that the plans for Operation Overlord must be recast to provide for an assault by five divisions instead of three. This involved extending the front by twenty-five miles, considerably increasing the scale of gunnery support, and the Royal Navy were called upon to find a thousand more landing-craft, in addition to hundreds of additional warships and minesweepers. In the circumstances there was only one course open to the Allied Command, and the date for the invasion was put back by a month, from May 1 to June 5.

To the Wheezers and Dodgers the postponement came as a welcome relief. Before work could begin on building the 96 full-scale Bombardons required for the two harbours over 300 separate experiments had to be carried out with scale models to check the theory of wave-suppression by the new floating units and determine the towing and mooring data necessary for full-scale operations.

Most of these intricate tests were made in the tank at Haslar, where a miniature Mulberry Harbour was created. The mooring problem needed particularly careful study. Normally, when ships are moored in a line, gaps approximately the length of each vessel are left ahead and astern. Such gaps could not, however, be permitted between the Bombardons, for this would have allowed waves to pass through and build up again inside the harbour to as much as three-quarters of their original height. Eventually it was decided to compromise, using a 50-foot gap and mooring the units in pairs between buoys. To reduce the wave-movement inside the breakwater still further, D.M.W.D.'s plans called for two parallel lines of Bombardons, 800 feet apart. Tests at Haslar had shown that if this was done the energy of the waves would diminish to one-tenth of their original force.

The model tests indicated that a full-sized Bombardon breakwater would suppress the biggest waves predicted for the period of the Overlord operation, and the expenditure in material would be less than a tenth of that required for any alternative method. The problem it posed in both materials and manpower was, however, still formidable. Over 25,000 tons of steel were needed, as well as a thousand tons of nuts and bolts. The task of building the units, for which sites were allocated at Tilbury and the King George V Dock at Southampton, was to occupy a labour force of 1700 men for six months.

Before making their final plans the Admiralty closely examined all available production resources, and in view of the heavy demands of the other Services they decided that Bombardon would have to be built by mass-producing a prefabricated structure, the various components being bolted together in the final assembly. A bolted construction would not have been contemplated by a naval architect in peace-time, but now it was Hobson's choice; there was simply not the skilled labour available for riveting and welding.

Since there was little information about the behaviour of waves readily available Robert Lochner decided to set up an observation post on the Sussex coast. The Wheezers and Dodgers took over a lighthouse at Newhaven, special recording instruments were installed, and a pretty Wren Petty Officer, Mary Lee, who had worked on a wide variety of jobs for the department, was posted there as resident 'caretaker.' Unfortunately D.M.W.D. forgot to notify the Naval Officer in Charge, Newhaven, that they were setting up this mysterious establishment in his command, and the N.O.I.C., a retired Vice-Admiral, was greatly incensed. Before long, however, the strange researches proceeding in the lighthouse began to intrigue him, and he would arrive almost daily on the breakwater to inspect progress invariably accompanied by two disdainful pekinese dogs.

The wave calculations which interested him so much were registered by an electrical recorder. These statistics were supplemented by visual observation, and Lochner, Byng, Urwin, and Quick spent hours on the cliffs timing the duration of the waves with a stopwatch. Gradually heights and lengths were linked with wind speed and fetch, and then the distinguished figure of Penney descended on the establishment to analyse the data they had collected. His calculations fascinated the lighthouse team, who watched him cover page after page of his notebooks with graceful, curling wave symbols. When asked by a visiting R.N.V.R. officer to explain what Penney was doing Quick replied, "We're not quite sure, but we think he's composing a concerto!"

The first two prototypes of Bombardon were ready by the end of December. They were brought round to Newhaven and moored there for observation, but almost immediately came an unwelcome setback. A sudden gale sprang up, and the units broke their backs. Fortunately an initial structural weakness was soon tracked down. By the end of January Admiral Tennant was able to report that the floating units were being materially strengthened, and would shortly undergo more intensive trials in Weymouth Bay.

Newhaven was deserted in favour of Weymouth because conditions in the latter area more closely approximated to those on the Normandy coast. Fifteen Bombardons were now moored in the bay —an outer row of nine and an inner row of six—and elaborate arrangements were made for recording the height, length, and period

of the waves on either side of the breakwaters. For this purpose new
and complicated apparatus had to be specially devised. Two 70-foot
masts were erected on the sea-bed, and on these were mounted rows
of watertight float switches which gave a direct recording of each
individual wave. Other types of recorder were placed inside the
Bombardons themselves.

The first full-scale trial of the floating breakwater took place on
April 1–2. And it provided just the test for which Lochner had been
hoping. An onshore gale, with a Force 7 wind gusting up to Force
8, brought heavy seas, but the Bombardons cushioned the waves so
effectively that in the lee of the lines of steel bastions the crew of an
American minesweeper found it possible to lower a small boat, row
about, and then board the ship again without any difficulty. When
the gale subsided Captain C. N. E. Curry, R.N., whom the Admiralty had placed in operational control of Bombardon, signalled that
the floating harbour had successfully withstood for ten hours a stress
twice as great as the breakwater had been designed to meet, repelling
waves 8 feet high and 200 feet long.

While Bombardon was being prepared for this trial Admiral
Tennant had to grapple with many other problems assailing this
gigantic harbour enterprise. One hitch occurred when the time came
to try out the raising of the Phœnix caissons. The pumping plant on
which the War Office had been relying to expel the sea-water ballast
from these enormous hollow structures worked too slowly, and it
became necessary to make additional vent-holes in the concrete sides
of the caissons.

This crisis brought an SOS to the Wheezers and Dodgers, and
the job was tackled by Brinsmead, using specially shaped explosive charges. Ever since the Hedgehog days he had been
experimenting at Whitchurch with the focusing of explosives, and
he was able to operate quickly and successfully on the submerged
Phœnixes. He knew a great deal about the effect of explosives
on concrete, for he had long been concentrating on this very subject to overcome a problem which was worrying the Overlord
planners.

One of the vital invasion requirements was the capture, and use at
the earliest possible moment, of the major Channel ports, so that
supplies could keep pace with the advancing armies. The Mulberry
Harbours were essentially a short-term project; they could not compete with the potentialities of permanent ports like Cherbourg,
Boulogne , and Antwerp. It was, however, well realized that the
enemy would do everything in their power to deny the use of such
ports to the Allies, and the approaches would almost certainly be
blocked by concrete-filled wrecks.

A GENERAL VIEW OF MULBERRY B,
THE BRITISH-BUILT INVASION
HARBOUR AT ARROMANCHES

Swiss Roll, the Royal Navy's floating roadway,
can be seen on the right of the picture.

War Office official photograph

ADMIRAL SIR WILLIAM TENNANT, FLAG
OFFICER IN CHARGE OF MULBERRY
AND PLUTO

OBLIQUE VIEW OF MULBERRY B,
LOOKING TOWARDS THE SOUTH-WEST

A BATTERY OF ROCKET GUNS OPERATED BY A TEAM FROM D.M.W.D.
DURING FLYING-BOMB ATTACKS ON THE SOUTH COAST AFTER D-DAY

ONE OF THE SAME WEAPONS IN ACTION DURING A NIGHT RAID

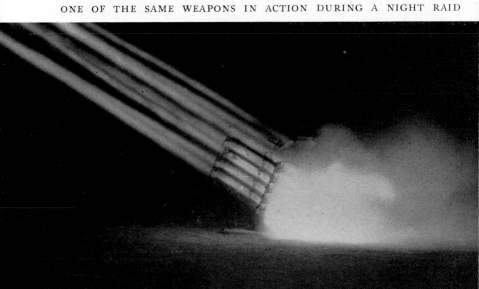

if they were turning to ice. To make matters worse the force of the explosion displaced his face-piece, with its breathing-tube, and instantly it filled with water.

For a long time after they had been brought ashore Pratt, Case, and Lieutenant Guy Boissard, R.N.V.R., an Australian who had asked to be allowed to take part in the experiments, all suffered from splitting headaches. It was therefore decided not to shorten the distance any further, for it seemed all too likely that they might be stunned, seriously injured, or drowned; but they carried on with the tests, trying each of the different suits in turn. As many as four times in a day they went down into the icy depths of the lake. The ordeal left them battered and tired, with excruciating aches in the knees, elbows, and shoulders. In time the pain spread to smaller joints like the wrists and fingers, and was to persist for several weeks.

The trials had to go on, for they still needed more data, and there was less than a month left. By now the three naval officers realized that if they were to continue the experiments unaided the physical punishment they were absorbing might soon affect their judgment and powers of observation. So a third series of underwater tests was launched with a fresh team of volunteers headed by a young New Zealander, Sub-Lieutenant W. J. L. Smith.

Like Boissard, Smith had been serving in submarines; and he shared the Australian's keen interest in applying scientific method to naval problems. The lake party now included two members of the Submarine Escape Training Section at H.M.S. *Dolphin*, Mr R. V. Rowkins, a Commissioned Boatswain, and Chief Petty Officer Watson; and a notable character in Chief Stoker George ("but me mates call me Barge!") Evans. On the technical side valuable assistance was given by Lieutenant-Commander W. O. Shelford, the Navy's greatest diving expert.

In bitter winds and chill water the hazardous work continued. Often when they were brought to the surface of the lake the battered and semi-conscious men had great difficulty in describing their strange new experiences to the waiting scientists. But they stuck to their task, and all the information which Pratt needed was finally secured.

It is not possible to recount the precise steps which were taken to neutralize the effect of explosions underwater, but the protective suit which was produced in time for use on the sea-bed at Cherbourg was triumphantly successful. Wearing it, the "P" Parties, as the frogmen who volunteered for this dangerous mission were officially known, searched over two million square feet of the port. Much of the time they were in total darkness, and had to fight their way through deep mud, with wreckage of all descriptions littering their path, but they located and destroyed hundreds of mines.[1]

Magnificent as their achievement was, the frogmen owed more than they knew to the self-sacrifice of that small band of scientists and sailors who had ventured into the unknown on the bed of Horsea Lake.

[1] In *Frogmen*, by T. J. Waldron and James Gleeson (Evans, 1950), occurs the following passage: "Not long before D-Day a special jacket had been invented to protect us against that terrible blast which can be experienced when a mine or shell explodes under water. Known as a Kapok jacket . . . it proved a most wonderful thing, and saved the lives of no less than three of my men."

25

THE MIRACULOUS PORT

As each part of the prefabricated harbours was finished it had to be towed from the construction berth to make room for the the next job. Finding suitable assembly areas for the vast conglomeration of harbour equipment was no easy problem, for there were 60 blockships, nearly 150 Phœnix caissons, some hundred sections of the floating breakwater, and miles of pier roadway.

To keep them safe until they were needed the Phœnix units were sunk on the bed of the Channel. This operation was not as easy as it sounded, for the concrete monsters were most particular about what they sat on. Unless the sea-bed was perfectly flat and in shallow water they were liable to crack and give endless trouble when the time came for the dispatching parties to pump them out and prepare them for their long journey.

Dungeness and Selsey were chosen as reception centres for the caissons, and as D-Day drew near they presented an amazing sight. The Phœnixes were as big as a block of flats. In Admiral Tennant's words it looked for all the world as if "some one had picked up Chicago and put it down on the Sussex foreshore." Additional parking areas were found for about five miles of pier roadway at Peel Bank and Marchwood, opposite Southampton, and the scene in the Solent was equally bizarre, the towering pier-heads suggesting that some vast factory had risen from the water.

The piers and pier-heads fitted together like a giant Meccano set, and their brilliantly ingenious design calls for some description. At the shore end the piers were secured to heavy ramps. As the metal roadway ran seaward over a succession of concrete barges, called Beetles, which supported it, every sixth span was telescopic to allow for the twist and sag of the pier in heavy weather.

At the seaward end the roadway was moored to "Spud" pier-heads—great floating platforms with steel legs at each corner. The inspiration for their design came from a certain type of dredger which had once ridden out a West Indies hurricane so violent that all other shipping in the area had been driven ashore to destruction.

The whole of this intricate equipment had been designed and produced under the direction of Major-General D. J. McMullen, the Director of Transportation at the War Office, and his able and forceful deputy, Brigadier Bruce White.[1]

With such an array of ships and strange marine objects assembling off the South Coast of England it seemed inconceivable that the enemy should remain ignorant of what was afoot. The naval forces alone taking part in Operation Neptune included 8 battleships and monitors, 22 cruisers, 93 destroyers, nearly 450 escorts and mine-sweepers, and 360 M.L.'s, M.T.B.'s, and kindred craft; the berthing overflow extended to Milford Haven and Harwich, the Humber, Belfast, and the Clyde.

To confuse the watchers on the enemy coast a cover plan was devised to suggest that the main landing would take place in the Pas de Calais, and the dumps of Phœnix caissons at Dungeness, easily visible from Boulogne, assisted in this deception.

In assessing the Allied intentions, however, the enemy were decisively handicapped by the inability of their air-reconnaissance units to maintain any proper survey over the South Coast of England as a whole. Days went by without a single report of any value reaching von Rundstedt's headquarters, and the Allied naval H.Q. at Southwick Park, a Georgian country house hidden in the woods near Portsmouth, remained undetected from the air. There the only signs of enemy activity were the flying bombs, which passed regularly overhead towards Southampton.[2]

Throughout this overture to Overlord the activities of the Wheezers and Dodgers were manifold. For months past Dove and others had been developing a variety of devices to confuse the enemy's radar from the moment the invasion fleet sailed. There were rockets and shells which emitted coils of aluminium wire to baffle the range-finding of the German coastal batteries. To draw the enemy fire away from major targets another group of objects was produced simulating forces which did not, in fact, exist at all. Different types of reflector again made quite small craft look like battle-ships on the radar screen, while cruisers appeared no bigger than fishing vessels.

D.M.W.D. designed special radar marking buoys to keep the Allied bombarding ships dead on course during their night approach

---

[1] Now Major-General Sir Donald McMullen, K.B.E., C.B., D.S.O. Brigadier Sir Bruce White, knighted for his services in 1944, was Director of Ports and Inland Waterways at the War Office.

[2] At this parkland headquarters it was forbidden to walk in the fields, for the trodden grass would have shown up plainly in aerial photographs. All the permitted entrance and exit routes were indicated by white pegs or painted lines. Over these paths camouflage netting was spread.

to the French coast. To the untrained observer these must have looked simple enough to make—just a large flag flying from a mast —but their effective operation depended on many highly technical factors, and the state of the sea, the height of the reflector above the surface, and the direction of the wind relative to the German radar sets all had to be taken into account.

Donald Currie was kept busy with the camouflage of Bombardon and Pluto and the concealment of small craft hiding up in rivers and creeks as they waited for D-Day. At Birnbeck a team headed by Coulson and Bruce was putting the finishing touches to Helter Skelter.

At the last minute the Army had asked for some means of speeding up the transfer of men and their equipment from troopships to the decks of the landing-craft. Scrambling nets, they had decided, were far from satisfactory.

So D.M.W.D. designed a tube from which stretched a long, rubberized canvas chute. The far end of this could be held quite easily by two men standing on the deck of a landing-craft; all that the soldier needed to do was to clamber in, feet first, and hurtle to the bottom.

They tried out the Helter Skelter at a factory in South London, and after several apprehensive workmen had been dispatched to earth from the fourth floor of the building without injuring themselves the device was taken to Birnbeck for more searching tests. There they soon discovered that modifications were necessary, for when it was used by some soldiers with full kit one man tore a strip clean down the canvas tunnel with the foresight of his rifle; the rest of his platoon, following close behind, all fell straight into the sea!

Bruce removed this hazard by inserting a bonded canvas lining inside the main chute. This embodied a safety-device to give prompt warning of any undue wear, and they now felt sufficiently confident to invite a detachment of American troops, quartered near by, to give Helter Skelter a thorough trial.

Fifty stalwart members of the United States Army paraded at the end of the pier, and to the N.C.O. in charge of them Bruce explained the object of the exercise. The men were to enter the tube in quick succession and dive forty feet into a small boat moored below.

Walking to the edge of the pier, the Sergeant took one look at the boat bobbing far beneath him, and declined Bruce's invitation with considerable emphasis! So Boswell and John Wide gave a demonstration. After that there was no holding the American Army, who spent the rest of the afternoon hurling themselves off the pier. They enjoyed themselves so hugely that Boswell had some difficulty in persuading them to return to their base.

The Helter Skelter was then passed for service, and Coulson supervised its installation on board a number of Castle Line troopships.

A few days before the invasion Admiral Tennant took Field-Marshal Smuts round the mass of landing-craft and other vessels lying off Spithead. Staring out over the crowded anchorage, Smuts remarked thoughtfully, "If this fails we shall have to start afresh, and perhaps take two years to build it all up again."

At the time Tennant could not envisage failure, particularly on the naval side, every facet of which he had been studying for months. Later he was to recall vividly what Smuts had said, but on this St Crispin's Eve the very scope and scale of the Allied preparations seemed to defy the possibility of disaster.

As far as the Wheezers and Dodgers were concerned the trials of Bombardon had been a complete success. They knew the floating breakwater would stand up to the weather conditions which the planners had specified. Robert Lochner, however, could not altogether rid himself of doubts about the safety-margin which had been set.

Bombardon was designed to contend with seas corresponding to winds of Force 6—no more and no less. Ostensibly this estimate was based on convincing weather statistics alone; while conceding that winds of much greater force often blew in the Channel, the meteorologists had reported that this rarely happened in the month of June. The planners therefore accepted this figure—but in point of fact they had no alternative. If they had called for a breakwater capable of withstanding any greater stress this would have complicated the constructional problem, and Bombardon might not have been built in time. Possibly, too, the view of the Army that *their* units could not be designed to stand up to Force 8 winds and seas had a bearing on the readiness of the planning staff to regard Force 6 as the desirable target figure.

The original estimate given to D.M.W.D. for a sea corresponding to a Force 6 wind set the maximum height of the waves at 8 feet and their length at 100 feet. Experiments at Newhaven and Weymouth showed this to be inaccurate, and the figures were increased to 10 feet and 150 feet. While the Weymouth trials had proved that Bombardon could stand up to heavier seas than this for a limited period, it was impossible to foretell what might happen if a prolonged spell of really bad weather occurred during the invasion.

From the start the Wheezers and Dodgers had recognized the obvious objections to mooring a floating object broadside on to the wind. If such an object was to withstand heavy seas over a long period Lochner maintained that it needed to be riveted and welded like a ship. This was particularly the case with the Bombardons, for, in view of the high rise and fall of tide off the Normandy coast and the deep draught of the Liberty ships using the harbours, the floating units would have to be moored in at least 70 feet of water. This placed a considerable strain on their moorings.

Voicing his anxiety to Admiral Wake-Walker, Lochner pointed out that during trials at Newhaven two of the units had broken apart. One was eventually washed up on the beach, and examination showed that the bolts had worked out. His request for a change in the method of construction was reluctantly but inevitably refused; there were not enough welders available to tackle the job. A modified design was, however, introduced, strips of iron being welded across part of the top, the side-fins, and the bottom of the breakwater units. It was only a compromise, but it was better than nothing.

Lochner asked for one further safety-measure. He wanted explosive cutters attached to the mooring cables at one end of each Bombardon. If a severe storm did come these cutters could be operated from the shore, and the floating units would then ride head to sea. Unfortunately, however, there was not time to incorporate this device.

The morning of June 4 brought warning of gales in the Channel, and after anxiously studying the 'met' reports General Eisenhower took his historic decision to postpone the invasion by twenty-four hours.

At 8.15 P.M. on the same day he issued a new order. The assault on the coast of France would be launched on June 6.

When the invasion fleet put to sea the first sections of the floating breakwater sailed with it from Portland. Before following their progress we must turn to other momentous events in which the Wheezers and Dodgers had a hand.

Five hours before zero hour a force of small craft left Newhaven and headed towards Dieppe, towing a number of the department's radar 'foxing' devices. By simulating an earlier attack to the eastward they hoped to draw off attention from the Bay of Caen, and the R.A.F. co-operated in this manœuvre.

Dove also had twelve minesweepers flying 'magic' balloons. These anchored off Selsey Bill until H.Hour arrived, and then went over with the heavy ships forming the bombarding force. When the cruisers opened up on the distant shore batteries the minesweepers circled in the smoke-screen to draw the fire of the enemy.

The assault force included 45 Hedgerows. The small landing-craft (L.C.A.'s) in which they were mounted were, unhappily, ill-equipped to face the conditions they encountered during their approach to France. Of one flotilla of nine, eight sank in heavy seas, but the Hedgerows which reached the beaches on time did magnificent work.

L.C.A. 712, commanded by Lieutenant R. Murray, R.N.V.R., had an adventurous passage. While still off the Isle of Wight she sustained damage from the rising seas; then there was difficulty in slipping the tow; and no sooner had they arrived on their assault station than the armoured doors were blown inward by a 6-inch shell. Under heavy small-arms fire Murray pressed home his attack, and saw his salvo of bombs explode half-way up the beach near Bernières Church.

L.C.A. 1071 (Sub-Lieutenant P. C. Lennard Payne, R.N.V.R.) had an even more eventful time. She shipped a considerable amount of water on the voyage, and the tow eventually parted. At 0745, however, she was in position off the enemy shore, and Payne sighted his target—a gap in the sea wall filled with sandbags and overlooked by a prominent landmark, a green house.

He held on his course, and, narrowly missing a beach obstacle with a mine attached to its top, he fired his Hedgerow. "As we turned I saw the bombs burst in and beyond the wall. Immediately we came under heavy small-arms fire from the green house and several bullets passed through our ensign." In seas which constantly threatened to capsize her L.C.A. 1071 struggled back to the rendezvous with her parent ship and was hoisted inboard.

L.C.A. 876 was taken in so close by her commanding officer, Lieutenant F. H. Penfold, Royal Marines, that she was almost aground when she fired. Her Hedgerow bombs blew a tremendous breach in the sea wall, and, as she withdrew, her crew watched Allied tanks forging through the gap.

Despite the heavy casualties they suffered these small craft and their formidable new weapons did great execution in this opening phase of the attack; Brigadier F. V. C. Knox, commanding the 69th Infantry Brigade, described them as invaluable in getting his men safely ashore.

Soon after 7 A.M. the cliff-scaling gear went into action. Three companies of the U.S. Rangers stormed ashore at Pointe du Hoe, three miles west of Omaha Beach, where an almost sheer cliff confronted them. At first sight it looked impregnable, and the Germans thinking that no one would be able to climb it, had left the immediate vicinity only lightly defended.

The Rangers shot up their Rocket Grapnels, and under covering fire from two destroyers they rapidly scaled the cliff-face.[1] A subsequent attack on the enemy's defensive positions from the rear enabled them to achieve a notable tactical success.

The Allies had expected to fight every inch of the way ashore on that morning of D-Day. In many sectors, however, the initial oppo-

[1] Wilmot, *The Struggle for Europe.*

sition was slight, and an officer on board H.M.S. *Mauritius* was able to describe the early proceedings as "a crashing anti-climax."[1] The tremendous bombardment by sea and air failed to destroy the well-protected enemy batteries, but it forced their guns' crews to take cover.

As a result Cooke's rescue vessel, H.M.S. *Hiker*, which had been made ready to act as a casualty ship, remained at anchor off the Isle of Wight. She was never called upon to fill this rôle.

The first of all the five thousand ships and craft to move in the invasion were the blockships. There were sixty of these, among them the old British battleship *Centurion*, the French battleship *Courbet*, the British and Dutch cruisers *Durban* and *Sumatra*, and merchant ships which had been launched as far back as 1903.

This veteran fleet, which was to form the Gooseberry shelters, was so old and so slow that many of the ships had had to begin their long journey from Northern ports six days before D-Day. Their best speed was less than 6 knots, but every one reached her destination on time. There was some anxiety whether they would go down on an even keel; if they turned over with their masts inward they might obstruct the harbour. So they were ballasted, and charges were placed in each hold. These were blown simultaneously, and each ship settled down at precisely the right angle.

By the time the last of the blockships were being sunk the Phœnix caissons were arriving. Their placing, too, was no easy matter. The tide had to be slack and the wind light. And when the sea-cocks were opened the tugs had to hold the monsters extremely accurately as they subsided on the bottom.

Each harbour had its planter, Commander R. K. Silcock, R.N., and Lieutenant-Commander A. M. D. Lampen, R.N., showing great skill in this highly specialized task. And the tugs were splendidly handled by their American masters.

The placing of the Bombardons was carried out by a fleet of carriers, net-layers, and Boom Defence vessels. The first lay took place on D plus 1; by D plus 6 the floating breakwater at Mulberry A was complete, and within twenty-four hours the Bombardons off the British harbour were also safely moored.

Although the laying of the units had proceeded without a hitch, the Wheezers and Dodgers were disturbed at a late decision to install the units as a single line, and not in double lines, as successfully tried at Weymouth. They were also anchored a good deal deeper than had been originally intended.

On the day after the breakwater at Arromanches had been finished

[1] Commander Kenneth Edwards, *Operation Neptune* (Collins, 1946), p. 134.

Lochner and Richardson crossed to France to examine it. It was blowing hard, and quite an appreciable sea was running, but the Bombardons were not pitching or rolling to any marked extent, and the water on the lee side was calm, the waves being cut down to as little as 18 inches. Above the long line of metal casings hung a cloud of spray rising to 20 feet—visible proof that the units were repulsing the oncoming waves—and while Richardson and Lochner rowed about, taking measurements of the sea inside and outside the break-water, unloading operations in the harbour were proceeding without interruption.

For the first fortnight the blockships and the floating breakwaters provided practically all the sheltered water used by the invading forces. During that period a great host of men and vast quantities of stores were successfully landed, and a supply position was established on shore sufficient to secure the bridgehead against any counter-attack which the Germans might launch.

The harbours, however, were not yet complete. In all, 1,500,000 tons of harbour equipment had to be brought across the Channel—an operation calling for 150 Allied tugs—and although by D plus 12 most of the Phœnix caissons were in position the weather had held up some of the more difficult tows. The massive sections of pier road-way gave the greatest trouble. They did not enjoy being towed unless the sea was nearly dead calm, and great struggles went on to keep them afloat during their 90-mile voyage.

At least seven miles of this pier roadway was still waiting on the English side, and with this problem on his hands Admiral Tennant was greatly relieved when Sunday, June 18, brought "a wonderful, calm summer evening . . . so calm in fact that I could follow a ripple right the way to the horizon."

As he left the beachhead in a destroyer a signal informed him that 23 tows of roadway, pier-head components, and Phœnix units had just been sailed for the French coast. "I remember thinking that my staff had done well to take prompt advantage of the new trend in the weather," he recalls; "the 'met' report was excellent, with a high barometer and a good forecast."

That very night, however, a sudden and disastrous change oc-curred. A warm front had been moving north from the Gulf of Lions, and without warning the great invasion fleet and the still unfinished harbours were struck by the worst gale the Channel had known for forty years.

Heading straight into the mælstrom, the mass of pier equipment still on its way to France had no hope of riding the storm. Only one and a half tows survived. Freshening all the time, a violent north-easterly wind drove mountainous seas on to the two Mulberries, and the spring tides aggravated the situation, for there was deeper water inside the harbours.

Hundreds of landing-craft managed to get under the lee of the blockships, and there they held on desperately, with little food, sleep, or even rest. Hundreds more, less fortunate, were driven ashore.

The American harbour at St Laurent suffered worst. Mulberry A had been built very quickly, but it had been placed in somewhat deeper water than the planners had intended, and it was, in any case, in a much more exposed position than the British harbour at Arromanches, the latter being partially protected by the Calvados Reef. To make matters worse the Americans had planted their blockships too hurriedly, laying both ends of the arc first and leaving huge gaps in the centre. This had been done to ensure easy communication with the shore for their assault craft, but the scheme greatly reduced the shelter which the line of blockships afforded. And it was these blockships which met the full fury of the gale.

Some, including the old battleship *Centurion*, broke their backs. As the sea scoured away the sand, which was deeper and more shifting than in the British harbour, other blockships settled right down on the bottom.

Although only four Phœnix units disintegrated at Mulberry B, the Americans' main caisson breakwater, sited at a different angle, suffered a frontal assault from the waves and rapidly broke up. The chaos of Mulberry A was multiplied by the fact that the harbour had been crammed to overflowing with ships. Many of these, breaking adrift, bore down on the Whale Piers, sinking the floating supports and crumpling the steel roadways like paper.

What of Bombardon? From the start of the gale these outer bastions of the two harbours were pounded by seas over 15 feet high and 300 feet long. The stress set up was far beyond that which they had been designed to meet. But for thirty hours the steel curtain stood this ferocious battering. Thereafter the gale made a clean sweep.[1]

The storm was still raging when Admiral Tennant sent Lochner

---

[1] In his account of the great gale (*Force Mulberry*) Commander Alfred Stanford, U.S.N.R., deputy commander of Mulberry A, has suggested that the floating breakwaters hastened the destruction of the American harbour. "Far out in the murk the worst possible hazard had occurred. The 200-ft. long, semi-submerged steel units of the Bombardon floating breakwater had torn loose. Flung by the sea, these long narrow steel objects Commander Ards had tended so faithfully had become battering rams. It was the Bombardons, torn loose and flailing against the Phœnix, which may well have breached the Phœnix wall."

The official report of N.O.I.C. Arromanches, dated August 19, 1944, makes it plain that in the British harbour, at any rate, the Bombardons there "damaged neither the few Phœnix then in place, nor the ships and craft, numbering about 500, sheltering under the lee of the Gooseberry" when they broke free and drifted ashore.

over in an M.L. to obtain an estimate of the damage. Lochner arrived with Byng to find ships galore piled up on the Calvados Reef. One end of Mulberry B was breaking up fast, but fortunately the British blockships had been planted almost entirely in the natural shelter of the Reef.

The ultimate failure of Bombardon there had apparently started with the collapse of the structure of one particular unit. After that the added strain on the bolted parts of the others had caused inevitable and progressive disintegration. At Mulberry A it seemed that a coupling connecting one of the Bombardons to its moorings had first given way.

After the gale had spent itself Tennant went over to confer with Rear-Admiral Allan B. Kirk, commanding the Western Task Force. They decided that it was out of the question to attempt to rebuild the American harbour in its original form; only 1200 feet of harbour components were left out of the one and a half miles they had laid down. The Americans therefore readily agreed to strengthen and expand the harbour at Arromanches with all the pier equipment which could be salvaged from St Laurent. Filling up and double-banking their own blockship breakwater, they converted Mulberry A into a two-fathom shelter.

In his *Struggle for Europe* the late Chester Wilmot raises an interesting point about the outcome of this decision:

> Undismayed, the Americans applied their talent for invention and organization. . . . During July they handled more than twice the tonnage of the British Mulberry. This achievement has led to the suggestion that the vast expenditure of effort and materials on the artificial harbours was unnecessary . . . the same effort could have been achieved far more economically with a few hundred more landing craft and ferries.

He goes on to point out, however, that the Allies were short of landing-craft when planning for Overlord began, and the possession of an artificial harbour gave us the freedom to land well away from heavily defended areas. It also gave confidence to the Allied High Command. At the time when the gale struck ammunition was running low ashore. Admiral Tennant therefore decided to carry on unloading, using what protection Mulberry B could still provide, and some 800 tons of stores and 1200 men were landed in a day.

When it was finally completed on D plus 40 the harbour at Arromanches was a truly remarkable enterprise. Two miles long by a mile broad, it was maintained by a force of over 5000 officers and men of the Royal Navy, and a fleet of hundreds of specialized craft, including port-construction ships, boom-defence vessels, tankers, ferries, floating cranes, and floating docks. The harbour was defended

against air attack by nearly 200 Army guns, as well as the guns of
the fleet; on the Eastern flank two miles of nets acted as a trap for
infernal machines, long-range torpedoes, one-man submarines, and
drifting mines.

The scale of the operations which it assisted is best conveyed by
cold statistics. In the first seven weeks the Allies landed 1,500,000
men with their arms, equipment, and supplies, as well as more than
322,000 vehicles and 1,500,000 tons of stores.

At Arromanches Swiss Roll was in continual use as the Royal
Navy's own pier for bringing ashore men and supplies. Hamilton's
floating bridge had, however, already played a far more important
part in the success of the invasion—as an instrument in the cover
plan for misleading the enemy over Allied intentions. The knowledge that this highly mobile type of sea bridge was in production
was one of many factors which contributed to German indecision
over the likely point of assault.

On July 23 the Prime Minister visited Mulberry B, and on his
return to England he paid his own eloquent tribute in a signal to the
Naval Officer in Charge, Captain Harold Hickling: "This miraculous port has played, and will continue to play, a most important
part in the liberation of Europe."

In the making of that port the Wheezers and Dodgers had played
their part, too. For them this was the last chapter. Mulberry Harbour
was the threshold of occupied Europe. And once the armies of liberation had crossed that threshold the end of the long struggle was in
sight.

D.M.W.D. had been born under the gunfire of Dunkirk. During
that last desperate stand on French soil a naval officer was flying
anti-aircraft kites in a vain endeavour to check low-level attacks by
the Luftwaffe on the beachhead.

Four years later the same naval officer—one of the founder members of the Wheezers and Dodgers—landed once again on the shores
of France on the morning of D-Day. He had just finished a mission
in which other more ingenious kinds of kite—this time created by
naval scientists and flown from craft under his command—had
assisted in the confusion of the enemy.

As he stood on the beach near Arromanches, watching the troops
and guns pouring ashore, a young officer in battledress shouted a
welcome. It was Ron Eades, who told him of the Rangers' success
with the Rocket Grapnel in their cliff assault farther to the east.

"What are you going to do now?" Eades asked.

"The war's just about over for me," said John Dove. "I think I
shall go back to England, get into plain clothes, and go fishing. What
about you?"

"I have to go to Bayeux, but I shan't be far behind you. See you later," Eades said to him.

He saluted in farewell, and Dove stood watching him as he strode quickly away up the beach to rejoin a party of waiting Americans.

Lieutenant Eades never came back. Later that morning he was killed in action as the Allied armies drove inland from the beachhead.

With many projects still under development D.M.W.D. continued to function as an Admiralty department until the autumn of the following year. Most of their work was then taken over by a new organization set up to deal with Craft and Amphibious Material.

"It seems unlikely that the scope of the development section will remain virtually unlimited, or that in peace-time it will be able to enjoy the unrestricted methods of working which have been so fruitful during its five and a half years of lively activity," ends a technical survey of D.M.W.D.'s achievements now in the Admiralty archives.

It would be, perhaps, unreasonable to expect that such an organization, essential in war, should be maintained under peace-time conditions. The urgency of war places a premium on speed. And to achieve speed of decision and execution it is often necessary to employ methods which might be quite impractical, financially and otherwise, for a Service department in days of peace.

It was the complete freedom to experiment, the freedom to tackle unorthodox projects in an unorthodox way, which was the basis of D.M.W.D.'s success. And it was greatly to the credit of the Admiralty that they allowed such a free hand to an organization whose approach to most problems must have seemed revolutionary in the extreme.

Writing to the author, Admiral of the Fleet Lord Fraser of North Cape, Controller of the Navy at the time when D.M.W.D. was a precocious newcomer to the Admiralty, and later First Sea Lord, said of the Wheezers and Dodgers: "Their job could only have been done if they were unhampered by routine work. A similar sort of weapon-thinking department will undoubtedly be required again should war ever come."

That was a verdict delivered a decade after D.M.W.D.'s end. In the rapid march of science in the development of the new Royal Navy it is perhaps not wishful thinking to imagine that something of the inspiration of the Wheezers and Dodgers lives on.

The value of the department was shown by the findings of the Royal Commission on Awards to Inventors, which, sitting long after the war was over, and sifting all the evidence with judicial impartiality, made substantial grants to many of its officers, including Goodeve, Richardson, Lochner, Terrell, and Goodfellow. To mention only

"I TRUST THE REQUIREMENT HAS BEEN MET, SIR"!

I.A/A.W.& D. — D.A.A.W. — D.M.W.D.

ADMIRALTY 1939/46

FIRST REUNION at SIMPSON'S-IN-THE-STRAND

Friday, May 8, 1953

In the Chair:
Commander Sir Charles Goodeve, O.B.E., F.R.S., R.N.V.R.

MENU CARD FOR THE FIRST REUNION DINNER OF THE
WHEEZERS AND DODGERS, SHOWING RUSSELL BROCK-
BANK'S IMPRESSION OF D.M.W.D. AT WORK!

T

one product of the department, Goodfellow's Wreck Dispersal Pistol alone was stated before the Commission to have saved the country some twenty million pounds.

What has happened to the Wheezers and Dodgers in the years since they went their separate ways?

Well, not long ago they held their first reunion at a restaurant in the Strand. The news of their gathering had somehow got about, and the restaurant's proprietors were a little apprehensive. Surely these were the eccentric scientists whose pockets were invariably crammed with high explosives? What would happen to their premises if Richardson or Lane brought with them a starshell or a P.A.C. rocket? Would Norway want to try out an improved version of the Great Panjandrum along their newly decorated corridor?

But when the guests arrived they all looked reassuringly respectable! The chair was taken by Charles Goodeve, now Director of the British Iron and Steel Research Association and a Knight of the British Empire for his scientific services to the Royal Navy. Supporting him were Richardson, head of the Nuffield Research Group at University College, and Nevil Shute Norway, whose countless best-selling novels had made him a household name.

Among the large company were Alec Menhinick, back from more recent adventures as a shark fisherman in the Seychelles; Jock Davies, retired from the sea and farming in Surrey; Purcell, soon to take up a new appointment as Chief Scientific Adviser to the Home Office; Guggenheim, Professor of Chemistry at Reading University; Laurie, now experimenting commercially with bubble harbours; and the indispensable Jamieson, still serving at the Admiralty, but additionally His Worship the Mayor of Twickenham—a dual rôle which, he claimed, was no more exacting than the administration of D.M.W.D.!

The waiters agreed among themselves that they had seldom seen a more dignified and decorous assembly, and all would have been well if the Chairman had not called upon Richardson for a speech.

"Gentlemen," said Richardson, "we were often accused—rather unjustifiably, I always thought—of endangering our neighbours in the Admiralty with unorthodox experiments. By a strange coincidence, only yesterday I found this in a drawer in my laboratory. . . ."

Rummaging in his pockets, he produced what appeared to be a small shell, and as he held it up his fellow-guests stared at it a trifle uneasily. "It's one of the old Mark VIII's, which, you may remember, gave us a bit of trouble towards the end of the war, and I thought it might be interesting to see if this one will still function after all these years. . . ."

Placing the object upright on the table in front of him, he raised the Chairman's gavel and struck it a sharp blow. With one accord the terrified waiters fled for their lives. And, since news travels fast, a knot of onlookers gathered in the street outside, waiting hopefully for a sight of the Wheezers and Dodgers using their cliff-scaling apparatus to reach the safety of the Strand.

But the explosion never came. A small sub-committee is now looking into the matter, and a resounding report is expected at the next reunion.

BIBLIOGRAPHY

The Second World War, by Winston S. Churchill, 6 vols. (Cassell, 1948–1954).

Science at War, by J. G. Crowther and Professor R. Whiddington, C.B.E., F.R.S. (H.M.S.O.).

The War at Sea, by Captain S. W. Roskill, Vol. I (H.M.S.O.).

Report by ANCXF on Operation Neptune, Vol. I.

Max Horton and the Western Approaches, by Rear-Admiral W. S. Chalmers, C.B.E., D.S.C. (Hodder and Stoughton, 1954).

Admiralty Weekly Intelligence Report, March–June 1946.

Operation Neptune, by Commander Kenneth Edwards, R.N. (Collins, 1946).

British Coaster 1939–1945 (H.M.S.O.).

The Epic of Dunkirk, by E. Keble Chatterton (Hurst and Blackett).

Above Us the Waves (Harrap, 1953).

The Dam Busters, by Paul Brickhill (Evans).

Die Wolfe und der Admiral, by Wolfgang Frank (Stalling-Verlag, Berlin).

Britain's Merchant Navy, edited by Sir Archibald Hurd.

Service Most Silent, by John Frayn Turner (Harrap, 1955).

Force Mulberry, by Commander A. B. Stanford, U.S.N.R. (William Morrow, New York).

Cornish Engineers (a history of Holman Brothers of Camborne), by Bernard Hollowood.

Wavy Navy, edited by Lennox Kerr and David James (Harrap, 1950).

Paper on the Bombardon Floating Breakwater (Lt.-Commander R. A. W. A. Lochner, M.B.E., R.N.V.R., Dr Oscar Faber, and Sir William Penney, K.B.E., F.R.S., M.A.) read at the Conference on War-time Engineering Problems, June 1947, and published by the Institute of Civil Engineers.

"Floating Wharves and Jetties," article by the late R. M. Hamilton, M.A., in the *Dock and Harbour Authority Journal* for April 1946.

"New England, Cradle of American Industrialisation" (address delivered under the auspices of the American Society of Civil Engineers and the Rhode Island Society of Professional Engineers by Antoine Gazda, April 1947).

Some Mechanical Features in Anti-submarine Weapons (paper by J. M. Kirkby, M.A., A.M.I.Mech.E., published by the Institution of Mechanical Engineers, 1948).

INDEX

[Note: *Titles and ranks quoted in this index are those held at the time of the events described.*]

Mount Union College Libraries
940.541242 P339s   MBO
Pawle, Gerald/The secret war, 1939–45

3 7048 00132 2409

WITHDRAWN
UNIV OF MOUNT UNION LIBRARY

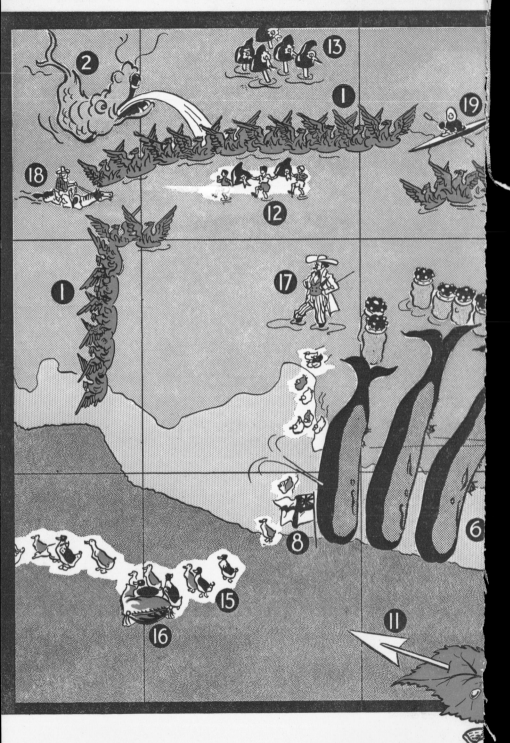

(*For key see page* 15.)